Japan's
Nuclear Option

John E. Endicott

The Praeger Special Studies program—utilizing the most modern and efficient book production techniques and a selective worldwide distribution network—makes available to the academic, government, and business communities significant, timely research in U.S. and international economic, social, and political development.

Japan's Nuclear Option

Political, Technical, and Strategic Factors

PRAEGER SPECIAL STUDIES IN INTERNATIONAL POLITICS AND GOVERNMENT

Praeger Publishers   New York   Washington   London

Library of Congress Cataloging in Publication Data

Endicott, John E
   Japan's nuclear option.

   (Praeger special studies in international politics
and government)
   Bibliography: p.
   Includes index.
   1. Japan—Military policy.   2. Japan—Defenses.
3. Japan—Foreign relations.   4. Atomic weapons.
I. Title.
UA845. E46   355. 03'35'52   75-3622
ISBN 0-275-05320-2

PRAEGER PUBLISHERS
111 Fourth Avenue, New York, N.Y. 10003, U.S.A.

Published in the United States of America in 1975
by Praeger Publishers, Inc.

Printed in the United States of America

To Michi

The study and research that have resulted in this book were an independent effort of the author and were not undertaken in connection with, or as a result of, his position as an officer of the U.S. Air Force. He has not had special access to official information or ideas and has employed in his subject only open-source material available to any student of the subject. The views and conclusions expressed in the book are those of the author. They are not intended and should not be thought to represent official ideas, attitudes, or policies of the U.S. Air Force, the Department of Defense, or the U.S. government.

The question of Japan's future course in the international system, and especially her role in Northeast Asia,
where she comes in direct contact with her immediate neigh-
bors--the Soviet Union, the People's Republic of China
(PRC), and the United States--is of continuing interest
to the policy-makers of those states. Increasingly, this
concern is shared by other actors of the international
scene, especially those with whom Japan played out the
drama of World War II.

Inherent in the overall question of future policy relationships is the issue that has become known as Japan's
nuclear option. Will Japan, no longer a subdued state,
seek that badge of sovereignty she has so long refused, or
will she continue to rely on some form of guarantee that
permits her a sufficient degree of security without re-
course to nuclear weapons?

This study examines the question of Japan's nuclear
option by attempting to review the main determinants that
are related to Japan and nuclear weapons. It is assumed,
as the general premise of this study, that only by faithfully inquiring into the international, domestic, technical, and strategic factors bearing on this question can a
fair appraisal be made relating to Japan's future nuclear
weapons policy. It is believed that an examination of any
one factor in isolation--for example, technical capability
--would lead to misleading conclusions that would serve
more to confuse than to clarify.

The method of presentation is one that describes system determinants as well as factors of societal will. The
author will attempt to set out the hypothesis that while
there are certain circumstances in the international system that support the notion that Japan should have nuclear weapons, the Japanese nation, while possessing a
clear-cut capability in a given time frame, will probably
postpone any decision to produce nuclear arms and supporting strategic delivery systems until there is a clear
threat to the very existence of the Japanese state itself,
which cannot be accommodated within the framework of existing bilateral or multilateral arrangements or procedures
of submissive accommodation. However, it is the position
of this book that, if a threat does materialize, public
opinion would support a reasonable response by the Japanese

government to include a program to attain a nuclear weapons deterrent capability. Such a force might first be introduced to the Japanese body politic in purely defensive terms with the use of nuclear arms limited to the interdiction of enemy forces in the act of invading the islands of Japan. As the self-abnegating nature of this policy becomes more generally recognized, Japanese deterrent objectives would probably settle on a desire to create a force capable of surviving a first strike and being able to inflict a limited degree of damage upon key urban industrial centers of an enemy.

In order to have the nuclear "crash program" as a viable option of defense policy, a requisite technological base must exist prior to a deterioration of bilateral relations. Whether intentionally or incidentally, extensive programs have been initiated in Japan that follow the November 18, 1964 recommendations of the Liberal Democratic Party National Security Research Council's policy report entitled "Policy That Our Country Must Take to Counter the Effect to the Security of Our Nation of the Chinese Nuclear Test as Well as Soviet Policies." When these projects are realized, Japan will be assured of possessing the technology of uranium enrichment, spent fuel reprocessing, rocket guidance and related aerospace skills, and nuclear maritime reactors. While some of the mentioned technical capabilities will be realiced in the late 1970s, it is clear that by 1985 an impressive base will exist that could support the creation of a sophisticated nuclear deterrent based on submarine-launched ballistic missiles, most probably on patrol in the Arabian Sea, if oriented toward the USSR, or in the Pacific, if oriented toward the PRC.

Even though all these skills will be attained by the end of the 1970s to early 1980s they will be subject to the very real constraints of internal determinants that exist on any Japanese government with regard to nuclear weapons, not the least of which are the opposition political parties, public opinion, the business community, legal proscriptions, and the policy of the leading party, which reflects the power of the mentioned groups.

In order to examine this hypothesis, the study is divided into six chapters. Chapter 1 reviews the recent significant bilateral diplomatic intercourse between Japan and her major neighbors in Northeast Asia. Stress, in this accounting of regional diplomatic relations, is placed on current unresolved issues, be they territorial, economic, or political, to provide an understanding of possible justifications for a nuclear weapons program. Also discussed

in the first chapter are other nonregional issues that are
of crucial Japanese national interest. Paramount are the
questions of Middle East oil and the future status of Japan
in Southeast Asia. It is suggested that in certain cases
these issues might develop significantly to be viewed as
bona fide casus belli.

Chapter 2 examines the situation of the nuclear question within Japan itself. It is the author's firm contention that, to date, the internal determinants of this issue have not been examined in appropriate detail by writ-
ers in the security studies field, who often have concentrated on the technological competence of the Japanese
state to produce nuclear weapons and have avoided coming
to grips with the nature of the dynamic and responsive interface of various domestic power groups. An attempt is
made to fill this void in Chapter 2, which generally finds
that the great public brake on the nuclear option continues to exist with one possible exception.

The third principal section, Chapter 3, addresses the
question of Japan's technical ability to build nuclear
weapons. An effort is made to show the possibility, but
worthlessness, of a psychological bomb, and the major questions that remain to be solved before a militarily viable
weapons program could be contemplated.

The question of building a bomb is followed (Chapter
4) with an in-depth examination concerning the Japanese
ability to deliver nuclear weapons. It is shown that a
considerable technological capability exists with regard
to guided missiles.

Chapter 5 considers the employment of a possible Japanese nuclear force against her closest neighbors, China
and the USSR. Possible target systems are created to determine, in a general empirical fashion, what strategic
results could be expected from a nuclear exchange. Generally, the study indicates that, under the circumstances
accounted for in the model, Japan would need to deploy a
submarine-launched ballistic missile system to be able to
inhibit possible actions by adversaries. While no one can
be certain, there appears to be a range of force levels
available to Japan that would afford her a deterrent capability. (The exact nature of the forces and deterrence
is explained in Chapter 5.)

Chapter 6 summarizes the principal findings of the
study.

Previous studies appearing in the United States or
Europe that considered, either directly or tangentially,
the issue of the nuclearization of Japan, have tended of-

ten to be more emotional than academic. It is the purpose
of this volume to strive for the latter. It will cite the
potential Japanese capability but do so in the context
and with an understanding of Japanese societal will. Where
it fails, it is none but the author's fault.

Japanese names are shown in Western style with given
name first, family name last. This is not the style used
in Japan but will be used, as it is the form most familiar
to our readers.

ACKNOWLEDGMENTS

This work owes much to many. The data presented reflect a research trip to Hokkaido in January 1969, a similar trip to Washington, D.C. in August 1972, a research/interview program conducted in Tokyo in February 1973, and two and one-half years of research under the tutorial guidance of Professors Geoffrey Kemp and Allan B. Cole of the Fletcher School of Law and Diplomacy, Tufts University.

Others to whom I am especially indebted are Hisahiko Okazaki, Information Counselor of the Embassy of Japan; Mr. Murata, Political Counselor of the Embassy of Japan; Colonel Mayuki Ichinomiya, Air Attaché, Embassy of Japan; Mr. Murakami, First Secretary and Science Attaché, Embassy of Japan; Ryukichi Imai, Adviser to the Foreign Ministry, Japan Atomic Power Company; Hisao Iwashima, Professor, National Defense College; Kobun Ito, of the Faculty of the National Defense College; Makoto Momoi, Director, International Relations, National Defense College; Osamu Kaihara, former Chief of the Secretariat, National Defense Council; Shunji Taoka, reporter, Asahi Shimbun; Michio Royama, Professor, Jochi University; Takuya Kubo, Director, Defense Bureau, Japanese Defense Agency; Jiro Hagi, Japanese Defense Agency; Tatsuo Arima, Foreign Ministry of Japan; Toshio Goto, Foreign Ministry of Japan; and Dr. Jun Tsunoda of the Diet Library.

On the American side, special gratitude goes to Billy Hill, U.S. Atomic Energy Commission; Lieutenant Colonel James Ling, Office of the Assistant to the Secretary of Defense for Atomic Energy; Peter Sheats, one-time Desk Officer, International Security Agency, Department of Defense; Lieutenant Commander James Auer, U.S. Navy; Raymond Aka, Mutual Defense Assistance Office; Norman Ng, Curator, Oriental Division, Air Force Cambridge Laboratory; Elizabeth Brociner, Massachusetts Institute of Technology Lincoln Laboratory Library; and the staff of the Fletcher School Library.

As always, a special note of thanks to my wife, Mitsuyo, who has patiently encouraged my study of Japanese society and its language through 15 years of married life.

CONTENTS

LIST OF TABLES

LIST OF FIGURES

Japan's
Nuclear Option

THE INTERNATIONAL
POLITICAL ENVIRONMENT

THE HISTORICAL PERSPECTIVE: SECURITY SYSTEMS OF NORTHEAST ASIA

While the notion that Japan could arm herself with nuclear weapons is not a new concept to those writing in 1974, it has gained acceptance as a serious option only as a result of perceptible changes that have taken place in the international environment, especially within the context of Northeast Asia (NEA).

The security structures in the NEA regional area have been marked by a discernible metamorphosis since the 20th Congress of the Communist Party of the Soviet Union in February 1956. From that time the deterioration in the Sino-Soviet relationship became evident.

The main security systems that existed in the area, the Sino-Soviet pact and the U.S.-Japanese alliance, had been formed within 19 months of each other. In the Sino-Soviet pact, signed on February 14, 1950, the USSR promised to protect the People's Republic of China (PRC) from attack by Japan or her allies and agreed to conform "with the principles of equality, mutual benefit and mutual respect for the national sovereignty and territorial integrity" of China.[1] The treaty was to last 30 years with a provision for a further five-year extension if not denounced one year before the expiration date.[2]

The Russian presence remained in Manchuria and the Liaotung Peninsula until the spring of 1955. For several years after that, until 1957, the two states managed to preserve a degree of socialist harmony, but following Nikita Khrushchev's denunciation of Joseph Stalin, the Chinese leadership began to reappraise China's foreign policy in the light of what was called Soviet revisionism. The two socialist powers gradually moved apart; the widening ideological split was marked by a series of events including in March 1958 unilateral cessation of nuclear testing by the USSR; Soviet inactivity vis-à-vis the revolt in Iraq led by General Abdul Karim el-Kassem, which toppled the government of Prime Minister Muri as-Said and resulted in the death of King Faisal II and the prime minister; Soviet reluctance to support the People's Republic of China in the early phases of the 1958 Taiwan Straits crisis; Khrushchev's visit to the United States; and border incidents beginning in 1959 in the T'ien Shan range area.[3]

Those events were followed by the termination of Soviet technical aid for China in 1960. During 1962 and 1963 relations became progressively strained as a result of the Soviet position regarding the Sino-Indian border dispute; the Cuban missile crisis, during which the Chinese had hoped for a more adamant Soviet policy; and the June 14, 1963 ultimatum from the PRC to the Soviet Union calling on the USSR to cease its revisionist ways.[4]

From 1963 onward, border incidents multiplied; Mao Tse-tung raised the specter that the territory to the north of China had been taken from the Chinese by 19th-century imperialist pressures.[5] Border clashes continued, became more serious, and resulted finally in the Damansky/Chenpao Island incidents in March 1969.[6]

These factors, plus the Soviet renewal of her alliance with Outer Mongolia, whose relations with the PRC subsequently deteriorated, and the reported movement of Soviet divisions into northeast Outer Mongolia were received by the Chinese with growing concern. The increase of Soviet forces along the entire joint border to a staggering 1.3 million further complicated the relationship.[7]

Soviet overtures to restore Sino-Soviet friendship to a semblance of its former status have been seen. In August 1970, Communist Party Secretary Leonid Brezhnev attempted to reach an understanding with China, but these overtures were to no avail, as the Chinese responded with an attack on "criminal schemes plotted by one or two superpowers"[8] or maintained silence except for comments to third parties. In October 1970 and again in 1973, the Soviets offered the PRC a nonaggression pact, but these proposals were rejected because the Chinese insisted on effective border agreements and reduction of forces on both sides of the border.[9]

Thus, in the 1970s the two socialist powers forming part of the security environment of Northeast Asia no longer represent a unified force but stand facing each other with the border areas ever ready to serve as a catalyst for peace or war. Chinese nuclear capability is growing month by month; whether or not the USSR will continue to permit this development remains a matter of intense speculation.[10]

The relationship is no longer simply between the PRC and the USSR; the United States, so recently the bête noire of the PRC assumed a new role in the summer of 1971. This role, plus the equally innovative policy of the fourth member of the NEA system, Japan, has resulted in a changed dynamism of Northeast Asian diplomacy.[11]

The U.S.-Japanese alliance, established to stem the eastward thrust of the Communist bloc, was consummated in the shadow of the Korean War and came only hours after the United States had signed the peace treaty with Japan that ended the state of war and recognized "full sovereignty of the Japanese people."[12] The security treaty noted that as Japan had no "effective means" to insure her defense from "irresponsible militarism," the United States would be willing to station "certain of its armed forces in and about Japan." These forces could be used to "contribute to the maintenance of international peace and security in the Far East and to the security of Japan against armed attack from without."

Under this security system, the United States had authority to intervene in internal disorders in the event of the "express request" of the government of Japan; veto any third party from obtaining similar military rights in Japan; and insist on a form of legal procedure that closely resembled extraterritoriality. The duration of this pact was not specified, only that it would expire when both governments believed alternative means for defense were available. The Americans, like the Russians for a time, maintained a physical presence on their allies' territory. As in the case of the Sino-Soviet relationship, the years since have brought considerable change.

The first of the changes in substance occurred in March 1954, when the U.S. Mutual Security Act of 1951 was made applicable to Japan. From this point onward began an unbroken chain of events that have resulted in a significantly modified security relationship between the United States and Japan. One of the major events that marked this transition was the 1957 negotiations conducted by Prime Minister Nobusuke Kishi in Washington, D.C. These provided for evacuation of U.S. ground troops; return of numerous U.S. base facilities to Japanese jurisdiction;

3

increased Japanese legal jurisdiction over certain types of criminal cases; release of the few criminals still in custody; and establishment of an intergovernmental committee "to study problems arising in relation to the Security Treaty."[13]

Another event of major bilateral significance was the revision of the Security Treaty itself in 1959-60, which altered many of the remaining aspects that detracted from the sovereignty of Japan. Some of the more salient changes were allowance for prior consultation before major changes in troop strength or weapons could occur; establishment of a 10-year duration for the treaty--after which, either side could abrogate following a year's notice; elimination of U.S. authority to intervene in internal disorders; and termination of U.S. veto power over third parties gaining military access to facilities in Japan.[14]

By the end of 1960, the major question between Japan and the United States was the status of Okinawa and the Bonin Islands. In 1968 the Bonins were returned, and significant progress had been made toward a mutual agreement concerning Okinawa.[15]

The U.S. involvement in Vietnam during the 1960s brought little evidence of support from the articulate Japanese public; however, the government of Japan maintained an official attitude of support or at least understanding. During this war, Okinawa was seen by the United States as the "keystone of the Pacific" and had become a vital logistical center in support of operations in Southeast Asia (SEA). It was clear that as long as the United States actively prosecuted the war in SEA, Okinawa would remain under U.S. jurisdiction.

With the election of President Richard Nixon in November 1968 came a significant shift in U.S. Pacific policy. At Guam in 1969, Nixon redefined the U.S. attitude toward defense objectives in the Pacific Basin. This new policy, on the one hand, reaffirmed that the United States would keep its treaty commitments and would provide a nuclear shield to allies and friends in need of such levels of protection; however, in "other types of aggression" the United States would provide equipment and economic assistance rather than ground troops.[16] The United States was announcing a scaling down of efforts in SEA. Shortly after this historic statement, the president met with Prime Minister Eisaku Sato to chart a new course for the relationship between the United States and Japan. With an eye on 1970 and a possible Security Treaty crisis, the United States agreed to return Okinawa to Japan by 1972, and in the joint communiqué Japan seemed to indicate its interest in the security of the NEA region, especially South Korea and Taiwan. In fact, it appeared that Japan finally had accepted the U.S. concept of regional defense responsibilities.[17]

As the major problems of the previous decade seemed to disappear before the hand of skilled statesmanship, other problems related to economic matters began to foster new controversies. These included the textile quota matter in which the United States attempted to encourage Japanese industry to restrain textile exports to the United States, U.S. access to the Japanese market and investments in Japan, and a growing trade imbalance. These developments seemed to reduce beyond all proportion the significant achievements made in removing older diplomatic irritants by both nations.* It was becoming evident that, inevitably, differences of interest between the allies, now dealing in more spheres as equals, would tax their statesmanship to avert adversary attitudes. Such changes have been properly recognized as aspects of the emergent polycentric system.

As economic debates continued and preparations for return of Okinawa progressed, there occurred what have come to be called the "Nixon shocks" of the summer of 1971. The nightmares so often recounted by Ambassador Koichiro Asakai had come true.[18] The United States had moved for rapprochement with the PRC and had done it in a manner likened by some Japanese observers (with some exaggeration) to the "Affair of 1939," when Soviet Russia and Germany concluded the startling nonaggression pact, causing the Hiranuma cabinet to fall.[19] The security system built partially on nonrecognition and containment of the PRC had been rocked by its very architect, the United States. The Japanese, not to be outdone, embarked on diplomatic initiatives of their own and by September 29, 1972 had recognized the regime of Mao Tse-tung before the United States had set up its first liaison office.

Thus, both the Sino-Soviet and U.S.-Japan security systems have undergone changes, significant and seemingly

---

*The textile issue became quite serious, causing some Americans to accuse Sato of failing to follow through on a "promise" made during the Nixon-Sato talks of November, 1969. See particularly the Mainichi Daily News of June 26, 1970 at the time of the collapse of negotiations for an indication of the depth of ill feelings that arose.

irreversible in the case of China and the USSR and, at
least, far-reaching in the case of the United States and
Japan.

THE EMERGENCE OF A MULTICENTRIC SYSTEM
AND JAPAN'S RESPONSE

The Japanese responded to the increased dynamism in
Northeast Asian regional relationships with a searching
assessment of the probable impact of multicentrism on
their policy planning. Particular emphasis in this assessment has been placed on the question of nuclear weapons
and how best Japan can obtain security in an era marked
by the declining importance of ideology and general obfus-
cation of former relationships.

Several theses as to Japan's future course have
emerged. Generally, there is a feeling that U.S. credibility and the U.S. nuclear guarantee have been denigrated to
some degree and that Japan will have to compensate for
this in some way. This declining faith in the U.S. guarantee was pointedly suggested by the conservative essayist
and political critic Takeshi Muramatsu.[20] He saw a changing role for Japan and cited William Kintner's "five polar"
interpretation and Robert Scalapino's call for Japan to
be given permanent membership on the UN Security Council
as evidence that foreign observers also see a changing role
for Japan as well as the United States.

Muramatsu, in noting the fairly universal recognition
of declining U.S. relative power, advocated a further examination of the security relationship. He was deeply
concerned (as were other Japanese defense analysts) regarding the reported March 1971 statement by General Bruce
Holloway (former commander of the U.S. Strategic Air Command) to the effect that if Europe were threatened, the
United States would not necessarily respond in certain
circumstances. In Muramatsu's opinion, the implications
of this statement are far more serious for Japan than for
Europe as the United States has many more historical connections with Europe than Japan. Japan would probably be
sacrificed in any nuclear encounter, according to Muramatsu.

This critic, typical of one school of thought, also
referred to the view that the U.S.-Chinese rapprochement
was born out of weakness rather than strength and maintains that the force that brought the two states together
was mutual fear of the USSR. The result, according to
Muramatsu, will be increased instability in Northeast Asia.

Regarding the role of nuclear weapons, Muramatsu pointedly made reference to the fact that under the administration of President Lyndon Johnson strong pressure was placed on Japan to ratify the Nonproliferation Treaty (NPT); however, he maintains that the current Republican administration has not made it an issue.*

In another article by the same author, three nuclear options for Japan are cited as possible ways to compensate for the change in U.S. power. It was suggested that Japan could arm with nuclear weapons unilaterally, do so jointly with the United States, or adhere to the NPT and allow China to become the leader in Asia.[21] Of the three possible courses, he favors the second and believes that Japan's optimum contribution can be made in concert with the United States.[22]

Whereas the school of thought represented by Muramatsu sees a possible nuclear role for Japan in the changing environment of Northeast Asia, Junnosuke Kishida, a noted press commentator and respected representative of one of the schools of "progressive" political thought, argues at length in three articles[23] that Japan can never be a military power in the nuclear sense of the term due to her geographical liabilities and concomitant vulnerability to nuclear attack. Kishida foresees an Asian security system (post-1975) on the following lines:

> (1) A fundamental, external framework based on a tacit recognition by the United States, the Soviet Union and China, the three nuclear powers in the region, of their common responsibilities.
> (2) An inner framework permitting an expanded political, economic and social role for a non-nuclear Japan, within the context of the stabilized, three polar military system outlined above.
> (3) An additional inner framework designed to promote regional cooperation and facilitate crisis management in Asia.[24]

The "withdrawal of American military power from Asia under the Nixon Doctrine" is welcomed by Kishida; he suggests that the U.S. hegemony can be replaced by a balance between the three great powers excluding Japan. For Japan, Kishida calls for "equal distance" diplomacy. Japan, in essence, should not be closely aligned with any of the three big powers and should retain her non-nuclear status basing her security on the knowledge that Japan could, if required, rapidly achieve the military forces needed.

7

Thus, according to Kishida's plan, Japan would place her faith in potential nuclear power rather than a costly and dangerous armed establishment; her productive role could be in the "political, economic and social coordination in Asia." Her main role would be that of flexibly contributing to equilibrium. This would be another reason for some loosening of the alliance with the United States.

The concept for a "denuclearized zone" is also advanced by Kishida for Japan and Korea. This is a scheme under which "the Korean peninsula would become a stabilized zone and Japan's three non-nuclear principles--non-possession, non-production, and non-introduction of nuclear weapons--would become international principles." Kishida feels that the Japanese desire for international activism could be oriented toward economic and social development of the underdeveloped states of Asia.

In a third article, appearing in early 1973, the same author placed increasing emphasis on the fact that Japan in her current non-nuclear, but near nuclear, position has already gained all the political advantages possible and has not incurred the "economic and political costs of going nuclear."[25] Kishida cautions that public opinion in Japan must be built up to guard "against any trend toward nuclear armament." In a direct criticism of one segment in Japanese business circles (which represents still another approach to the problem of nuclear security), he insists that Japan has no "responsibility for paying for the protection provided by the nuclear umbrella.[26] He notes that "since the super-powers have established the umbrella of their own volition, they cannot force any country to pay for the protection it affords."[27]

Kishida advises Japan to escape from the threat of nuclear arms by getting the nuclear powers to sign no-first-use agreements and to denuclearize Northeast Asia.[28] While some military analysts might find the above policy recommendations bordering on irresponsibility, Kishida is one of the most articulate spokesmen for a non-nuclear Japan, and what he writes should be taken as being representative of the opinions of a significant number of the Japanese body politic.

Professor Hisao Iwashima of the Japanese Defense College has drawn attention to the forecasts emanating from the United States to the effect that Japan will join the nuclear club.[29] These forecasts in U.S. newspapers became so frequent in July 1971 that Senator Hubert Humphrey sent a letter to Secretary of Defense Melvin Laird to express his alarm. Humphrey noted that any such action by Japan

would be in violation of the NPT.[30] Another such forecast, but of a far more serious nature due to its reported
origin, occurred during the Sato-Nixon meeting of January
1972 at San Clemente. The U.S. news commentator Jack
Anderson made public reportedly secret data based on a
report of the U.S. Embassy in Japan to the White House.
In part, the release indicated that the U.S. government
was quite concerned about the prospect of Japan going nuclear and had decided to justify the U.S.-Japanese Security
Treaty, in talks with Chou En-lai, on the grounds that it
was an effective brake on nuclear armament moves by Japan.[31]

Iwashima contends that Japan will not develop nuclear
weapons "in the near future or, for that matter, even in
the remote future, as long as the present level of international order is maintained." This "present level of international order," however, in Iwashima's own words would
be threatened if "the American nuclear capability were to
be lost or weakened considerably, and other Asian nations
began to develop their own nuclear forces."[32] Thus, the
"external pressures imposed by the international environment" become critical as determinants of future Japanese
policy, and in this respect, the role of the United States
vis-à-vis Japan is of prime importance. In a sense, this
commentator is calling on the United States to stand by
its protégé of the past 25 years and provide a measure of
reassurance instead of continuing cries of alarm.

Other Japanese analysts, including Yonosuke Nagai
(professor at Tokyo Technical University), Hidekazu Kawai
(professor at Gakushuin University), Hiroharu Seki (professor at Tokyo University), Masamori Sase (assistant professor at Seikei University), and Osamu Miyoshi (editorial
writer for the Mainichi Shimbun)[33] have contributed to the
discussion of policy options advancing ideas such as: the
threat of "intimidation of the weak" (the idea that Korea
and Taiwan could attempt to take undue advantage of the
U.S. withdrawal from Asia in light of Japan's weak military); the need for independent diplomacy to avert a U.S.-
Chinese arrangement to confront a resurgent Japan; association with the United States is most dangerous for Japan
as the United States still has a first-strike strategy
against China, leaving Japan the prime target for China
to strike; rapid termination of the U.S. security system
would militate against the Japanese and have untold results
on the national prosperity--so keep the system and make
necessary accommodations with potential enemies from within
the system; the only way for the Nixon doctrine to succeed
in Asia is for Japan to assume the U.S. role; and the

United States would be Japan's "most dangerous potential enemy" in the 1970s; thus maintenance of the security system is advisable until 1975, when a revision might be possible.

Professor Nagai (Tokyo Technical University) followed his January 1972 article with the concept of the historic U.S.-Japanese adversary relationship. He feared that the United States might make Japan a "scapegoat" for the realignment of the old alliance systems and that the pattern of prewar cooperation with China at Japan's expense might recur.[34]

Assistant Professor Jun Eto (also of the Tokyo Technological University) advanced the theory that as Japan was recovering Okinawa it had become an "anti-status quo country." This status would make it, automatically, an "unlovable country" in the eyes of the United States. As "unlovable" had connotations of adversary, Eto offered the following countermeasures. Japan should (1) open its doors as soon as possible and make itself an indispensable market for the U.S. economy; (2) promote cultural exchange with the United States; (3) inform the world that Japan has changed from the "export-first" policy to one that places the "people's livelihood-first."[35]

The period after President Nixon visited China brought still additional policy recommendations from the Japanese press. The prestigious Nihon Keizai declared it was "urgently necessary for Japan to start wide-range diplomatic activities" not only with China but with such countries as North and South Korea, Taiwan, the Philippines, Thailand, Malaysia, Burma, India, and Pakistan.[36]

Even the Security Research Council of the Liberal Democratic Party (LDP) almost on the eve of the election of a new prime minister to replace Sato, noted in its deliberations that other concepts for security existed besides the Japan-U.S. Security Treaty, and mentioned, in particular, Asian collective security systems and bilateral nonaggression pacts with the USSR and China.[37]

The most far-reaching demonstration of Japan's response to the emerging multicentric system occurred in September 1972, when then Prime Minister Kakuei Tanaka visited the People's Republic of China. Restoration of diplomatic relations was achieved during the visit, but the debate concerning Japanese security policy only intensified. The principal opposition parties argued that the normalization of Japanese-Chinese relations negated the requirement for the U.S.-Japanese Security Treaty;[38] certain groups called for the establishment of a non-nuclear zone for Asia, while some remained firm in the belief that the security treaty was needed as an interim guarantee of nuclear secutiry.[39]

Although the responses to the changing international environment have been varied, there has been one common thread of concern: the status of the U.S. nuclear guarantee and the manner in which Japan might offset any degradation of the guarantee's effectiveness. This concern for security arrangements has not, however, inhibited the government in giving vent to a "new diplomacy" now recognized for its initiatives in North Vietnam, North and South Korea, Mongolia, and Bangladesh.[40]

The overall course of Japanese foreign policy and, of course, security policy is being decided now. The ultimate direction of this policy will be based on an appraisal of those issues that make up the political, economic, and military milieu between Japan and the other primary actors of Northeast Asia: China, the USSR, and the United States. What specific role nuclear weapons could play in future relations will be discussed at a later point in the paper.

NORTHEAST ASIA: THE PRIMARY ACTORS

Chinese Political and Economic Relationships with Japan

The state of war, or more precisely, the "abnormal state of affairs" that existed between Japan and China ended on September 28, 1972 with the publication of the Sino-Japanese communiqué of that date.[41] This joint declaration was realized almost 80 years after Japan began its involvement in Manchuria, a process that led to eight years of undeclared war and untold suffering, eventually to both sides.

The post-World War II political relationships between China and Japan can only be described as having been cyclic in nature. Generally the tone of the dialogue has been set by the Chinese side; the Japanese have reacted depending on domestic political considerations. No attempt will be made here to trace the fascinating fluctuations of Sino-Japanese relations since late 1970, but recent events that contributed to the creation of the current diplomatic environment of détente, along with certain economic and military matters, will be presented.

Indications that a basic reorientation of Japanese policy toward China was being contemplated surfaced in late 1970. Shortly after Prime Minister Sato reaffirmed his opposition to PRC membership in the United Nations, he said, "This state of affairs could not go on forever."[42] In early November, only days after the above statement, the Chinese Problem Subcommittee of the Foreign Affairs Research Council of the LDP began deliberations to develop a new China policy to "suit Japan's national interest."[43] The 30 Liberal Democrats who attended the first meeting indicated that restoration of diplomatic relations with China would be "high on the agenda."[44]

These events were followed in early December by the formation of a suprapartisan Dietmen's League for Accelerating the Restoration of Japan-China Diplomatic Relations. There was widespread support for this body as was indicated by the 379 Diet members who joined. All political parties were represented, including the LDP. The inaugural declaration of the group stated, "The Government insists on recognizing Taipei as the sole legal government for the whole of China. This stand is anachronistic, and is injurious to the present and future interests of our nation."[45] While this group did not immediately begin a program within the Diet, its establishment was a harbinger of future events.

The Japanese popular press in 1970, according to some observers, was active to the point of adoration in its coverage of the PRC and no doubt helped establish an environment conducive to the movement for normalization. The fact that the newspapers' coverage might serve some parochial interest was dramatically revealed by Osamu Miyoshi, a newspaper reporter, who stated that the Japan-China reporter exchange consummated in 1968 had a "secret" quid pro quo--namely, the major newspapers reportedly agreed to accept Chou's Three Principles and to self-regulate articles that might otherwise be critical of the Chinese side in order to have special correspondents assigned to cover China.[46]

In April 1971, "ping-pong diplomacy" emerged during the meeting of the World Table Tennis Athletic Association in Tokyo. U.S. participants were invited to China, and soon thereafter, Henry Kissinger, then special adviser to the president, visited Peking. Kissinger's visit was followed by the U.S. announcement of the scheduled trip of Nixon to China.

After these events, Japan was seen to redouble its efforts toward normalization, Prime Minister Sato, only two days after his "Nixon shock," remarked that he "looks forward to development of negotiations on a government level with China."[47] Only four days later, while addressing the Budget Committee of the House of Councillors, he said that he was ready to make a visit to Peking. On July 23 he underlined the importance of his previous statement by saying that it should be taken "as an official appeal to China by Japan."[48]

Throughout the course of the next year, the Japanese attitude was seen to grow in its accommodating characteristics toward the PRC. The indicators coming from Tokyo were unmistakable and numerous. Actions demonstrating that Japan was seeking to open a new relationship with Peking were typified by the following: the joint declaration of the Dietmen's League for Normalization of Japan-China Relations;[49] the "Hori Letter" sent by Liberal Democratic Party Secretary General Shigeru Hori to Chou En-lai stating "we recognize the Government of the Peoples' Republic of China";[50] the Japanese Foreign Ministry's "Three Principles" for normalization of Sino-Japanese relations introduced in January 1972;[51] and a most revealing omission of any reference of Taiwan in the foreign policy "Blue Book" that appeared in March 1972.[52]

While these overtures from the Sato government were by no means inconsequential, they did not seem to interest the PRC, and the replies from T'ian An Square reflected no desire to change the Sino-Japanese relationship as long as Sato was head of government. However, upon the formation of the Tanaka administration in July 1972, the political environment took on a decidedly new character.

On becoming prime minister, Tanaka clarified his position, saying that he would attempt to hasten talks between Japan and China,[53] and the LDP formed an ad hoc committee, the Japan-China Diplomatic Relations Normalization Consultative Council, with Zentaro Kosaka as chairman, to adjust the intraparty opinions regarding this volatile issue.[54]

This activity was echoed in the PRC by a series of "Chou statements" reportedly welcoming "the new Tanaka Government."[55] By September 1972, the historic "Tanaka-Chou" talks had occurred and on September 28, 1972, the Sino-Japanese communiqué was issued. A summary of the main points follows:

> 1. The state of war between China and Japan was terminated.

2. Japan recognized the PRC as the "sole legal government of China."

3. Japan noted that it "fully understands and respects" the position of the PRC that "the government of the People's Republic of China reaffirms that Taiwan is an inalienable part of the territory of the People's Republic of China."

4. Diplomatic relations were established between Japan and China from September 29, 1972.

5. China renounced its demands for war indemnities from Japan.

6. Japan recognized the principles of peaceful coexistence as the basis for relations and both states agreed to settle disputes by peaceful means.

7. No third country was seen as the object of the normalization, and both countries agreed that they "should not seek hegemony in the Asia-Pacific Region." Both voiced their opposition "to efforts by any other country or groups of countries to establish . . . hegemony."

8. Negotiations to bring about a treaty of peace and friendship would be held.

9. Negotiations for other agreements on trade, aviation, etc. would also be held.[56]

In a period of less than 100 days, from July 5 to September 28, 1972, Prime Minister Tanaka had dramatically moved the Japanese government along a program that resulted in normalization. It was a splendid accomplishment, but one very difficult to top.

It is often profitable to inquire as to the reasons for the sudden change in the attitude of policy-makers; it should not be less so in this case. As for Japan, it became clear after the Nixon visit to China, and China's entry into the United Nations, that there was nothing to be gained from continuing a "hard" pro-Taipei position. In fact, when commercial competition with U.S. business interests in China was considered, much was to be lost by any hesitant position. Moreover, control over Okinawa had been achieved on May 15, 1972. There was no longer need for Japan to fear "complications" on that scene, and such dynamic action by Tanaka gave the impression of a "new diplomacy," which was popular with the public. The affair also must have been conceived as being rather productive for the domestic political interests of the LDP.

In China, other but equally important factors propelled the leaders of the PRC toward normalization of relations with its one-time foe. Basically, a fear of international isolation in the face of possible USSR military action to settle ideological and border disputes between the two powers must have been instrumental. Ancillary to the above point seems to have been a desire to impress upon the Japanese, especially the Socialists, the necessity for a realistic defense posture in Northeast Asia.

Other contributing factors might have been the desire to gain more leverage over Japan in order to influence the pace of joint Soviet-Japanese development of Siberia. (In this regard, the Chinese have already "warned" the Japanese that participation in the Tyumen oil field development scheme with the USSR "runs counter to China's national interests."[57] The PRC also might have desired to preclude further Japanese advancement into Taiwan in the light of the past Japanese colonial association with that island; or perhaps there was a desire to have greater access to the industrial and financial might of Japan--that is, export-import funds, to aid in the development of Chinese industry.

While these factors probably contributed in some way to the bilateral decisions to proceed rapidly with normalization, events since have indicated that completion of the supplementary agreements to make normalization meaningful have progressed at a surprisingly slow pace in light of the initial rush. For example, the Japan-China Aviation Agreement, which was slated for conclusion before any other operational agreement, was not finalized until April 20, 1974, even though formal negotiations were started in early March 1973.[58] Progress was deadlocked over the question of China Airlines (the Taiwan line) flying into Heneda Airport, and some observers were noting that, in certain aspects, a "two-Chinas" situation was being realized.[59]

Opposition to an air accord came primarily from pro-Taiwan Liberal Democratic members of the Dietmen's Discussion Group on Japan-Taiwan Relations who were concerned that such a move not be made at the expense of the national dignity of the Republic of China (Taiwan).

When the agreement was finally realized, it was accompanied by a statement made by then Foreign Minister Masayoshi Ohira that the "'emblem' on the Nationalist aircraft would not be recognized as a 'national flag' and that the China Airlines operating from Taiwan would not be considered as representing a state."[60]

This statement brought Nationalist retaliation in the form of the discontinuance of the Taipei-Tokyo air link and disdain from the pro-Taiwan members of the LDP. Such was the anger of these members that 50 of them absented themselves from the House of Representatives when the pact was unanimously approved in early May.[61] Included in the group opposed to the slight to Nationalist China were 21 of the 31-member right-wing group Seirankai, and of the 50 who stayed away some 30 were said to be members of the faction belonging to Takeo Fukuda.[62]

The above major step in restoring normal commercial intercourse between the two nations was followed on April 26, 1974 by ratification of a Japan-China trade agreement that replaced the Memorandum Trade Agreement that had been scheduled to expire at the end of 1973.[63]

Pending items that have been on the agenda since the Sino-Japanese communiqué include a fishery agreement; a peace and friendship treaty; a maritime transportation agreement; and a cultural agreement.

The status of these agreements, as of this writing, indicates that those who advocate caution in the normalization of all facets of Japan-PRC intercourse are having some impact. Fishery talks were begun on May 23, 1974 in Peking to supersede a private agreement set to expire on June 22.[64] These talks ran into "rough sailing" soon after their initiation and were suspended on June 19.[65] The private accord was continued temporarily, but agreement could not be reached concerning the status of Pohai Bay. Peking insisted that the area was a military region, and Tokyo wanted it as part of the treaty area.[66]

Talks concerning a maritime transportation agreement began on July 8, 1974[67] but were suspended after approximately three weeks when the PRC demanded that ships from the Republic of China remove the Taiwan flag when in Japanese ports.[68]

Hopes for an early peace and friendship treaty between the two states were dashed when Tokyo held the position that the substantial operational agreements should be fairly well along to completion before initiating peace treaty talks.[69] The Chinese side, in opposition, unofficially indicated its desire to proceed with peace treaty and operational agreement negotiations simultaneously as early as July 21; the Japanese did not respond in a clear manner until September 5 that this was acceptable.[70] On that date, during a session of the Foreign Affairs Committee of the lower house, Foreign Minister Kimura stated, "If an agreement is reached between the Japanese and Chinese governments, Japan is willing to begin negotiations to conclude a Japan-China peace and friendship treaty in conjunction with the negotiations on the marine transport and fishing agreements."[71]

It would appear that little chance exists to see this pact consummated before 1975; however, some concrete developments have resulted concerning a cultural agreement. A program for exchange of Foreign Ministry language students has been implemented, and a broader exchange of scholars is being studied.[72]

While some positive progress is being registered, the right-wing newspapers have picked up the fact that progress has been slow and that Taiwan connections, other than political, have been treated in high regard.[73]

A brief look at the statistics of trade for 1961 to 1970 will reveal that, as the political relations slowly developed between the two states, economics and politics have been separated in large measure. The items of trade and their scope will help us understand the economic dependencies involved in the bilateral relationship. Main exports to China have consistently been fertilizers, iron and steel, and machinery, while imports from the PRC have been concentrated in soybeans, oil seeds, and pig iron. Generally the trade relationship has favored Japan by a considerable margin.[74]

Although the development of the multicentric system has possibly lessened the threat of major conflict in the world, by allowing national politics to be based on interest rather than ideology, in theory a diffused system offers ample opportunity for armed disputes at a more regional level. Be that as it may, this study must turn to one of the realities of world relationships: the existence of military power and the propensity to use it to influence the outcome of international disputes.

The Chinese Military Threat to Japan

In the fluid political situation of Northeast Asia, the world has just witnessed a period of détente between two former enemies. The first anniversary of the formal ending of the state of war is not long past, and a peace and friendship treaty is in some stage of preliminary draft. It would seem to some that in such an atmosphere the thought of "threat" is misplaced. If an examination is conducted beneath the surface of the image of tranquility, it is soon realized that certain concepts remained unchanged. One of those concepts concerns the defense of the Japanese Islands.

17

Japanese defense planners conceive of and plan against three specific contingencies that could threaten Japan in a military sense. These three are attack by Soviet or Chinese nuclear forces; a direct invasion by hostile forces using conventional arms, most often, admittedly, seen as coming from the USSR; and, finally, "indirect aggression" taking the form of massive internal disturbances with leadership provided by Japan-based communists with support from either the Soviet Union or the PRC.[75]

The Chinese military establishment of regular forces numbers approximately 2.9 million personnel; however, of the estimated population of 800 million, males in the 15-49 age bracket and considered fit for military service number 105 million. Approximately 8.5 million reach military age each year.[76] While the army consists of 2.5 million troops, only five of the 140 divisions are armored. One hundred and ten divisions are infantry, approximately 20 divisions are artillery, 3 are cavalry, and 2 are airborne. Heavy equipment include Soviet JS-2, T-34, and T-54 tanks as well as Chinese-made T-59 and T-62. Generally, the ratio of heavy mechanized equipment is lower than is characteristic of major industrial states, and, as might be expected under such circumstances, mobility if limited.[77]

The navy is primarily oriented toward coastal defense, having only four destroyers and four destroyer escorts; over 30 conventional submarines are believed in the inventory. However, "at least one nuclear-powered submarine appears to be under construction."[78]

The army or the navy do not present a significant threat to Japan;[79] however, the Chinese missile force and Chinese air force present a different picture. The air force has as many as 100 TU-16 medium bombers with a combat range of more than 1,650 miles. These bombers are being produced in the PRC with estimates varying as to monthly output. (One estimate runs as high as five TU-16s per month.)[80]

Of greater concern to the Japanese defense forces is the nuclear weapons program and the developing missile delivery capability of the PRC. It has been estimated that the gaseous diffusion plant located in Kansu Province was producing enriched weapons-grade uranium as early as 1963. The estimate of yearly output now stands at 272 kilograms with a projected capacity by the mid- to late 1970s of 363 kilograms (kg) annually. The available stockpile is estimated at 1,818 kilograms.[81]

The supply of plutonium is also reported to be sizable. The Yumen reactor is estimated to produce 205 kilo-

grams of plutonium 239 per year.[82] As this particular
plutonium-producing reactor has been in operation since
1967, it is believed that China has a "potential to deploy
nearly 300 nuclear warheads" if the capabilities of both
uranium and plutonium plants are combined.[83] The problem,
however, is somewhat complicated, as of the successful
tests to date, four have been in the three-megaton range,
three in the 200-to-300-kiloton (kt) zone, and the remainder 20 to 30 kilotons.[84] Perhaps as much as 200 kilograms
of U-235 has been expended in the tests to date; however,
using the available figures as to uranium and plutonium,
it soon becomes clear that China's problem is not one of
weapons but delivery against a concentrated target system
as in Japan. The actual number of warheads, of course,
would depend on the yield desired.

   If it can be assumed that China has the capability
to produce at least 300 20-kt warheads weighing less than
2,000 pounds, the delivery systems required to make this
power meaningful must be examined. The TU-16 bombers, already mentioned, dropped five 3-megaton (mt) devices during the test series[85] and offer a subsonic delivery capability covering all of Japan. It provides a credible
threat against Japan's air surveillance system, which reportedly is still manually operated for a major portion
of each day.[86]

   While the manned aircraft threat is fairly well perceived, the picture with regard to missiles is not quite
so clear. In January 1967, then Secretary of Defense
Robert S. McNamara indicated that the Chinese would have
"an initial intercontinental ballistic missile capability
in the early 1970's, and a modest force in the mid-70's."[87]
In a report of the Department of Defense (DOD) dated February 17, 1972, Secretary of Defense Melvin Laird indicated that the state of the PRC missile program appeared
"difficult to assess."[88] Alice Langley Hsieh, of the Institute for Defense Analysis, and William Wilson, of the
RAND Corporation, appearing before the Foreign Relations
and Foreign Affairs Committees of Congress indicated that
stress would probably be placed on medium-range ballistic
missiles (MRBMs) rather than ICBMs.[89] It is currently believed that 20 to 30 MRBMs have been deployed in northwest-
ern and northeastern China along with perhaps 15 to 20
intermediate-range ballistic missiles (IRBMs).[90] A 3,000-
mile IRBM is reported to be in some stage of testing.

   The exact status of ICBM development is now known,
but Secretary of Defense Laird estimated that 10 to 20
ICBMs could be deployed by mid-1976.[91] More recently an

independent researcher indicated that an operational ready date of 1978 would be possibly more feasible,[92] and the annual Defense Department report issued by Elliott Richardson estimated that, at the earliest, an initial capability by the end of the decade."[93]

The main implication for Japan, of course, is the possible further erosion of the U.S. nuclear deterrence once U.S. cities can be placed at risk by Peking decision-makers. According to U.S. Department of Defense estimates, the first ICBMs will be liquid fueled; however, a solid propellant plant reportedly has been constructed for second-generation missiles.[94] Any attempt to establish a second strike capability by producing Polaris-type submarines is felt by the DOD to be a decade away.[95]

For the near term, the TU-16 will be the mainstay of the Chinese delivery system operating from an adequate and dispersed air facility system. However, in the face of the U.S. nuclear deterrent, the Chinese will have to depend on "no-first-use" diplomacy, as it is the strategy of the weak. One is tempted to wonder, and possibly speculate, about the Chinese desire to realize an operational ICBM. As long as China does not threaten the United States with a viable long-range missile force, the U.S. guarantee to Japan remains theoretically credible. The day that China threatens the United States directly must be the time Japan looks very seriously at her long-postponed nuclear weapons option. As China with a 3,000-mile IRBM can threaten European Russia as well as the Indian subcontinent and Alaska,[96] it could be imagined that Peking is in no rush to force the issue and compound her encirclement as well as her nuclear defense.

It would not be beyond reason, given the sophisticated attitude of the Chinese toward nuclear weapons, which has been manifest since the Cultural Revolution, to credit Peking with a deliberate policy of delaying an operational ICBM so as not to pressure Japan into a weapon program.

Soviet Political, Military, and Economic Relationships to Japan

The breaking of the Russo-Japanese Nonaggression Pact in the final days of World War II, and the capture of South Sakhalin and the tiny islands of Etorofu, Shikotan, Kunashiri, and the Habomais ensured that the postwar relationship between Japan and the Soviet Union would eventually assume an irredentist character. This, of course, was not immediately important due to the status of Japan as an occupied state, but it has become an increasing ir- ritant to Japanese-Soviet relations and has become enmeshed in efforts to conclude a peace treaty, secure certain fish- ing rights, and jointly develop Siberian resources. In essence, Japan claims all four of the islands just north- east of Hokkaido while the USSR is willing to return two upon conclusion of a peace treaty, but not all four.[97]

The Northern Territories issue (as it is referred to in Japan) is not merely comprised of claims of ownership over the territory of the four islands mentioned above but also of the problem of fishing in the adjacent waters. Incidents between Soviet patrol boats and Japanese fishing trawlers entail obvious destabilizing features. According to the Japanese Foreign Ministry, since 1946, a total of 1,336 fishing boats have been captured in the contested waters. A total of 11,316 fishermen manning these boats were seized, and of the boats and men, 826 boats were re- turned with 11,265 fishermen. Twenty-two boats sank and 32 men were killed. In 1970 alone, 22 boats and 190 men were captured.[98]

In January 1972, as world attention turned toward the U.S.-Chinese détente, and the Japanese newspapers were filled to overflowing with items concerning China, Foreign Minister Andrei Gromyko visited Tokyo and was so unusually charming that his mission was immediately entitled one of "smiling diplomacy." During the course of his short visit, it was decided that the premiers of both nations would exchange visits but, more important, that peace talks would be held later in the year.[99]

The promised talks were held between Foreign Ministers Masayoshi Ohira of Japan and Gromyko of the Soviet Union in Moscow during the latter part of October; however, the two representatives ended their conversations deadlocked over the issue of the four islands. Japan continued to demand all four islands; the Soviets repeated their offer to return Shikotan and the Habomais. Further talks put off until 1973 also proved nonproductive.[100]

The Diet has gone on record calling for return of all four islands as a condition for a Japan-Soviet peace ac- cord, and according to former Prime Minister Tanaka, "even if the reins of Government are taken by any other politi- cal party than the LDP, the reversion of the northern ter- ritory will become the pre-condition for conclusion of a Japan-Soviet peace treaty."[101]

A related issue, possibly more important to the fu- ture of Soviet-Japanese relations than the ultimate outcome of the territorial issue, is the possibility for growing economic interdependence between the two states as envisaged in the various schemes for development of Siberian resources.

In 1970, Shigeo Nagano led a Japanese delegation to Moscow to attend the Fourth Annual Japan-Soviet Economic Committee meeting.[102] Significantly, at that meeting, the two sides pledged efforts toward development of Siberian resources. The Japanese were initially interested in natural gas from Sakhalin but were directed to the larger and more "suitable" gas deposits of the Yakutsk area.[103]

Talks concerning Siberian development have continued intermittently with occasional announcements by the Soviet trade representatives in Japan as to the "bright outlook for . . . cooperation."[104] Current areas of mutual interest include construction of an oil pipeline between Tyumen and Nakhodka and delivery of oil to Japan, development of Yuzhno-Yakutsk coal and gas deposits, prospecting for coal in South Yakutsk, and prospecting for oil and gas on the Sakhalin continental shelf.[105] According to a "government source," the USSR will ask the Japanese government to extend a $5 billion loan for joint development of oil, natural gas, and coking coal in Siberia. Estimates available at this time show that $2 billion would be used in the Tyumen project, $600 million for the South Yakutsk coking coal, $2 billion for Yakutsk gas (reduced considerably since U.S. firms have shown interest), and $1 billion for Sakhalin.[106]

Thus far, the government of Japan has insisted that private business carry most of the negotiating burden, and Tanaka stated to the Soviet side, "if talks between the private circles are successfully concluded, the offering of credit will be properly handled."[107] This initial arm's-length attitude reportedly displeased Soviet officials and a scheduled August 1973 trip of Tanaka to Moscow was requested postponed until September, supposedly due to dissatisfaction of the Russian side with the slow pace of Japanese business circles.[108]

The measured, slow pace of the Japanese side, so obvious in 1973, quickened after the events of October-November 1973 in the Middle East. By the spring of 1974, a basic agreement was reached regarding the project to exploit the coking coal of South Yakut, which included a $450 million credit to the USSR in return for 104 million tons of coking coal over a 20-year period starting from 1979.[109] By mid-July 1974 the Soviets had indicated a desire to order some 4,500 vehicles for the project including dump trucks, bulldozers, power shovels, boring machines, and so on for delivery in 1975.[110]

Spring of 1974 also brought an exchange of memos concerning Sakhalin continental-shelf-oil development. This agreement provided that prospecting would be conducted on the northeast and southwest parts of the continental shelf of Sakhalin and that Japan would provide $100 million for prospecting, would pay on success of Soviet efforts, and would obtain 50 percent of oil production. The question of natural gas was put off until further research into the economics of the matter could be considered.[111]

Progress has been much slower with respect to the Tyumen oil and Yakut natural gas projects. In fact, in late August 1974, the possibility existed that Japan would "give up the idea of participating in a Japan-Soviet joint project to develop oil fields in Tyumen . . . due to good prospects of oil from CPR."[112]

Chinese supplies were seen as going as high as 10 million tons by 1975 with a potential supply of 30 million tons hoped for in a few years.[113]

As the United States continued to show its reluctance to join this venture, Japan was hesitant also. It appeared that Japan wished a little commercial insurance in this project and would not move further until a U.S. commitment to participate could be obtained.[114]

The project for development of Yakut natural gas appeared to be one that might see independent Japanese action. The Soviets are eager to have Japan "go it alone," and, indeed, there was speculation that Japan might start prospecting after the winter of 1974-75 as the military implications of such an independent course were held to be slight.[115]

The Soviet Union must realize that depending on Japanese resources for development of Siberia and adjacent areas might place extra bargaining power at Tokyo's disposal, and if it is possible to turn these projects into leverage regarding the Northern Territory issue, it probably will be done. Generally, the situation regarding the Soviet Union and Japan is one of a status quo state (the USSR) attempting to ward off the irredentist activities of its island neighbor. The future course of Soviet-Japanese relations will not be easy to project, but it could be rationally suggested that with her European borders becoming more secure, the USSR might be willing to yield on the two remaining islands in return for wholehearted Japanese cooperation in Siberia. One must speculate that Japan's need for the oil and gas of Siberia and Sakhalin in the face of inordinate dependence on Mideast oil will tend to undermine her bargaining position vis-à-vis these islands for the near term. It is most likely that the dispute will go unresolved into the era of the 1990s.

The Soviet Military Threat to Japan

Until the unlikely day that Japan "tilts" toward the USSR in Northeast Asian power relationships, the military might of the Soviet Union remains a most formidable part of policy considerations. The "threat" of attack from Soviet forces is probably that contingency around which defense plans of the Japanese Self-Defense Force (JSDF) are based.[116] The total armed forces of the USSR stand near a figure of 3,375,000. Of these, 33 divisions (slightly over 500,000) are deployed along the regions adjacent to the Sino-Soviet border.[117]

Any direct invasion attempt of Japan would necessarily rely on the capabilities of the air and naval components to transport forces and maintain a favorable air and sea environment. Currently, the USSR has some 105 landing ships and numerous landing craft; the air force has approximately 1,700 transport aircraft as well as more than 800 troop-carrying helicopters. These facilities represent the beginning of a growing capacity for movement. The seven airborne divisions supported by tactical nuclear missiles, which are incorporated into the forces generally, would represent an exceedingly grave challenge if successfully delivered to Hokkaido beachheads.[118]

Former Director General of the Defense Agency Nakasone has stated his belief that a conventional landing on the home island would be defeated by the JSDF. Of course, the Japanese do not claim, at this point, to be able to defeat an all-out concerted attack on Japan. The strategy is for a capability to hold against such an all-out (conventional) attack for 15 to 30 days. Upon completion of the Fourth Defense Build-up, the capability will be extended somewhat further.[119]

While a conventional land attack supported by conventional air and sea forces must always present a serious problem for Japanese military planners, the ominous missile capability of Soviet Russia can, at present, only be countered by the U.S. commitment. The existence of this commitment was restated by ex-President Nixon at Guam in 1969, when he said, "We shall provide a shield if a nuclear power threatens the freedom of a nation allied with us.[120] This resolve was reiterated by the then president in his foreign policy report in May 1973.[121]

24

According to the International Institute for Strategic Studies, of the 700 MRBMs and IRBMs in the Soviet inventory, approximately 70 are programmed against targets in China and Japan. The Soviet Union could also designate a portion of available submarine launched missiles (currently totaling approximately 440) for Japanese targets as well as have available approximately 210 medium- and long-range bombers stationed in the Far East.[122]

The threat and continued presence of Soviet airpower is made manifest to the Japanese population on a regular basis. The so-called Tokyo Express and other less colorfully titled reconnaissance flights occur in a frequency range of from 50 to 150 times a year in the air space adjacent to Japan.[123] In the spring of 1970, in a rather clumsy but effective manner, the capabilities of the Soviet Far Eastern Air Arm were dramatized. On March 28, 1970, approaching bombing drills were announced by the Soviet Ambassador Oleg A. Troyanovsky.[124] These practice runs were scheduled to bracket the Japanese Islands to the north, west, and south. Certainly, if the Soviets could practice delivering conventional weapons in an area some 200 nautical miles off Shikoku Island, they could place at risk any target in Japan. After severe protests were made by the Foreign Office, the drills were finally canceled, on April 1, 1970.[125]

The largest number of Soviet planes ever to penetrate the Japan Air Self-Defense Force (JASDF) defense zone as a body was on May 16, 1973 when seven reconnaissance aircraft were observed over the Pacific and Japan Sea sides of Japan. The aircraft were TU-95s, AN-12s, and TU-16s.[126] This kind of constant probing contributes to a general awareness that is not lost on the Japanese people or their leaders.

The United States and Japan: The Changing Relationship

The account of U.S.-Japanese relations since World War II is a study that records the step-by-step efforts of Japan, first, to regain her internationally recognized sovereign status and, second, to enter into "genuinely equal relations" with the United States while remaining within the shelter of the U.S. nuclear umbrella. Events of the early 1970s clearly indicated that the goal of equality had been achieved. A long chain of events marked at intervals by the conclusion of significant treaties and occasionally by the retrocession of former Japanese territory preceded the fact of genuine equality, but the pact for the reversion of Okinawa in May 1971 followed by the initiatives of President Nixon in July of the same year were historic notices that equality had been achieved.

Equality did not come without certain costs to the bilateral relationship. Japan evinced a growing skepticism concerning the U.S. resolve to honor its nuclear defense commitment while some Americans criticized the so-called free ride Japan was getting regarding defense expenditures. Frequent discord occurred over economic and trade matters during this same era, and on occasion even the highest elected officials of the two nations appeared to have doubts about the nature of the alliance.

The principal event that can be considered the watershed in dividing the old era from the new took place in November 1969. At that time President Nixon met Prime Minister Sato, and the U.S. president promised to return Okinawa to Japan. In the joint communiqué issued on November 21, the two leaders "agreed to consult with a view to accomplish the reversion during 1972."[127]

If this 1969 meeting was immediately successful regarding Okinawa, it did not quite form a foundation for rosy cooperation. A major economic issue centering on the textile industries of both countries had developed over the large quantities of woolens and synthetic textiles entering the United States. The U.S. textile industry had taken a position favoring import quotas and had argued their case so effectively that then Commerce Secretary Maurice Stans had attempted to obtain voluntary controls by European and Asian producers. These initial efforts were to no avail, but U.S. pressure continued to be applied, especially toward Japan. As Japan was providing 29 percent of the textiles imported into America at that time, it became plain that to induce Japan to restrain its output might have beneficial effects on other producers.

Reportedly, at the summit, Nixon and Prime Minister Sato reached a basic "understanding" on this matter.[128] According to the Japanese press, Sato said, "It is strange that there should be so much fuss over the textile issue. I'll take care of it."[129] Whether the translator gave the correct emphasis and nuance to Sato's words is not known, but the textile dispute was not resolved until October 15, 1971 and caused much ill feeling.[130]

While difficulty was being experienced regarding the textile issue, progress was made with respect to Okinawa; a reversion agreement was concluded between the two governments and was based on the joint communiqué of November 1969. The knotty problem of nuclear weapons and Okinawa was solved by extending the three non-nuclear principles of Japan to Okinawa making it impossible to possess, manu- facture, or introduce nuclear arms into its territory.[131]

Practically one month after the Okinawa Reversion Agreement was signed and while the textile issue still served as a "serious irritant in . . . relation[s]," the United States announced the president's intention to visit Peking. The Japanese reaction to this has been described in the opening section of this paper. The incident be- came known as the first of the "Nixon shocks" of 1971, and set off a train of events resulting in the first of two yen revaluations.[132] Sato, who had described the Okinawa agreement as "the birth of a new era" for the United States and Japan had obviously not realized that the "child" would grow up so soon.

By the time January 1972 arrived, the leaders of the two states obviously had things to discuss. At San Cle- mente on January 6 and 7, 1972, Sato and Nixon met and de- cided on the final date for Okinawa's return to Japan.[133] Conversations also were held covering subjects such as the scheduled trips to Peking and Moscow by Nixon, the question of the U.S. failure to consult Japan prior to the announce- ment of the Peking trip and the ever pressing economic mat- ters.[134]

On May 15, 1972 Okinawa officially regained its status as part of Japan,[135] and soon thereafter (July 5, 1972) Sato retired and was replaced as prime minister by Kakuei Tanaka.[136] Tanaka pledged to continue efforts to normalize relations with China as well as to solve the outstanding international economic problems.[137] His task was made somewhat easier when two giant economic organizations of Japan (Keidanren and Kankeiren) publicly announced that they were pressing the new government to correct the trade imbalance with the United States as soon as possible.[138]

President Nixon met with the new Japanese prime minis- ter in Hawaii from August 31 to September 1, 1972. The two agreed to relieve the trade problems (through emergency purchases of $1.1 billion of U.S. goods) and discussed Tanaka's scheduled trip to Peking.[139]

While the session seemed rather successful with the cited measures being taken to mollify the trade imbalance, which had been in Japan's favor since 1965, Nixon, in the May 1973 U.S. Foreign Policy Report, repeated the theme that Japan must perform as an economic and political equal of the United States.[140] In particular, he stated,

The easing of the Cold War military confrontation
has brought other aspects of power--economic, in
particular--to the forefront of the international
political stage. U.S. military protection no
longer suffices as the principal rationale for
close partnership and cooperation.

Japan's emergence is a political fact of
enormous importance. Japan is now a major factor
in the international system, and her conduct is
a major determinant of its stability.[141]

The presidential report continues, "Our abandoning
our paternalistic style of alliance leadership meant not
that we are casting Japan or any ally adrift, but that we
took our allies . . . as full partners."[142] Nixon emphasized that the United States was no longer the status quo
power with regard to the U.S.-Japanese relationship but
that the United States itself was determined to embark on
a drive to correct the "enormous imbalance in our bilateral trade."[143]

Although grateful for the achievements reached concerning synthetic textiles, steel, and access to markets
besides agreements for increased purchases from the United
States of agricultural goods, civil aircraft, uranium enrichment services, and military items, Nixon was obviously
pressing for a complete equalization of the economic sector. He asserted, in the report, that the "U.S. can only
place the highest importance on the carrying out of these
policies,"[144] and in one of the most striking comments of
the report noted that, "without conscious effort of political will, our economic disputes could tear the fabric of
our alliance."[145]

The Japanese press, for so many years the outspoken
critics of the security treaty, were disturbed by the report, and the foreign minister was reportedly "shocked by
the Nixon Report."[146] Nevertheless, he set the Foreign
Ministry to work to produce a study, similar to the U.S.
report, as a sophisticated answer to the questions raised
in the study.

In a most penetrating understatement concerning the
report, Foreign Minister Ohira said, "America, in spite
of its close relationship with our country, does not understand us so well."[147] The obvious purpose of the May foreign policy report was once again to emphasize to the leaders of Japan, and all the informed public, that Japan was
in actuality no longer a junior partner. The entire series
of "Nixon shocks," blunt economic dialogue, and seemingly

insensitive political actions by the Nixon administration
were attempts to destroy the old "special relationship"
that existed between teacher and star pupil in order to
create a newer, more appropriate relationship--the kind
that comes of graduating with honors.

Has this new relationship resulted in a weakening of
the security community that has existed between the two
countries? The exact nature of a security community has
been defined by Karl Deutsch and K. J. Holsti as "those
areas where relationships between independent or integrat-
ing political units are predictably peaceful, and where
conflicts are resolved by compromise, avoidance, and
awards rather than by force."[148] Further, the main indications of the presence of a security community are said to
be "(1) where the policy-makers of two or more political
units, and their societies in general, cease to contemplate
the possibility of mutual warfare, (2) where the two or
more states cease to allocate resources for building military capabilities aimed at each other," and " mutual acceptance and vigorous observance of certain rules of international law and bilateral treaties when collective objectives of the units are not in harmony."[149]

The bilateral relations of the United States and Japan
have paralleled the above criteria in an absolute fashion.
Especially noteworthy was the action of the United States
to carry out the return of Okinawa during the period of aggravated disharmony over economic matters and the ancillary
positive reaction of the Tanaka government toward measures
to remove the trade imbalance. While this imbalance cannot be eliminated overnight, the Japanese resolve to cooperate with the United States has been indicated by two yen
revaluations, a liberalized capital investment principle,
large agricultural purchases, and a promise to reduce the
trade imbalance by at least $2 billion a year.

The conclusion must be that the U.S.-Japanese security
community continues to exist and may have been made stronger
as a result of the maturing relationship. Very real benefits are to be obtained by its long-term maintenance. It
offers extensive markets for both nations, which are now
first and third in gross national product (GNP) in the
world. It affords to Japan a nuclear guarantee within the
U.S.-Japanese Security Treaty permitting that country to
spend less than 1 percent of its GNP for defense. It provides the United States with access to South Korea and
Taiwan and a stability in Northeast Asia that has permitted
a gradual withdrawal of U.S. forces from the area.

Bilateral trade, which increases yearly, stood at a total of 4,139,783,000,000 yen by 1970. Main categories of exports to the United States were fish and fish preparations, raw silk, plywood, silk fabrics, pottery, iron and steel, machinery, clothing, and toys. The principal imports were wheat (unmilled), soybeans, cotton (ginned), iron and steel scrap, coal, heavy oil, and machinery.[150]

The mutual dependencies that exist regarding bilateral trade and the mutual benefits to be gained by a continuation of the security structure, plus the growing similarities in both societies help to create an environment that is indicative of a long-term relationship of mutual gain.

It would seem that most scenarios incorporating a Japanese nuclear weapons program must also consider some deterioration of the existing security community. Realistically a nuclear weapons program could not be attempted by Japan without either (1) abrogation of existing U.S.-Japanese Atomic Cooperation treaties or (2) full cooperation of the United States. If full cooperation were to be expected, it would be far easier for the Japanese to buy the requisite number of warheads and fit them to the applicable delivery systems, but this would imply the complete disintegration of the current U.S.-Soviet détente, and the existence of perhaps a completely altered international system. Abrogation of existing atomic power agreements also could not be contemplated unless significant system changes had occurred due to Japan's extreme dependence on the United States for uranium and enrichment services. (The nature of this dependence will be addressed at length in Chapter 3.)

Comments thus far have concentrated on presenting a general review of the nature of political, economic, and military relationships among the primary actors of Northeast Asia. It is conceivable that nonregional factors could have an even greater impact on future Japanese policy decisions than matters limited to her regional relationships. It is appropriate, before turning to an examination of the nuclear question on Japan's domestic scene, to review some of the nonregional questions that could be of vital concern to the national interests of Japan.

JAPAN IN HER NONREGIONAL ENVIRONMENT

Dependence on Mideast Oil

Japan is dependent on foreign countries for 99 percent of its crude oil and on international petroleum capi-

30

tal for 90 percent of its crude imports. Eighty-seven percent of all this oil comes from the Mideast, and the total amount of crude oil that Japan can obtain without going through the gigantic international corporations is a mere 10 percent.[151] The oil over which Japan has some control comes mainly from Arabia Oil and North Sumatra Petroleum Development; however, some small domestic capability is included. This autonomously developed oil will amount to approximately 34.7 million kiloliters in 1972-73.[152]

The crude oil requirements for 1973 were seen as reaching 282,594,000 kiloliters, only 900,000 kiloliters of which is domestically produced. The fiscal year 1974 stockpile was set at 41,076,000 kiloliters, or enough to meet demand for 55 days.[153] The average annual increase in overall crude oil requirements was seen at 10.4 percent from the fiscal year 1972/73 base.[154]

The importance of oil is magnified when it is realized that the yearly capacity of hydroelectric power plants is decreasing in relation to overall electric requirements. Atomic power plants have only recently begun to contribute to generation capacity. Five atomic power plants are on line at present.

The above statistics have led some analysts to conclude that the politics of oil will be far more crucial in determining Japanese defense and nuclear policy than the degradation of the U.S. nuclear umbrella or the development of trade, economic, or political conflict in the NEA arena. One school of such defense thought in Japan, in line with such concern for energy resources, has called for a greater capability to defend Japan's vulnerable sea lanes that stretch from the Persian Gulf through the Straits of Malacca to Japan. In particular, the crucial issue of the continued use of the Malacca Straits has been debated widely with the costly detour through the Straits of Lombok becoming almost common knowledge.[155] This issue itself surfaced when Indonesia announced it would require tankers of more than 200,000 tons to "detour through the Lombok and Macassar Straits." The government of Japan responded by expediting a Japanese financed survey of the passageway so that greater safety measures might be taken.[156]

During the 1973 Middle East war, Japan assumed a policy that definitely supported the Arab side, hoping to gain relaxed restrictions on the supply of Mideast oil.[157] However, she found that even in the face of her political precautions she was forced to take unusual austerity measures to reduce domestic demand.

While the cutoff of oil by Japan's principal suppliers can no longer be discounted, there is a general feeling that by the use of alternative sources of power, especially atomic, future dependencies can be reduced, though never eliminated. Great hope is placed in Siberian, Alaskan, Manchurian, Indonesian, and continental shelf oil reserves of Northeast Asia. (These latter reserves, of course, include those located in the vicinity of the Senkaku Islands currently claimed by Japan, the PRC, and Taiwan. It remains to be seen if the spirit of détente will extend to the exploitation of oil.)*

Japan and Southeast Asia

Southeast Asia and the nature of future Japanese policy, be it nuclear or non-nuclear, are linked in several ways. First, Southeast Asia is important to Japan, as the vital life-line of oil, as mentioned above, goes through the Malacca Straits. Japan desires that access to that water passageway be kept as secure and unhindered as possible. Second, Southeast Asia is important to Japan as a source of crude rubber, crude oil, tin, and other minerals, maize, and oil seeds; SEA also is an ever growing market for Japanese goods.

The relationship of trade with SEA to overall trade in 1970 was close to 10 percent for both exports and imports. As an area, SEA had a slightly unfavorable balance

---

*Some commentators have noted that U.S. needs for Middle East oil, which currently stand at about 3 percent of U.S. demand, could conceivably rise to 40 to 60 percent of U.S. consumption by the mid-1980s. This, coupled with Japan's dependence on Middle East oil, which stands at 87 percent, places the two energy-consuming powers on a collision course. Japanese editorial comment has gone so far as to say, "If the current trends continue unabated, the possible outbreak of a future 'Japan-U.S. war over Middle East oil' cannot be completely ruled out." (Asahi Evening News, January 16, 1973.) The U.S.-Japanese agreements of January 1973 to work jointly on solving energy questions, and the November 1973 "Operation Independence" program announced by then President Nixon to provide the United States assured sources of energy by the mid-1980s tend to reduce the likelihood of such a collision, in the view of this observer.

of trade with Japan in 1970.[158] However, in some states, Thailand in particular, reaction to the nature of the imbalance has been increasingly critical. (Thailand registered a 2.59-to-1 ratio in 1969, and a 1.93-to-1 in 1971.[159] The most significant demonstration of this growing irritation with lopsided trade occurred in the period November 20-30, 1972, when university students in Thailand sponsored a nationwide boycott of Japanese goods.

News of the boycott was received in Tokyo with concern and, of course, much national self-examination. The situation was viewed as serious enough to send the Minister of International Trade and Industry, Yasuhiro Nakasone, to the January 1973 meeting of the Japan-Thai Trade Committee.[160]

The boycott and other unfavorable press coverage of the activities of individual Japanese in Southeast Asia gave rise to speculation that similar anti-Japanese sentiment could one day possibly result in significant loss of life to a Japanese business community abroad. In such a situation it was hypothesized that an aroused Japan would rise up as one and militarily crush the wrongdoers, be they in Bangkok, Manila, or Singapore.

Whether such a scenario is valid will not be debated at this point in the paper, but it is introduced to indicate the nature of current Japanese-SEA relations and the fact that areas of discord and potential conflict do exist.

Thailand is not the only SEA nation that is unhappy over the degree of Japanese business enterprise. In May 1971, a "high trade official" in the Philippine government went so far as to charge Japan with "economic aggression."[161] He lamented the fact that Japan was "turning the archipelago into a source of raw material supply for Japanese industry."[162]

There also is much dissatisfaction among all the SEA nations concerning Japanese aid and the manner in which it is given. Criticism centers on three significant points: (1) official development aid provided by Japan is scanty; (2) technical cooperation is the lowest among all aid-giving nations in the Development Assistance Committee (DAC); and (3) terms are attached to the aid.[163]

As alarming as this presentation might seem, the Japanese relationship with SEA is still sound, with local attitudes toward Japan "generally favorable" in such countries as Singapore, Malaysia, the Republic of the Philippines, and Indonesia, as the influx of Japanese business has been somewhat better controlled than in Thailand.[164] However, there are obvious reasons for not taking Japanese-

33

SEA relations for granted, as nationalism in this area is high and the Japanese find themselves often far too visible. The violent reaction to Tanaka's "goodwill" tours of Southeast Asian states in 1974 only underlines the critical nature of Japanese relations with these essential suppliers of raw materials. In this environment, the area that has been called the Balkans of the Orient could indeed give Japan serious moments. (This writer must be extremely skeptical, however, when it comes to linking SEA with the main impetus for a nuclear weapons policy by Japan.)

The data in this chapter have attempted to reveal, however sketchily, some informed Japanese perceptions of the changing international environment and Japanese impressions as to the possible role of nuclear weapons to ensure Japan's security. Additionally, a glimpse of the major political, economic, and military relationships existing between Japan and the principal powers of Northeast Asia has been presented to show the current and possible future nature of bilateral relations with Japan. Finally, comments have been introduced concerning Japan's admitted dependence on overseas sources for the natural resources demanded by a modern industrial society, especially oil.

While these external factors may be significant in causing Japan to select a nuclear option, it must be stressed that, without reviewing the nature of this question as a domestic issue, the analyst would not be operating with all of the critical factors. Next, therefore, the domestic political context of the nuclear question will be discussed.

NOTES

1. Harold C. Hinton, Communist China in World Politics (Boston: Houghton Mifflin Company, 1966), pp. 85-86.
2. Winberg Chai, The Foreign Relations of the People's Republic of China (New York: Capricorn Books, 1972), pp. 123-30.
3. Thomas W. Robinson, The Sino-Soviet Border Dispute: Background, Development, and the March 1969 Clashes (Santa Monica, Calif.: RAND Corporation, 1970), pp. 6-7.
4. Hinton, op. cit., pp. 41-44.
5. Robinson, op. cit., p. 9.
6. Ibid., pp. 33-43.
7. Chou En-lai reportedly holds the view that 1.3 million Soviet troops are on the Sino-Soviet border. The International Institute for Strategic Studies (IISS) lists

33 divisions in the Sino-Soviet border area and 28 in the Caucasus and West Turkestan, for a total of approximately 910,000. International Institute for Strategic Studies, The Military Balance 1971-1972 (London: International Institute for Strategic Studies, 1971), p. 6.

8. Mainichi Daily News, August 29, 1970.

9. Ibid., October 1, 1970.

10. For a recent alarmist account see Joseph Alsop, "Will Russia Attack China?" Readers' Digest, August 1973, pp. 77-82.

11. See particularly the Asahi Evening News, or Asahi Shimbun, of February 21, 1972.

12. U.S. Department of State, Treaties and Other International Acts Series (Washington, D.C.: Government Printing Office, 1952), no. 2491; and Dean Acheson, Present at the Creation (New York: W. W. Norton, 1969), p. 544.

13. Dan Kurgman, Kishi and Japan (New York: Ivan Obolensky, 1960), p. 326.

14. U.S. Department of State, "Treaty of Mutual Cooperation and Security with Japan," Department of State Bulletin, February 8, 1960, pp. 179-81.

15. U.S. Department of State, "U.S. and Japan Reaffirm Common Objectives and Pledge Continued Cooperation," Department of State Bulletin, December 4, 1967, pp. 745-47.

16. Richard M. Nixon, U.S. Foreign Policy for the 1970's (Washington, D.C.: Government Printing Office, 1970), pp. 55-60.

17. U.S. Department of State, "President Nixon and Prime Minister Sato of Japan Hold Talks at Washington," Department of State Bulletin, December 15, 1969, p. 556.

18. Takeshi Muramutsu, "Japan's Choice," a presentation delivered by Muramutsu in Philadelphia, Pa. at the 5th International Arms Control Symposium, p. 2. Ambassador Asakai reportedly dreamed, evidently quite often, that the United States would recognize China while he slept.

19. Ibid., and Minoru Omori, "First Danger Produced by U.S.-China Conference," Chuo Koron, June 1972, pp. 273-86.

20. Takeshi Muramatsu, "Is the Security Treaty Effective?" Jiyu, July 1972, pp. 10-19.

21. Muramatsu, "Japan's Choice," pp. 21-24.

22. Ibid.

23. Junnosuke Kishida, "Non-Nuclear Japan: Her National Security and Role for Asian Peace," an address delivered at the Peace in Asia Conference, Kyoto, Japan, June 1972, and "Japan Should Not Have Nuclear Weapons," Jiyu, April 1972, pp. 66-73. The third article was "Japan's

Non-Nuclear Policy," <u>Survival</u>, January/December 1973, pp. 15-20.

24. Kishida, "Non-Nuclear Japan," p. 1.

25. Kishida, "Japan's Non-Nuclear Policy," p. 16.

26. Ibid., p. 17.

27. Ibid., p. 18.

28. Ibid.

29. Hisao Iwashima, "Trends of Peace Research and Military Studies in Japan," an address presented at the Convention of the International Studies Association in Dallas, Texas, March 14-18, 1972.

30. <u>Yomiuri</u>, July 10, 1971, U.S. Embassy translation.

31. <u>Mainichi</u>, January 16, 1972, U.S. Embassy translation.

32. Iwashima, <u>Trends</u>, p. 8.

33. Yonosuke Nagai, "The Pitfalls of Allied Diplomacy," <u>Chuo Koron</u>, January 1972; Hidekazu Kawai, "The Tri-Polar Structure and Japan's Diplomacy," <u>Economist</u>, New Year 1972; Hiroharu Seki, "The End of the Era of Yoshida's Followers," <u>Chuo Koron</u>, February 1972; Masamori Sase, "The Foreign Policy Principles of a Medium Nation--Japan," <u>Jiyu</u>, March 1972; as summarized by Mitsuo Yagisawa, "In the Magazines," <u>Japan Quarterly</u>, April-June 1972, pp. 272-37; and Osamu Miyoshi, "Japan's Defense and the U.S. Troop Pullout," <u>Ryudo</u>, February 1971, as summarized by Misao Obuta, "In the Magazines," <u>Japan Quarterly</u>, April-June 1971, pp. 226-28.

34. <u>Bungei Shunju</u>, February 1972, U.S. Embassy translation.

35. Ibid.

36. <u>Nihon Keizai</u>, October 3, 1972, U.S. Embassy translation.

37. <u>Yomiuri</u>, June 15, 1972, U.S. Embassy translation.

38. <u>Nihon Keizai</u>, October 4, 1972, U.S. Embassy translation.

39. Ibid.

40. Richard M. Nixon, <u>U.S. Foreign Policy for the 1970's</u> (Washington, D.C.: Government Printing Office, May 3, 1973), p. 95.

41. <u>Survival</u>, November/December 1972.

42. <u>Mainichi Daily News</u>, October 27, 1970.

43. Ibid., November 19, 1970.

44. Ibid.

45. Ibid., December 11, 1970.

46. <u>Chosa Geppo</u>, January 1973, p. 7.

47. <u>Asahi Evening News</u>, July 17, 1971.

48. <u>Mainichi Daily News</u>, July 23, 1971.

49. *Asahi Evening News*, October 5, 1971.

50. Ibid., November 12 and December 9, 1971.

51. Ibid., January 17, 1972.

52. Ibid., July 1, 1972.

53. *Asahi*, July 19, 1972, U.S. Embassy translation.

54. Ibid.

55. *Mainichi Daily News*, July 22, 1972.

56. "Sino-Japanese Communiqué," *Survival*, November/December 1972.

57. *Sankei*, March 27, 1973, U.S. Embassy translation.

58. *Japan Times*, April 21, 1974.

59. *Nihon Keizai*, March 6, 1973.

60. *Japan Times*, April 23, 1974.

61. Ibid., May 8, 1974.

62. Ibid., May 10, 1974.

63. Foreign Broadcast Information Service (FBIS), April 29, 1974.

64. *Yomiuri*, June 10, 1974, U.S. Embassy translation.

65. *Tokyo Shimbun*, June 20, 1974.

66. *Sankei*, June 21, 1974, U.S. Embassy translation.

67. *Kanagawa Shimbu*, July 9, 1974, U.S. Embassy translation.

68. *Daily Yomiuri*, July 28, 1974.

69. *Asahi*, July 21, 1974, U.S. Embassy translation.

70. Ibid., September 6, 1974.

71. Ibid.

72. *Yomiuri*, June 11, 1973, U.S. Embassy translation.

73. See especially the *Yamato Shimbun*, May 16, 1973, U.S. Embassy translation.

74. *Japan Almanac 1972* (Tokyo: Mainichi Newspapers, 1972), p. 450.

75. Martin E. Weinstein, *Japan's Postwar Defense Policy, 1947-1968* (New York: Columbia University Press, 1971), pp. 111-12.

76. U.S. Department of State, *Issues-Profile of Mainland China* (Washington, D.C.: Government Printing Office, 1969), p. 4.

77. The International Institute for Strategic Studies, *The Military Balance, 1972-1973* (London: IISS, 1972), pp. 41-42.

78. Ibid.

79. U.S. Senate, "U.S. Security Agreements and Commitments Abroad, Japan and Okinawa" (Washington, D.C.: Government Printing Office, 1970), part 5, p. 1208.

80. IISS, *Military Balance*, pp. 40-42.

81. Charles H. Murphy, "Mainland China's Evolving Nuclear Deterrent," *Bulletin of the Atomic Scientists*, January 1972, p. 29.

82. Ibid.

83. Ibid.

84. Chosa Geppo, September 1973, p. 33.

85. Ibid.

86. Michael Bryant Hughes, "Japan's Air Power Options: The Employment of Military Aviation in the Post-War Era," Ph.D. Dissertation, Fletcher School of Law and Diplomacy, Tufts University, August 16, 1972, p. 336. Hughes explains that the system is operated at its optimum for only 10 to 12 hours per day. The major limitation seems to be computer support, which may be upgraded during the current build-up plan.

87. Robert S. McNamara, "A 'Light' ABM System," in Readings from the Scientific American: Science, Conflict and Society (San Francisco: W. H. Treeman and Company, 1969), p. 341.

88. Melvin R. Laird, National Security Strategy of Realistic Deterrence (Washington, D.C.: Government Printing Office, 1972), p. 44.

89. U.S. Senate, ABM, MIRV, SALT and the Nuclear Arms Race, Hearings before the Subcommittee on Arms Control, International Law and Organization of the Committee on Foreign Relations, 91st Cong., 2d sess. (Washington, D.C.: Government Printing Office, 1970), p. 150; and U.S. House of Representatives, United States-China Relations: A Strategy for the Future, Hearings before the Subcommittee on Asian and Pacific Affairs of the Committee on Foreign Affairs, 91st Cong., 2d sess. (Washington, D.C.: Government Printing Office, 1970), p. 129.

90. IISS, Military Balance, p. 44.

91. Laird, op. cit., p. 45.

92. Murphy, op. cit., p. 32.

93. Elliott Richardson, DOD Annual Report FY 1974 (Washington, D.C.: Government Printing Office, March 29, 1973), p. 37.

94. Laird, op. cit., p. 46.

95. Ibid.

96. Richardson, op. cit., p. 37.

97. Ministry of Foreign Affairs, Japan: The Northern Territories Issue (Tokyo: Ministry of Foreign Affairs, 1970), p. 20.

98. Mainichi Daily News, February 2, 1971.

99. Asahi Evening News, January 28, 1972.

100. Ibid., October 24, 1972.

101. Tokyo Shimbun, June 15, 1974; and Mainichi, July 4, 1974, U.S. Embassy translations.

102. Mainichi Daily News, February 18, 1970.

103. Ibid., March 13, 1970.
104. Asahi Evening News, November 6, 1971.
105. Sankei, June 18, 1973, U.S. Embassy translation.
106. Ibid.
107. Yomiuri, June 6, 1973, U.S. Embassy translation.
108. Ibid.
109. Asahi Evening News, May 22, 1974.
110. Nihon Keizai, July 15, 1974.
111. Nikkan Kogyo, July 13, 1974.
112. Daily Yomiuri, August 30, 1974.
113. Ibid.
114. Asahi Evening News, August 13, 1974.
115. Ibid.
116. See Asahi Evening News, December 7, 1973, for re-inforcement of this hypothesis.
117. IISS, Military Balance, p. 6.
118. Ibid., p. 7.
119. Yasuhiro Nakasone, The Defense of Japan, Japan Defense Agency, October 1970, p. 86. See the book Nihon Retto Shubitairon (Tokyo: Asagumo Sha, 1972) by Osamu Kaihara, for a realistic appraisal of current Japanese capabilities to fight a major land battle. Most of his criticism is based on the inordinately low stocks of ordnance (ammunition) to accompany the relatively sophisticated weaponry available. His dismay is substantiated to a certain extent when the weapons and ammunition procurement figures are reviewed for fiscal year 1973. Only sixty 750-pound bombs are scheduled for the Japan Air Self-Defense Force for the entire year! (Boei Tokushin, May 15, 1973.)
120. Nixon, op. cit., p. 55.
121. Ibid., p. 110.
122. IISS, Military Balance, pp. 5-7.
123. Nihon no Boei, p. 77.
124. Mainichi Daily News, March 28, 1970.
125. All Japanese newspapers from March 28 to April 1, 1970 devoted significant coverage to this incident. See especially the Asahi Evening News for the period involved.
126. Nihon Keizai, May 31, 1973, U.S. Embassy translation.
127. U.S. Department of State, "President Nixon and Prime Minister Sato of Japan Hold Talks at Washington," Department of State Bulletin, December 15, 1969, p. 556.
128. Mainichi Daily News, March 4, 1970.
129. Ibid., December 15, 1970.
130. About this matter President Nixon wrote, "This issue, which had important political and economic aspects in both of our countries, had become a serious irritant in

our relations. After many months of hard negotiations which admittedly had an adverse effect on the general atmosphere between us, the agreement of October 15 resolved this vexing issue." Department of State Bulletin, March 13, 1972, p. 342.

131. Mainichi Daily News, June 18, 1971.
132. Department of State Bulletin, December 18, 1972.
133. Ibid., January 31, 1972, p. 118.
134. Ibid., p. 119.
135. Ibid., June 12, 1972, pp. 809-10.
136. Asahi Evening News, July 5, 1972.
137. Ibid., July 7, 1972.
138. Ibid.
139. Department of State Bulletin, September 25, 1972, pp. 329-40, and Asahi Evening News, September 1 and 2, 1972.
140. Nixon, op. cit., pp. 94-105.
141. Ibid., p. 96.
142. Ibid., p. 99.
143. Ibid.
144. Ibid., pp. 101-02.
145. Ibid., p. 102.
146. See especially Yomiuri, May 5, 1973; and Mainichi, May 14, 1973, U.S. Embassy translations.
147. Yomiuri, May 7, 1973, U.S. Embassy translation.
148. K. J. Holsti, International Politics (Englewood Cliffs, N.J.: Prentice-Hall, 1967), p. 478.
149. Ibid., p. 479.
150. Japan Almanac 1972, pp. 455-56.
151. Ibid., pp. 140-41.
152. Ibid.
153. Nihon Kogyo, March 13, 1973, U.S. Embassy translation.
154. Ibid.
155. Tokyo Shimbun, May 5, 1972, U.S. Embassy translation.
156. Ibid.
157. Asahi Evening News, November 22, 1973.
158. Japan Almanac 1972, p. 448.
159. Asahi Evening News, January 23, 1973.
160. Ibid., January 22, 1973.
161. Ibid., December 9, 1972.
162. Asahi Evening News, December 9, 1972.
163. Ibid., December 2, 1972.
164. Ibid., November 27, 1972.

2

THE DOMESTIC
POLITICAL ENVIRONMENT

The internal factors that contribute to the characteristics of societal will regarding the nuclear question in Japan are extremely important and must be thoroughly evaluated in any attempt to assess future Japanese nuclear policy. In this chapter, several key elements have been selected for review. First, the legal barriers are described that stand in the way of those who would pursue the nuclear option. Second, attitudes and policy of the major political parties are examined. And finally the positions of business and the informed public are reviewed.

LEGAL BARRIERS

When speaking in terms of a nuclear option for Japan, one of the first obstacles that must be dealt with by any proponent of nuclear weapons is Article IX of the Constitution of Japan, dealing with war potential. This article binds the government of Japan to renounce war as a means to resolve disputes. Article IX reads as follows:

> Aspiring sincerely to an international peace based on justice and order, the Japanese people forever renounce war as a sovereign right of the nation and the threat or use of force as means of settling international disputes.
>   In order to accomplish the aim of the preceding paragraph, land, sea, and air forces, as well as other war potential, will never be maintained. The right of belligerency of the state will not be recognized.[1]

Since 1957, the government of Japan has interpreted this restriction as pertaining only to offensive weapons, thus allowing the potential development of defensive nuclear weapons. This position was stated by Prime Minister Nobusuke Kishi on May 7, 1957 and was reaffirmed before the House of Councillors Special Korea Committee on December 3, 1965.[2] The chief of the Legislative Bureau, while testifying before this body, said,

> If it is a weapon with the justifiable objective of defense of the nation and it is not possible to cross borders [with it], the Constitution does not prohibit its possession. It is clear that the Constitution does not permit possession of nuclear weapons like atomic bombs because of their general characteristics. However, at the same time, if, for argument's sake, there is a nuclear weapon that conforms to the above characteristics, for the advancement of scientific technique, etc., in that case, theoretically possession would not violate the Constitution.[3]

This position was restated in the October 1970 Defense Agency White Paper "The Defense of Japan." This document, which remains in effect, not having been superseded, states:

> With regard to nuclear weapons, we adopt the three point non-nuclear principle. Even though it would be possible to say that in a legal and theoretical sense possession of small nuclear weapons, falling within the minimum requirement for capacity necessary for self-defense and not posing a threat of aggression to other countries, would be permissible, the government, as its policy, adopts the principle of not attempting nuclear armament which might be possible under the Constitution.[4]

Most recently (March 1973), the issue of defensive nuclear weapons was discussed by then Prime Minister Tanaka. The subject was raised at a Budget Committee meeting of the Lower House on March 13, 1973, at which the prime minister had stated, "Nuclear weapons are offensive weapons and against the Constitution."[5] However, the next day, the government of Japan presented its unified view on the matter saying that the Constitution did permit tactical nuclear weapons.[6]

Several days later, at the Budget Committee of the Upper House, Tanaka was interpellated regarding the statement, much preferred by the "progressive" Diet members present, that "nuclear weapons are offensive weapons, and our country's possession of nuclear weapons runs counter to the Constitution."[7] The reply given by the Prime Minister follows:

(1) If within the scope of self-defense, nuclear weapons will not run counter to the Constitution, (2) however, since nuclear weapons are considered to be offensive weapons, generally, they run counter to the Constitution, and (3) the Government will firmly maintain the Three Non-Nuclear Principles and will not carry out nuclear armament.[8]

On March 20, at the same forum, Tanaka, in response to further interpellation stated, "We will firmly maintain the policy, based on the three non-nuclear principles. . . . We will not be able to hold offensive nuclear weapons, but it does not mean that we will not be permitted to hold nuclear weapons at all."[9]

The Cabinet Legislative Bureau Director General was reported to have said at the same meeting, "It is difficult to judge whether they [nuclear weapons] are offensive or defensive weapons."[10] However, he indicated that a device such as a nuclear mine to defend against forces landing in Japan would be defensive. Japan Defense Agency Defense Bureau Director General Takuya Kubo added that "nuclear mines and anti-air missiles against attack by another nation can probably be called defensive weapons."[11]

The government, by insisting it possesses the necessary constitutional authority for defensive nuclear weapons, has thereby indicated that a constitutional amendment would not be required to initiate a limited nuclear program. Such a position seems to be based on the pragmatic awareness of the extreme difficulties associated with accomplishing a constitutional amendment under the present political climate, which witnesses almost yearly the gradual erosion of the Liberal Democratic Party (LDP) plurality.

Amendments to the constitution are technically possible but must be initiated by the Diet and be approved by two-thirds or more of all the members of each house. If concurrence of the Diet is obtained, the issue is submitted to the electorate and requires a majority of all votes cast.[12]

43

While the call for revision of the constitution has
been a dead issue almost since the merger of the Liberal
and Democratic parties, on occasion it reappears. In
October 1969, it was repeated by Takeshi Sakurada, an influential businessman, and, more recently, by Yasuhiro
Nakasone. Nakasone (the current minister for International
Trade and Industry) on June 21, 1971, while at the Officer
Candidate School of the Ground Self-Defense Force (GSDF),
was quoted as saying in his then capacity as director of
the Defense Agency:

> In view of international conditions, the reversion
> of Okinawa does not necessarily mean the termina-
> tion of the post war period. There is the China
> problem and the problem of revising General Mac-
> Arthur's reforms again. There is an indication
> that the Constitution, as one of his big reforms,
> will be re-examined and revised in the future,
> though not at the present moment. It is natural
> that the Constitution should be re-examined after
> our one million compatriots are returned to the
> fatherland.[13]

While the constitution, even as interpreted by the
government of Japan can stand as a most formidable obsta-
cle to any groups that advocate an offensive nuclear capability for Japan, the Atomic Energy Law leaves even less
room for interpretation:

> Article 1. The objective of this Law should
> be to secure energy resources in the future, to
> achieve the progress of science and technology
> and the promotion of industries by fostering the
> research, development and utilization of atomic
> energy and thereby to contribute to the welfare
> of mankind and to the elevation of the national
> living standard.
> Article 2. The research, development and
> utilization of atomic energy shall be limited to
> peaceful purposes and performed independently un-
> der democratic management, the result therefrom
> shall be made public to contribute to international
> cooperation.[14]

It becomes apparent from a reading of Article 2 that
any program, defensive or offensive, that included proposals to develop a nuclear capability for nonpeaceful ob-

jectives would contravene the intent of the Atomic Energy Basic Law. Preliminary to such a program a revision of this law would be necessary. Whether this would be possible even though the LDP has consistently held more than 55 percent of the seats in the lower house will become more apparent in the following chapter.

Finally, while constraints on the nuclear option are being considered, there are some additional policy statements made by representatives of the government of Japan that should be recalled. On January 30, 1968, Prime Minister Sato at the 58th Regular Session of the Lower House announced the Kaku yon Seisaku (Four Nuclear Principles) Policy.[15] The four points announced as government policy were (1) the Three Non-Nuclear Principles (not to manufacture, possess, or allow the importation into Japan of nuclear weapons), (2) efforts toward nuclear disarmament, (3) dependence on the nuclear deterrent power of the United States based on the U.S.-Japanese Security Treaty, and (4) peaceful use of nuclear energy.[16]

Subsequent to the enunciation of the Three Non-Nuclear Principles as government policy, they were incorporated into a Diet Resolution. This occurred on November 24, 1971 and was part of an agreement between the LDP and opposition parties to resolve basic misgivings of the opposition over the Okinawa Reversion Agreement between the United States and Japan.[17] Only the LDP, Komeito, and Democratic Socialist Party (DSP) took part in the vote; the Japan Socialist Party (JSP) and the Japan Communist Party (JCP) absented themselves.[18]

Prime Minister Sato, while in office, maintained that the Three Non-Nuclear Principles were not only a policy of his cabinet but had been "established as . . . national policy to be retained by my successors."[19] Indeed, in his first speech as Chairman of the Japan Atomic Energy Commission in July 1972, on the event of the Tanaka Cabinet's inauguration, Nakasone stated, "The Government will continue to abide by the three Non-Nuclear Principles."[20] This policy was also reconfirmed by Prime Minister Tanaka et al., in the March 1973 united government position noted previously.

All regulations are subject to interpretation by public officials in the course of implementation or execution. This interpretation is then scrutinized by the body politic. If reaction is passive enough, or even enthusiastic in support, the interpretation stands. The record is clear enough concerning the gradual development of ground, sea, and air "defense forces" in Japan. Whether such a similar development would ever occur in Japan with respect to the production of a "peaceful" nuclear device will depend on the domestic political situation. An analysis of the political climate and some of the internal political considerations that contribute to the determinants of decision-making follows.

THE LDP AND THE NUCLEAR QUESTION

A clear understanding of the internal dynamics of Japan's governing party, including a perception of the various power centers within the party, is necessary in order to assess adequately future trends concerning the nuclear option. The LDP has governed Japan since the merger of the Liberal and Democratic parties on November 15, 1955[21] and, in all likelihood, will continue to govern throughout the era of the 1970s, barring any unforeseen factional conflict leading to the collapse of the historically effective coalition.

As pointed out in the excellent surveys of the conservative party of Japan by Thayer, Hellmann, and Fukui,[22] the key to the study of the LDP is precise data regarding the factions that abound within that party.

Factions in the LDP

After the general elections of December 1972, the relative factional strength was as follows: Fukuda faction, 55 members; Tanaka faction, 48 members; Ohira faction, 45 members; Nakasone faction, 37 members; Miki faction, 36 members; Shiina faction, 18 members; Mizuta faction, 13 members; Funada faction, 9 members; Ishii faction 9 members; Hayakawa affiliated group, 3 members; Fujiyama affiliated group, 2 members; and 7 members nonaligned, including Eisaku Sato.[23]

Fukuda's faction, the largest, has many senior Dietmen among its membership; it has an average age that approximates 61 years. In the July 1972 party election for the three-year term as president of the LDP, which in essence means prime minister, Fukuda lost in a head-on battle with Kakuei Tanaka. By virtue of this loss in the party election, the Fukuda faction became an anti-mainstream group (the opposition within the LDP) but was asked to participate in the cabinet to aid in healing the very strained relations that had developed.

46

Going into the December 1972 lower house elections, the Fukuda faction had a strength of 65. Possibly overstepping its capabilities in order to increase factional strength, it backed 78 candidates in the election. Of these 78 only 55 were elected. The losses suffered were probably not a result of a lack of funds, as the Fukuda faction in 1971 received 947 million yen in contributions from Japanese business interests, which made it the wealthiest faction in the LDP in 1971.[24]

The Tanaka faction is the second largest in the LDP, with 48 members. The average age is 52 years, which places it second in terms of youthfulness in the party. Tanaka, as stated above, won the July presidential election by forming an alliance with the Ohira, Miki, and Nakasone factions. Although not the chosen successor of Prime Minister Sato, Tanaka was able to obtain the support of some 75 percent of the 62 members of the former Sato faction[25] and is probably the richest of all groups today. In 1971 it was reported that 855 million yen was given by business interests to this faction and its related study groups.[26] In the December elections, 59 candidates ran with Tanaka's backing and 48 were elected. This represented a net gain of five and demonstrated considerable strength in view of the total LDP showing in December 1972.

The Ohira faction in 1972 had 45 members. Due to its early support of Tanaka in the LDP presidential election, the Ohira faction generally feels that it has an advantage for the next presidency of the LDP. This faction received the third largest amount of money from business in 1971, but due to its rather large membership the per-member sum amounted to only 11.7 million yen; this is rather less than other major factions on a member basis. The Ohira group supported 52 candidates in the December 1972 elections and was successful in 45 cases, for an increase of one.

The Nakasone faction is the youngest group, with an average age somewhat under 52 years. Its leader is the outspoken and dynamic Yasuhiro Nakasone, who moved to support Tanaka in his bid for the party presidency in the summer of 1972. His support was given to Tanaka, even though Fukuda comes from the same prefecture as Nakasone, and the failed opportunity to establish a Gumma ken "dynasty" was not lost on the voters of that particular prefecture.

The "bullishness" of Nakasone has become a cause for concern among members of the faction that has a collective leadership composed of Umekichi Nakamura, Yoshio Sakarauchi, Sadanori Yamanaka, and Buichi Oishi, in addition to Nakasone. As competition within the faction increases, so will its centrifugal tendencies.

One very encouraging indicator for the Nakasone faction has been its improving relations with business and general access to financial contributions. Total contributions during 1971 were 438 million yen, which computes to 12.8 million yen per member. While this total sum is fifth among the 10 factions, it represents a 166 percent increase over funds raised in 1970.[27] Further, this faction backed 47 candidates in the 1972 elections and 37 were successful, producing an overall gain of three. With rising success at the polls, its increasing ability to attract financial support, this faction, if it can survive the aggressive style of its leader, seems to be destined to enjoy a decade of prosperity.

The Miki faction, consisting mostly of former Progressive Party members, has an average age of almost 56 years. It is currently in the mainstream but is rather weak in its connections with business financial sources. Contributions amounted to 445 million yen in 1971 or 11.1 million yen per member, somewhat less than the average.

In the 1972 elections this faction suffered a setback second only to that experienced by the Fukuda faction. Starting with 40 members in the Diet the faction supported 52 candidates but was successful in only 36 cases. One of the main characteristics of this faction is that most members are not former bureaucrats.[28]

The remaining four factions, led by Funada, Mizuta, Ishii, and Shiina, have a total of 45 members. They demonstrate varying degrees of success in obtaining financial support from big business, running from the enviable 29.1 million yen per member for the Funada group to the relatively meager 4.6 million yen per member for the Shiina faction. (The small amount garnered by the Shiina faction did not prevent it from increasing its membership in the 1972 elections by one, whereas the Funada group was reduced by one.)

Although there is not necessarily a direct correlation between amount received and relative political power, it is interesting to note that business confidence in a faction seems to go hand in hand with the contribution provided. The policies that prompted the contribution, however, may differ. With the Fujiyama faction, the forward-looking position of this ex-businessman on normalization of relations with China might have been important, but that same factor did not seem so helpful to the other small factions that espoused a similar line. The 166 percent increase over 1970 is also an interesting phenomenon in the case of the Nakasone faction. The policies pursued by Nakasone that prompted this sudden inflow could be associated with his strong advocacy of Japan-developed armaments, his program of autonomous defense, or the unusual magnetism and general nationalism of the man.

To compensate for the fact that factional association does not necessarily mean ideological compatibility in all areas, suprafactional groups are continuously being organized. Some spring up to deal with one specific issue; others are more long-term and general in nature. The most important of these suprafactional groups as far as this study is concerned is the body called the Soshinkai (Pure Hearts Society). This society stresses nationalism and anticommunism and has particularly high representation from the "Sato, Fukuda and Ishii factions."[29] This organization has been adamantly opposed to ratification of the Nuclear Nonproliferation Treaty (NPT), and, on occasion, has played a significant role in slowing--almost stopping--any forward movement toward reaching consensus on the ratification of the NPT within the LDP.[30]

Other examples of factional organizations aligned on interest or ideological grounds are the Shishikai and the Shoshikai. The Shishikai, an organization originally based on Diet tenure, was formed by 47 first-year Dietmen in 1971. This group has had a decidedly hawkish or conservative outlook and has worked hard for the Yasukuni Shrine Bill.[31]

The Shoshikai, on the other hand, was formed in reaction to the Shishikai by approximately 22 first-year Dietmen who were characterized as rather dovish in policy orientation. The Shoshikai was formed as a policy research organization.[32]

In the last several years, this "doves" and "hawks" cleavage has been particularly significant in relation to the considerable debate that has developed over the U.S.-Japanese Security Treaty in relation to the Japanese government's moves toward accommodation with China. The "doves" in the Security Treaty debate have stressed the point that the agreement is part of a treaty system that was a product of the cold war and that, in the light of recent international developments, the treaty structure should be weakened.

The "hawks" fear that, since the Taiwan-Japan Treaty has been abrogated by Japan, the security treaty must not be changed substantially. To do so, argue members of this group, would be to risk a major Far East security crisis.[33]

Generally it appears that members of the 1970 Problems
Research Council with Chairman Kosaka and a "young peoples'
group" including Ohira and Nakasone are indicating that
the reexamination of the security treaty is necessary
while an "older group" centered around the Anzen Hosho
Chosa Kai (the National Security Research Council) with
Chairman Kaneshichi Masuda wishes to concentrate policy
toward the realization of a state secrecy preservation law
and studies on the relationship of the UN Charter to the
Constitution of Japan.

While it is admittedly difficult to make categorical
classifications as to policy preferences of the various
factions, certain long-time observers of the Japanese political scene have identified the Tanaka, Fukuda, and
Ishii factions with certain right-wing policy goals. Some
of these are connected with establishing a greater defense
capability for Japan, support for the U.S. alliance, and
the desire to realize the restoration of traditional values
of nationalism.*

The Ohira faction has been called centrist[34] and the
Nakasone, Shiina, Funada, and Mizuta factions have been
called "middle-of-the-road factions."[35] The old Matsumura
faction, now reduced to one member, Shigetaro Susayama,[36]
was considered furthest left.[37] Yoshikazu Sunata, writing
in the Mainichi Daily News in 1970 summed up the true position of ideology in factional alignment:

> There exist, indeed, differences of opinion among
> the various factions on important problems . . .
> but it is nonetheless quite rare for all the mem-
> bers of one faction to entertain opinions entirely
> different from those held by other factions. Such
> differences of policy matters are not necessarily
> important when compared with the intensity of per-
> sonal antagonism and rivalry in the incessant
> power struggle.[38]

Leadership of the current factions has changed markedly even compared with the July 1968 accounting found in

---

*Two issues will illustrate what is meant by "restora-
tion of traditional values": (1) The absence of any legal
base for the continued use of the imperial era dating system has caused concern among some of the LDP; and (2) the
bill calling for the nationalization of Yasukuni Shrine
are two examples.

Nathaniel B. Thayer's record of the LDP leadership role in Japan.[39] The reader's attention is directed to the Fukuda, Tanaka, and Ishii factions (total current strength, 112) whose members are attracted particularly to the suprafactional conservative organizations.

Defense Policy and the
Policy-Making Process in the LDP

What has emerged from interfactional interface as the basic LDP view toward defense and particularly the question of nuclear weapons? Over the years, the factions with good business connections and large financial contributions have tended to advocate strong defense positions for Japan while those not so positive on defense (the Miki faction, for example) have found access to funds not as readily available. Some observers of the Japanese political scene have indicated that this has resulted in those "poorer" factions being forced into a more compromising position than they might prefer.[40]

The LDP, as the party in power, has called consistently for the gradual modernization of the Japanese Self-Defense Forces (JSDF); it has desired that the U.S. alliance be maintained, although increasingly delimited to achieve increased autonomy for Japan and greater delineation of U.S. responsibilities. Regarding the nuclear question, the LDP supported enactment of the Basic Atomic Energy Law, which, as mentioned previously, restricts atomic power to peaceful uses and requires that everything connected with the atomic energy program be open for public review. It has supported the Three Non-Nuclear Principles articulated by former Prime Minister Sato as well as the signing and ratification of the Antarctic Treaty (1959-60), the Partial Test Ban Treaty (1963-64), and the Outer Space Treaty (1967). The signing of the Nonproliferation Treaty was accomplished on February 3, 1970,[41] but consensus within the party to allow ratification has not developed. The Treaty Banning Military Utilization of the Sea Bed was signed February 11, 1971, and ratification was completed on June 21, 1971.[42]

In addition to these rather well-known accomplishments, the Japanese government with LDP approval has been extremely active in the UN Conference of the Committee on Disarmament (CCD). In meetings of this group, both Ambassadors Hiroto Tanaka and Masahiro Nishibori have advocated the conclusion of a treaty for the comprehensive prohibi-

tion of nuclear weapons tests.[43] The position advocated
in these meetings is that "realization of the comprehensive
prohibition of nuclear weapons tests is the crux of nuclear
disarmament."[44]

Ambassador Nishibori directly addressed the question
of underground nuclear weapon tests in a presentation of
March 28, 1972, maintaining that "even small-scale underground nuclear tests" can be detected.[45] Theoretically,
he indicated that is is "possible to detect even an underground nuclear test of about one kiloton in hard rock."[46]

The position of the LDP, because at its apex it is
also the government, with respect to defense policy generally and nuclear weapons policy specifically can be demonstrated as indicated above. The party has been quite em-
phatic in its opposition to offensive nuclear weapons both
on the domestic scene and internationally.

The Determination of Policy

The process of policy formulation within the LDP has
been treated in a comprehensive fashion by Nathaniel Thayer,
Donald Hellman, and Paul Langer in their books. In this
study, as it relates primarily to the question of the
nuclear question, major emphasis will be placed on those
agencies in the LDP that have responsibilities in the security national defense field.

Within the LDP, two bodies, the National Defense Division (Kokubo Bukai) and the National Security Research
Council (Anzen Hosho Chosa Kai) are charged mainly with
defining security problems for the party, assessing alternatives, and making recommendations concerning possible
countermeasures or courses of action.[47] This is not to
say that only these two groups touch such matters. Other
committees or investigation councils obviously have overlapping interests; for example, the Japan-China Diplomatic
Normalization Consultative Council, the Foreign Affairs
Council, the Special Committee on Military Base Problems,
the Committee on the Nuclear Nonproliferation Treaty, and
others, all consider problems related to national security.
The confusion that could attend such an organization is reduced somewhat by joint sessions, as occasionally members
belong to more than one committee interested in the subject.

The actual party organization for policy formulation
is keyed around the Policy Affairs Research Council (Seisaku Chosa Kai) whose present chairman is Zentaro Kosaka.
All decisions or recommendations of the National Defense

52

Division and the National Security Research Council must
be processed through the Policy Affairs Research Council
and its chairman. He ranks as one of the top four men in
the LDP besides the president, who is also the prime minister when the party is in power. The chairman of the Public
Affairs Research Council has five vice-chairmen, usually
filled by one member each from the major factions. Within
the Policy Affairs Research Council are 15 divisions each
with its own chairman and three vice-chairmen.[48]

In LDP policy formulation, policy recommendations
flow upward from the divisions, special committees or investigative commissions to the Deliberation Commission,
which, upon approval, submits its findings to the party
Executive Council. The Executive Council seldom reverses
a Deliberative Commission recommendation. From the Executive Council the policy goes to the cabinet for final approval.[49]

The 61-member National Security Research Council, under
Kaneshichi Masuda as chairman,[50] has become the primary
sounding board for the intra-LDP security policy debate
with almost all LDP policy statements dealing with security
bearing its stamp. This council considers a broad range
of policy topics, and in 1972 its agenda included questions
relating to the U.S. 7th Fleet, Korea, Taiwan, the northern
territories and the security of Japan, the threat of nuclear
attack against Japan, and the NPT. Other, more general
matters are also matters of interest, such as creation of
an all-encompassing security policy, enhancement of national defense awareness, consolidation and strengthening
of an autonomous defense structure, resolution of relationship of the UN Charter and the constitution (can troops be
dispatched overseas to participate in UN actions?), the
creation of a Japan-U.S. Defense Committee, the enactment
of a state secrecy preservation law, consolidation and
strengthening of a central information agency, and so on.[51]

While the National Security Research Council has assumed a major role in policy formulation on these grand
matters, the 43-member National Defense Division (NDD)
under the chairmanship of ex-general Minoru Genda considers
the more technical, less policy-oriented questions of national defense.[52] Due to the basically controversial nature of defense matters in Japan, only Diet members with
an interest in defense are attracted to membership in the
Defense Division. This situation tends to produce a group
of individuals most sympathetic to the requests of the
Defense Agency and less critical than might be warranted.
This leads frequently to National Defense recommendations

that must be diluted at higher party levels to make them palatable to the party and nation as a whole (this also happens on occasion in the National Security Research Council).[53]

The National Defense Division is responsible for reviewing "all proposed legislation concerning military matters; all structural, organizational, and administrative changes affecting the Self-Defense Forces; all questions relating to military equipment; and--most important among the NDD responsibilities--all budgetary matters."[54] Of course, this last function encompasses the review of the annual budget draft and the various five-year plan requirements.

The NDD suffers from an ailment common to most advanced representative governments. With the ever advancing technical nature of defense, the members of the National Defense Division do not possess the expertise nor the time actually to initiate measures but have come to rely on the experts of the Defense Agency.[55] This dependence on the military for technical advice does not seem as marked in the National Security Research Council, since generally the measures considered by that body deal with broad policy considerations.

By examining some of the past policy reports of the LDP, primarily originating in the National Security Research Council, it may be possible to gain a clearer insight concerning the LDP defense policy formulating process, as well as examine the evolution of this policy especially as it concerns nuclear arms.

LDP Policy Statements

The LDP since its founding in 1955 has held steadfastly that the U.S. alliance be maintained, although it has consistently advocated the achievement of increasing autonomy and delineation of U.S. responsibilities. With the same amount of consistency it has attacked the JSP position of unarmed neutrality as unrealistic. As an example of a particularly scathing attack on the JSP during the era of the great debate on the revision of the Security Treaty, the LDP Policy Affairs Research Council accused the JSP of advocating a policy that was contradictory and recommended that the JSP leaders observe the real condition of the world, where even Sweden, Switzerland, and India had military forces. The policy statement pointed out that even little Iceland was in NATO.[56]

While calling for an increased defense establishment and following through with the First through Fourth Defense Build-Up Plans, the LDP has also been quite clear and consistent regarding the question of nuclear weapons for Japan. In 1963, for example, the National Security Research Council of the LDP in an interim report entitled "Research Related to the Guarantee of Security" stated a thesis quite in line with the no-war provisions of the Japanese Constitution when it held that it was no longer suitable for a state to use war as a means of prosecuting national objectives, since war had become accompanied by total national mobilization and use of nuclear weapons. A war, the report stated, would be a catastrophe for civilized mankind.[57]

The report was preceded by some information that provides a valuable insight into the decision-making process. Evidently the function of reviewing security policy and defense-related questions was being accomplished by ad hoc groups composed of volunteer members who periodically gathered in roundtable discussions to research and exchange points of view. In 1962, the introduction to the report states, this ad hoc characteristic was deemed inappropriate in view of the serious nature of the problems involved, and on March 27, 1962, a formal apparatus was established within the Political Affairs Research Council. The National Security Research Council was established; its first meeting was held on April 20, 1962. After more than 30 "enthusiastic" meetings and deliberations, an interim report was approved for release in July 1963. Consensus was obtained, evidently, neither quickly nor quietly.[58]

The advent of a successful Chinese nuclear test on October 16, 1964[59] brought about a period of keen introspection on the part of the LDP. In December 1964, the LDP National Security Research Council published its position vis-à-vis this new dimension of the nuclear age, and some anxiety was apparent. The report revealed more information regarding the internal mechanism of joint meetings and the time required for the various levels of party hierarchy to approve policy recommendations. Entitled "Policy That Our Country Must Take to Counter the Effect to the Security of Our Nation of the Chinese Nuclear Test as Well as Soviet Policies,"[60] the report was the result of a decision of the National Security Research Council on November 18, 1964. A joint session of the Foreign Affairs Division (sectional meeting), National Defense Division (sectional meeting), Special Committee for Public Peace and Order Countermeasures, Diplomatic Affairs Research Council, and the National Security Research Council was held on December 8 and approved the recommendations. On the next day (December 9, 1964) the Deliberation Commission accepted it, and the Executive Council of the LDP approved it on December 18, 1964.[61]

Although no date was indicated to reveal the total deliberation period, it can be assumed that the meetings of the National Security Research Council started after the October 16 nuclear test in China.

The policy proposal called for a wait-and-see attitude toward the Chinese program and offered the comforting advice that "it would require many years before Chinese nuclear weapons could be a major force."[62] The report, above all, called for no hasty outcry from Japan and proposed as countermeasures the following four points:

> 1. Make the belief in liberal democracy stronger.
> 2. Strengthen the security guarantee structure within Japan.
> 3. Hold on to the Japan-American security structure.
> 4. Lecture the people so they will not panic in the event of a nuclear threat from China or the USSR.[63]

Through the countermeasures, it was hoped the following would be produced:

> 1. An increased national understanding and support of the policy.
> 2. A situation which would not produce an inferiority complex toward China or the USSR while going ahead with peaceful development of space satellite, rocket and atomic power technology.[64]

Six months later a meeting of the National Security Research Council was held that was attended by well-placed bureaucrats of the Foreign Office, Defense Agency, and others, plus one U.S. visitor. Specifically, giving their opinions on the subject "The Far East Situation and the Security of Our Country" were the U.S. Bureau Chief and China Section Head from the Foreign Ministry, Public Safety Research Agency Vice-Chief, Chairman of Joint Staff of the Defense Agency, and the one U.S. visitor, State Department Policy Planning Chief Walt W. Rostow.[65] From the composition of the speakers at this particular meeting, the extremely important role played by the bureaucracy in data input for policy consideration can be readily seen.

This session's orientation was not directly toward the nuclear question, but it did suggest six points for increasing the overall security structure of Japan:

1. Strengthen the policy of the LDP.
2. A law for the protection of secrets must be enacted.
3. Establish a Security Guarantee Conference and dissolve the National Defense Conference.
4. Strengthen the central organization for information publicity.
5. Create a Japan-American joint Defense Committee for investigation of joint defense plans.
6. Strengthen the police power for defense and public security.[66]

While the measures recommended above are based on broad security interests, the report toward the end is more specific regarding nuclear policy; it recommends that the country should hold to the U.S.-Japanese Security Treaty and "rely on that to be effective militarily." It also suggests that "Japan should take a warning from the state of nuclear development of China and the strategic nuclear forces of the Soviet Union."[67]

It is evident that by mid-1965 the LDP was concerned with the growing threat from a nuclear China and the USSR. In a policy statement of June of that year by the National Security Research Council, a bipartisan foreign policy was urged for the nation in order to meet the threat of Soviet/ Chinese forces. It was realized that it would be no small task to achieve consensus, since all parties would have to consolidate attitudes independently.[68]

The report met the nuclear issue directly and concluded with policy recommendations that were surprisingly candid. The Research Council observed that Japan must hold firmly to the Japanese-U.S. security structure for "if Japan attempted to defend the nation's security by itself in the environment of Chinese nuclear development and expansion of the nuclear war power of the Soviet Union, it would eventually be necessary to produce nuclear weapons."[69] It further noted that if the number of nuclear-weapons-producing states increased after China's entry into the nuclear club, then the necessity of Japan's producing nuclear weapons would increase.[70]

Having considered or at least mentioned unilateral defense and the nth-country dilemma, the council recommended that Japan attempt, by diplomatic means, to halt the tendency toward nuclear spread and observed that Japan "must surely be exempt from nuclear threats from other countries," as it would remain under the nuclear umbrella of the United States and maintain the U.S.-Japanese Security Treaty.[71]

In June 1966, another interim report was issued by the National Security Research Council. In explaining the gathering of the data the council noted that it had concluded scheduled hearings by the end of April but, at that time, was surprised by the unexpected publication of the JSP andthe DSP policy positions during the first part and middle part of May respectively. Because of the publication of the opposition policy the council felt it necessary to proceed as fast as possible. It noted that in the writing of the report numerous opinions were gathered from inside the party and that from the beginning it had sat in general session and requested that all LDP Diet members state their opinions frankly and without reservations.[72]

As hearings continued a subcommittee of three persons drafted the report; in this manner, the council believed that the maximum possible progress in the deliberations was accomplished. According to the introduction, the meetings continued at a very enthusiastic level, for example, three committee meetings at the climax of the debate took place in the "dead of night." The report was finally issued on June 22, 1966, a period almost two months from the end of hearings and some eight months from initiation of the study.[73]

From the above it is obvious that there were some differences of opinion and that some of these were felt keenly. Additional data on what actually constituted the main differences are available concerning this particular policy report.[74] Evidently the interim report was drafted by the "rightist faction" (not further identified but possibly the Soshinkai) of the LDP, and attributed to Vice-Chairman Zenshiro Hoshina of the council. The draft took a very strong position on rearmament and incorporated the following proposals:

1. The Security Treaty be extended for another 10-year period and be so revised after the expiration of the period as to continue to hold good by five years automatically
2. Article 9 of the Constitution be amended so that Japan can maintain a self-defense force to cooperate with an international peace system of self-defense purposes,

3.   That introduction of nuclear arms into
Japan be admitted [suggestion].
4.   That an anti-espionage law be enacted and
a central counterintelligence organ be established.[75]

During the course of arriving at a consensus for the
interim report, the participants included only the first
point, a 10-year extension of the security treaty. Some
oblique reference to nuclear arms was made in relation to
policy options that included armed neutrality, but there
was nothing like that called for in point 3 of the Hoshina
draft.[76]

The section of particular relevance to this study was
entitled "The Guarantee Against the Threat of Nuclear Aggression."[77] In this portion the reliance on the U.S.
nuclear umbrella was reiterated.

The security of Japan has been affirmed by the Sato-
Johnson joint communiqué as well as the provisions
of Article 5 of the Japan-U.S. Security Treaty that
U.S. nuclear power [will be used] against the
threat of nuclear aggression, apprehension of which
has been increasing in our country. By this U.S.
guarantee there is not a degree of doubt that
U.S. deterrent power is the principal means to
prevent a nuclear attack against our country before anything happens.[78]

The release of the interim report resulted in some
criticism by the "neutrals" or "leftists" of the LDP.[79]
A draft counterpolicy was issued under Kosaka's name and
contained the following points:

1.   That automatic extension of the Security
Treaty is more recommendable, since it will remain
in force for an indefinite period.
2.   That . . . confronting the leftist camp
by perpetuating the Security Treaty for another
10 years will provoke the crisis of 1970.
3.   That establishment of a Japan-U.S. Joint
Defense Commission . . . is unnecessary.
4.   That the policy for securing the nation's
safety should not be limited to its military phase,
but elimination of poverty should serve as . . . a
new system of national security.[80]

In this series of events it is possible to see the complete process of the LDP right and left interaction. The latent power of the rightists was demonstrated when the nuclear question and constitutional revision issues were placed on the draft interim report. However, it seems more significant that the ultraconservative LDP members did not possess the power to halt a temporizing revision.

In 1968 the National Security Research Council published a 547-page book entitled Trends Toward the 1970s.[81] In this report the committee addressed various subjects such as "The Situation in North Korea" and "The Condition of the Soviet Military." Of specific interest to the scope of the present study was the chapter dealing with "The Ability of Japan to Produce Nuclear Weapons." This 1968 study points out the real problems to be faced by any Japanese program. For example, the report examines Japan's ability with respect to warhead production, availability of uranium and plutonium, and development costs and problems of missile fuel.[82] The program costs for a five-year ICBM development program were estimated to be $1.464 billion with $139 million for a uranium enrichment (gaseous diffusion) plant.[83]

The analysis, presentation of technical difficulties, and cost estimates, made in 1968 dollars, certainly do not indicate an attempt to consider lightly the difficulties involved; however, the costs do seem a bit optimistic.

In 1969 the basic adherence to the Three Non-Nuclear Principles of Prime Minister Sato by the LDP was reiterated in a policy release in April. In the article, under a section entitled "Nuclear Weapons and Autonomous Defense," the LDP position was again made quite clear. It was, in essence, to base nuclear defense on the U.S.-Japanese security system and continue with conventional arms for Japanese forces.[84] This position was restated in July 1970.[85]

During the campaign for the House of Representatives at the close of 1972, the LPD's platform, or party pledge, on foreign policy and defense was as follows:

It shall be the basis of foreign policy to deepen peaceful and friendly relations with various nations of the world and ensure the peace and security of our country. However, under the present situation where the easing of tension is not in a stable condition, it is insufficient to ensure peace and security with diplomacy alone. There-

fore, while maintaining the Security Treaty structure with the United States, we will possess effective defense power of our own.[86]

It is possible to make some broad observations from
the information presented of LDP nuclear policy since the
early 1960s. The LDP recommendations relative to defense
have been made after a high degree of bureaucratic input,
both civil and military; they have been made after broad
LDP Diet-member participation; they have often been accompanied by keen debate; they have taken place primarily
in the National Security Research Council, which appears
strongly conservative in nature; they must be approved by
the Deliberation Commission of the Policy Affairs Research
Council and the Executive Council of the LDP; and arriving
at a consensus can take, as seen in the above cases, from
several months to a year or more.
    The agreed-upon policy has been characterized by two
interrelated points: dependence on the U.S. alliance to
provide an acceptable Northeast Asian environment, and
within that context, a firm resolution by a majority of
the party not to advocate the development of nuclear weapons or to allow their possession or importation into
Japan. This latter policy has been followed in the face
of the proponents of more rapid rearmament or even nuclear
arms for defense.
    The proponents of such a policy within the LDP tend
to be, as demonstrated in the 1966 draft report, older men
with military or bureaucratic training. (Hoshina was an
ex-vice-admiral.) Of course there are exceptions such as
Shintaro Ishihara, who, although not backed as an official
LDP candidate in the 1972 elections, ran as an independent,
was reelected, and later rejoined the LDP Parliamentary
Party. He is reported to have very close ties with the
Nakasone faction.[87] This young man, with anything but a
military or bureaucratic background (he is a popular novelist), has advocated strongly the development of nuclear
weapons by Japan for use in diplomatic bargaining. Ishihara has written[88] that Japan is not covered by the U.S.
nuclear umbrella, which, he considers, in actuality, covers
only the United States and a part of Canada. He feels
that, when China obtains ICBMs, Japan will become a medium-
level nuclear state such as France with the most likely
force being built around nuclear-powered submarines carrying multiple independently targeted reentry vehicles
(MIRVs). Ishihara contends that to base the security of
Japan on weak treaties is not only stupid but may bring
about treasonous results.[89]

Another individual, who is not quite as flamboyant as Ishihara, is former Chief of the Air Self-Defense Force General Minoru Genda, long-time head of the National Defense Division and member of the House of Councillors. Genda's position on nuclear arms has been explained to this writer as quite cautious; however, he is reported to have maintained that as a military man he can see certain advantages to possession but recognizes possible political and economic drawbacks.[90]

Former Prime Minister Kishi is also seen as a leader of the heavy rearmament school of thought.[91] (Whether in his case that includes advocacy of nuclear arms is not clear.) He caused a national sensation in 1957 when he indicated in the Diet that defensive nuclear weapons would not contravene the consitution.[92]

Yashuhiro Nakasone, one-time Director of the Defense Agency and current head of the influential Ministry of International Trade and Industry was once described in a Japanese Who's Who as the "most radical advocate of rearmament and the man who advocated the so-called 'Atom Pile Budget.'"[93] In 1971 he was reported to have said (while director of the Defense Agency) that "there can be introduction of nuclear weapons at a time of emergency."[94] When asked about this statement in the Diet, Prime Minister Sato replied that it could not occur as he would be the responsible official and would veto it.[95] (Nakasone does not advocate nuclear weapons--he came to this conclusion in August 1969[96]--but one wonders how closely he has read the three non-nuclear principles.)

While not in the LDP Parliamentary Party, others who act as advisers to various factions in the LDP and, of course, appear at hearings of the investigative committees do take a prodevelopment position. Akio Doi, a former general and now the head of a Tokyo-based research group, the Continental Problems Research Agency, takes a position very similar to Ishihara in that such weapons would be useful diplomatically.[97]

In April 1968, in the book The New Strategy and Japan, he wrote that for a defensive country like Japan, nuclear weapons are best. Holding the option that ABM and other weapons systems have demonstrated the defensive nature of nuclear weapons, Doi advocated such weapons for Japan as they have inherent deterrence value and will also contribute to assisting any U.S. defense of Japan. The particular attributes of tactical nuclear weapons were stressed--for example, their value to defeat a large army with a good small one, their capability against human-wave tactics and any attacks coming from the sea, and so on.

Doi emphasized the value of tactical nuclear arms but also indicated that for true deterrence, strategic weapons are needed. If the United States will not provide such weapons, Doi recommends as alternatives joint possession with countries such as Australia or the Philippines or independent ownership by Japan. The advantages of a joint program with Australia, for example, are that expenses and test sites can be shared.

The time frame for possession envisaged by this nuclear advocate is by the middle 1970s; Doi comments that Japan's being the third largest industrial nation in the world is reason enough for having nuclear weapons.[98]

In 1966 Shigeru Fukutome, a former vice-admiral, wrote several well-conceived articles advocating nuclear weapons. In the first, written in April, he recommended that the U.S.-Japanese Security Agreement be revised so that, according to circumstances, authority could be given for introduction into Japan of U.S. nuclear arms. He also suggested that careful consideration be given to nuclear armaments for Japanese Self Defense Forces. In July of the same year he wrote, "The nuclear umbrella held by the U.S. must surely be useful, but for complete faith there is the nuclear umbrella opened by oneself."[99] He noted that it is "disheartening" to place deterrent power in the hands of another country, even though it is an allied power.

Fukutome expanded his theme slightly in the third article written in September to advocate more conclusively that Japanese forces might be able to use autonomously any nuclear weapons introduced into the country by U.S. forces. This would contribute to the military power of the U.S.-Japanese alliance. Of course, he indicated that an autonomous nuclear weapons development program would be desirable but difficult to realize under the conditions of 1966. Fukutome cautioned his readers that if any such autonomous program were attempted in direct conflict with U.S. desires, the security system would be affected. For long-term considerations, Fukutome recommended that the potentiality of an autonomous weapons program be encouraged and that thus promotion of peaceful nuclear uses must occur; he recommended the fast realization of nuclear-powered submarines; and, finally, he stressed the development of rocketry. Noting that there would be some political problems resulting from possession of nuclear arms by Japan, as far as the U.S.-Japanese security system was concerned, he felt that if these hurdles could be overcome there would be "possibilities enough."[100]

One other military critic who also advocates nuclear weapons is Hideo Sekino, a former navy commander. In the November 1970 issues of the magazine _Reformer_, he wrote a very sophisticated article advocating tactical nuclear arms for Japan. Basically, Sekino argues that in a large-scale conventional attack against Japan or in the event the opponent uses tactical nuclear weapons, the possibility that the United States would respond by using strategic nuclears would be slight, and in such an exchange Japan would suffer. The possibility of the use of U.S. strategic arms being slight, the effectiveness of deterrence also becomes slight. To fill this gap and provide an additional option besides the mutual destruction of the United States and the USSR from a strategic exchange, Sekino sees the value of tactical nuclear weapons for fighter bombers. As the capability of China to strike the United States increases and a level of mutual deterrence is reached between those two powers, Sekino believes the creation of an English-size limited nuclear retaliatory force would be necessary during the period of the 1970s.[101]

An interesting indication of attitudes of LDP candidates, which may or may not be related to the question of nuclear weapons but which does indicate overall changes in security concepts, was obtained by the _Yomiuri_ in December 1972. A poll conducted among LDP candidates asked specifically if they supported "continuation of the Security Treaty."[102] The poll revealed that only 44.5 percent of the candidates supported continuation, and those who favored revision or gradual abrogation totaled 47.8 percent. This represented a marked change from the 99 percent of LDP candidates who stood for continuation of the treaty in 1969.[103] As the LDP has indicated in past policy statements, reliance on the Security Treaty has obviated the requirement for Japan's own nuclear weapons, this change in attitude could be very significant. Further, it should not be forgotten that reliance on the Security Treaty was one of Prime Minister Sato's "Four Nuclear Policies" enunciated in 1968.

Additional LDP Policy with Possible Defense Connotations

The Question of Civilian Control

As a result of a government "oversight" in January-February 1972, the Fourth Defense Consolidation Plan had not been submitted to the National Defense Council when the Diet began studying the draft fiscal year 1972 budget. This budget included funding allocations for Fourth Defense Consolidation Plan line items, but that particular plan had not been approved by the National Defense Council, which, under Article 62 of the Defense Agency Law, must approve long-range planning before initiation of the plan.[104] Needless to say when the JSP, Komeito, and DSP interpellators discovered this in the course of questioning Prime Minister Sato and his Finance Minister Mikio Mizuta, a political crisis of the first magnitude resulted. (It did not help when both LDP officials indicated there was no connection between the budget and the Fourth Plan.)[105] Finally a compromise was reached, which, among other things, provided, "The Government will take from its own side necessary measures for effective 'civilian control' in the light of the circumstances this time."[106]

Soon thereafter, on February 10, 1972, the first LDP proposal regarding civilian control was released. It proposed that, in addition to the current members of the National Defense Council (the prime minister, deputy prime minister, foreign minister, finance minister, Japan Defense Agency director general, and Economic Planning Agency director general) there would be one representative each from the House of Representatives and House of Councillors.[107]

By May, this idea had been dropped, and in its stead was a proposal to add the International Trade and Industry minister, Science and Technology Agency director general, National Public Safety Agency chairman, and the chief of the Cabinet Secretariat.[108] This was the final group added to the National Defense Council and from the surface would appear to increase the potential for civilian control if, in fact, matters of long-range planning are submitted to it. However, there is an aspect of the double-edged sword in that if the director general of the Science and Technology Agency is acting concurrently as the chairman of the Atomic Energy Commission, there occurs a concentration of military, political, and scientific leadership, which, as pointed out by several members of the scientific community, could provide a possible focal point for manipulation of scientific R and D toward military ends. For example, coordinated, long-term programs that fulfill civilian requirements might be better managed by such a group to provide increased military utilization.[109]

Diet members Yoshio Miki (JSP) and Kenjiro Yamanaka (JCP) were among those who objected, noting that results obtained from peaceful development programs could be used

for military purposes. In a classic, if somewhat opinion-
ated, appraisal they commented, "We cannot but say that
the Tanaka Cabinet has disclosed its true character. We
feel as if we have seen a piece of armor under the priest's
robe."[110]

Industrial Dispersal

In a book published by Kakuei Tanaka shortly before
he became prime minister, Rebuilding the Japanese Archipelago, the idea of removing "factories from excessively con-
gested industrial areas along the Pacific Coast to less
developed areas" was advanced.[111] The concept of industrial
dispersal was accompanied by proposals to build medium-size
cities with populations around 200,000 and supporting these
cities with a massive extension of the communication and
transportation network to permit any part of Japan to be
reached in one day. Some specific goals of the plan were
to "reduce the ratio of industrial areas along the Pacific
Coast in total production from the present 73 percent to
50 percent by 1975, . . . extend the length of expressways
from 709 km to 10,000 km, . . . and increase the highspeed
rail net [Bullet Trains] to 9,000 km."[112]
While the objective of the plan is to create a "better
living environment, rectifying the overcrowding in urban
areas,"[113] which no one would deny to the Japanese people,
it will have certain obvious strategic advantages to Japan.
Primary among these advantages will be the possible reduction of the impact of the specter that disturbs most Japanese defense analysts, that of a hostage Tokyo and a cap-
tive Osaka.*

The LDP and the NPT

On February 3, 1970, the government of Japan signed
the NPT. When it did, it accompanied the act of signing
with a statement that indicated clearly that it was not
satisfied with the treaty as it stood. The following are
the main points of the Japanese position:

1. The Government has confidence that the
NPT is the first step toward nuclear disarmament

---

*The precipitous increase in land prices that accom-
panied the publication of this book, helped to bring about
Tanaka's resignation in late 1974.

and desires the participation of as many nations as possible.

    2. Especially it desires the participation of the Chinese People's Republic and France, which do not seem to have the intention of participating as nuclear weapons states.

    3. The discrimination between nuclear weapon states and non-nuclear weapon states must be dissolved by the eventual removal of nuclear weapons. To this end, the nuclear weapons states must bear an awareness of this special responsibility.

    4. The non-nuclear weapon states will not be hindered in any meaning whatsoever in the experimentation, development, and research of the peaceful uses of nuclear energy and will not receive discriminatory treatment from any source.[114]

With regard to disarmament as well as national security the Japanese statement listed several points that needed to be resolved.

    1. The Government of Japan thinks it necessary for the realization of the objectives of the NPT that the nuclear weapons states take concrete nuclear disarmament measures to comply with the pledges of Article 6 of the Treaty.

    2. The nuclear weapon states must not threaten the use or use nuclear weapons against non-nuclear weapon states.

    3. The Government of Japan desires to continue thorough investigations into measures that are effective for providing security for the non-nuclear nations, and [gives] serious consideration to the declarations of the U.S., U.K., and the USSR, which indicate [they] desire speedy action of the Security Council in the event there is the threat or aggressive use of nuclear weapons.

    4. The Government of Japan, in the period until treaty ratification, will investigate cautiously the rest of the problems which must be seriously considered in order to secure national prosperity and will pay attention to the circumstances of execution of the Security Council resolution and the transition of the disarmament negotiations.

>   5.   The Government of Japan notes the provi-
> sion of Article 10 of the Treaty, "There is the
> right of withdrawal . . . when it is recognized
> that [the treaty] has endangered the supreme in-
> terests of the nation."[115]

The translated positions were taken along with others of a
scientific and technical nature dealing with access to
nuclear data and formulation of safeguards.

This basically negative, much hedged, adherence to
the NPT preceded the entering into force of the treaty by
slightly more than one month (the effective date was March
5, 1970),[116] and there was considerable pressure to make
the dealine as a "charter member" for negotiating purposes.
With opposition to ratification of the treaty rather high,
even in the opposition parties, forward progress toward
ratification since April 1970 has not been readily apparent. More important, support for ratification has been
lacking from the LDP itself.[117]

In January 1972, as preparations were made for the
U.S.-Japanese summit talks at San Clemente, California,
the U.S. columnist Jack Anderson made public a reportedly
secret memorandum of the U.S. Embassy concerning Japan's
probable future course in Asia. The report warned that
"Japan may come to nuclearize itself autonomously, leaving
the nuclear umbrella of America."[118] This release precipitated considerable outcry as to Japan's nuclear intentions
and may have been related to the establishment of the Nuclear Nonproliferation Treaty Committee by the LDP on March
2, 1972 within the Foreign Affairs Research Council.
Yoshitake Sasaki was appointed chairman, and it was reported that this newly formed group would "steadily study"
questions relating to the NPT.[119]

The committee, besides Chairman Sasaki, had 26 Lower
House members and 7 Upper House members. At its first
meeting, on March 10, the director of the Foreign Ministry's UN Bureau addressed the members concerning the NPT
and its problem areas. Further sessions were planned to
hear opinions of representatives of the electric utilities
and manufacturers who would be affected by any safeguards
agreement. Of special significance to this study was the
composition of the "working group" established by the committee, which included Foreign Office, Science and Technology Agency, and Japan Atomic Industrial Forum representatives.[120]

Shortly after the establishment of the LDP committee,
the newspapers carried a report that the United States

"has started taking the posture of not positively request-
ing Japan to ratify the Nuclear Nonproliferation Treaty
quickly."[121] This report was denied by the U.S. State Department a full six days later, but the space given to the
original story was considerably greater than that given to
the refutation. The fact that it took six days to deny
the original report probably did not go unnoticed by those
interested in the subject.[122]

In May 1972, Atoms in Japan, the monthly magazine of
the influential Japan Atomic Industrial Forum, took a very
interesting position regarding the NPT. The editor cau-
tiously stated that "the Atomic Industrial Forum of Japan
may soon recommend to the Government that the NPT should
be ratified quickly." Having said "quickly" he then noted
that the recommendation would probably be "conditional"
based on "the policy of the U.S.A., developments between
EURATOM and IAEA, and the policy posture of the ruling
Liberal Democratic Party of Japan."[123]

The editor noted that little had been done since 1968
to prevent vertical proliferation and that the MIRV only
presented the world with "over-kill squared." He was
critical of efforts to assure a free exchange of technical
information and pointed out that there was "no discussion
that acceptance of safeguards will qualify NNWS for receiving such information." It was noted further that the
nuclear weapon states (NWS) had not really developed a
system to protect non-nuclear weapon states (NNWS) from
nuclear attack or nuclear threat.[124]

In reference to the political situation surrounding
the ratification of the NPT, the editor indicated that the
"NPT is undeniably an unequal treaty." Commenting on its
relation to the nuclear option, he stated, "giving up the
nuclear option as a policy requires clear appreciation of
the future development of political, military and other
implications in the Pacific Basin."[125]

While the stated objective of the recommendation in
favor of NPT ratification was to "clarify industry's position on this complicated issue," it was wrapped with so
many reservations that the final suggestion came as a surprise: "the long term position of Japan's nuclear technology, industry, and resources will be better if the treaty
is ratified before very long."[126]

Of particular interest to the atomic industry is long-
term access to uranium, technological exchanges, enrichment services, and so on, which could be jeopardized if
ratification is delayed too long. It would be natural to
assume that the atomic industry, as well as the electric

power industry, in order to obtain needed materials for the generation of electric power, would lobby in favor of the NPT. It is surprising to note a slightly more than ambivalent view on the part of Atoms in Japan.

A position that reflected the above view was taken before the LDP-NPT Committee in one of its hearings by representatives of the Japan Atomic Power Company and the Tokyo Electric Power Company. The witnesses stated, with respect to safeguards that, "the nuclear industry of Japan is willing to pronounce NPT safeguards as no longer unacceptable."[127] The atomic power industry had served notice that, from their point of view (those most affected by safeguards inspections), the NPT could be ratified. One of the major points of contention had been removed. Or had it?

Shortly after the May position taken by the power interests, two government officials, also high in LDP circles, commented on the NPT. On June 2 at a Lower House plenary session of the Diet, Foreign Minister Fukuda stated, "Now that Japan has signed NPT, Japan cannot but ratify it. But we have no idea yet on when to ratify NPT."[128] In early July, in fact on the day the Tanaka cabinet took office (July 5, 1972), the second comment was made. Yasuhiro Nakasone, newly appointed minister of International Trade and Industry, director general of the Science and Technology Agency, and chairman of the Atomic Energy Commission, made the following statement to the press:

> The Government will continue to abide by the three Non-Nuclear Principles. But the ongoing controversy over treaty ratification is only "hypothetical," and the time is not ripe [for ratification of the Nuclear Nonproliferation Treaty]. In view of stringent [IAEA*-proposed] conditions of inspection, industrial circles may be motivated to favor [ratification]. But the time is not yet when early ratification should be undertaken at the sacrifice of the Japanese position. Careful study is needed from the standpoint of our national interests . . . the nuclear powers should make a non-use declaration first, to assure the non-nuclear countries that they will not be threatened. After that, it will not be too late for Japan to ratify the treaty.[129]

---

*International Atomic Energy Agency.

Such a statement coming from a highly placed political and governmental official on the first day of the Tanaka cabinet's life was a clear indication that opposition (of a political nature) to rapid ratification must have been keen. Another point, not to be forgotten with regard to the Nakasone statement, is the fact that he cannot be considered one of the extreme "rightists" in the LDP. Therefore, opposition to ratification in July 1972 must have been a rather general phenomena within the LDP.

In January 1973 a "government source" indicated to a newspaper reporter that the reservations noted in February 1970 when Japan signed the NPT had yet to be satisfied, and the government of Japan would be "shelving" the effort to ratify it for another year. It was indicated that Japan feels especially strong about a safeguards agreement and would not tolerate unfavorable or discriminatory treatment from the IAEA. Since the European Atomic Energy Community (Euratom) concluded a safeguards agreement with the IAEA in April 1973, which permitted Euratom to carry out inspections largely independently, Japan can be expected to demand no less.[130] As the Euratom Security Measures Agreement permits extensive use of the autonomous inspection system in Euratom, Japanese observers noted immediately the need to perfect the control system existing in Japan to make it so reliable that it will be accepted by the IAEA as in the Euratom experience.[131]

Another reason for the continued procrastination on the part of the government was cited as "strong opposition, within the LDP."[132] The Soshinkai position of "Do not close a way to nuclear armament in the future" was noted as "gaining strength." Once again the notion that the United States was not pressuring Japan for rapid ratification was repeated; however, an interesting variation was introduced by adding the Soviet Union to the host of disinterested parties.[133]

In February 1973, additional indications of an increasing disinclination to act on the NPT were noted. The Atomic Power Industry was reported as less outspoken for ratification. The reported decline in spirit was attributed to current site acquisition problems facing the industry.[134] However, in March 1973 at the annual meeting of the Japan Council of Atomic Energy Industry a statement urging the government to "an earlier ratification" of the NPT was endorsed.[135] In order to evaluate adequately the comparative time element in the phrase "an earlier ratification," more data on the total NPT "game plan" of the government must be known; is it earlier than 1974, 1975, or, indeed, 1980?

71

In conversations with Japanese officials on this matter the author was informed that the government of Japan was watching with keen interest the actions of West Germany with regard to ratification of the NPT. When West Germany ratifies, "Japan will make her move."

West Germany's Bundestag, now that a Security Measures Agreement exists between Euratom and IAEA did, in fact, ratify the NPT;[136] however, another disturbing point was raised after the June 1, 1973 establishment of the Association for Centrifuge Enrichment (ACE), with the Netherlands, West Germany, and Great Britain as members. A point was made that two of the members of ACE are non-nuclear nations, while Britain is a nuclear nation. This arrangement places valuable techniques within West Germany's grasp, but not Japan's. Japan could be the only advanced nation thus placed "in an unfavorable position as to inspection,"[137] and this was cited as reason enough to reexamine the entire question of NPT ratification.[138]

Other reports were much more optimistic regarding the Japanese position and indicated that the government of Japan, after meeting with representatives of the IAEA in early June 1973, saw clearly the points at issue. Reportedly, once the control structure could be tightened in Japan, an international inspection agreement would be concluded rapidly. The time frame for such an agreement was estimated as September-October 1974.[139] While this date now appears to have been overly optimistic, hope does seem real for the spring or summer of 1975.

Events overtook the measured game plan for ratification in the fall of 1974 when a sixth nation, India, exploded a nuclear device. In fact, India's underground nuclear test, announced on May 18, 1974, produced political shock waves, which grew in intensity as they reached Japan. The major newspapers were unreserved in their condemnation of the blast. The Asahi was shocked that a country of such poverty could be so irresponsible as to allocate valuable, and scarce, resources in an attempt to gain some kind of international prestige. This newspaper, in the face of this unexpected development, called for greater efforts on the part of the Japanese government to ratify the NPT.[140]

The Yomiuri, another major daily, was concerned how the test would be received by the PRC and opined that it might "increase tensions" not only with China but also with "other neighboring countries." The paper felt that it might result in a weakening of the fragile Indian economy.[141]

First responses from official Japanese sources came from the Defense Agency and the prime minister's office. An unidentified Defense Agency source offered a rather optimistic assessment by citing that since the test was for peaceful purposes, "the underground nuclear experiment will not readily lead to nuclear armament." In this light, no major change was anticipated in the military balance in the Far East.[142]

Of greater interest to this study, however, were the comments of the first attributed government spokesman Susumu Nikaido, chief cabinet secretary. In his statement, little good could be found in the test; it "ran counter" to the desires for cessation of nuclear proliferation, weakened the movement for détente in South Asia and was irreconcilable with the Japanese opposition to any nuclear test.[143]

The principal opposition parties, the Japan Socialist Party, the Japan Communist Party, and the Komeito, promptly castigated the Indians for the test and called for complete prohibition of nuclear weapons, including abolution of current stocks.[144]

The rightist of the LDP (the Soshinkai and the Seirankai) were seen as seizing on this development to more strongly oppose any moves toward NPT ratification.[145]

While shock or perhaps, more accurately, dismay seemed to be the Japanese immediate response, especially as the event impacted on proliferation and the implications for Japanese ratification of the NPT, the question arose internationally as to how India was able to accomplish it.

The United States quickly denied it had provided any of the fissionable material used in the Indian blast. A spokesman for the U.S. Atomic Energy Commission pointed out that while the United States had provided some 141,000 kilograms of slightly enriched uranium since 1969, the material had been under control of the IAEA safeguard system. A more likely source was indicated to be the Canadian/Indian natural uranium research reactor in Trombay. It was seen to have a capability to produce weapons-grade material needing only separation from waste products of the reactor.[146]

Japanese official reaction took a more precise form on May 23, when the lower house of the Diet passed unanimously a resolution protesting the Indian development. The resolution, in fact, was backed by the LDP and all the opposition parties.[147]

Calls were heard for some kind of concrete indication of Japan's displeasure, which gave rise to suggestions to reduce the amount of economic assistance provided to India.[148]

The picture of general condemnation of the Indian move painted thus far was not appropriate for all shades of Japan's political spectrum. Bin Akao, head of the rightist Nihon Aikokuto, harangued anyone who would pause for a moment in front of his sound truck located in busy downtown Tokyo. His was a nationalist plea for Japan also to join the nuclear club, but how many Tokyoites shared his desire for a nuclear Japan was readily apparent from the apathetic response.[149]

A first indication of the man in the street's reaction came from the May Sankei 1,000 public opinion poll. This poll revealed that while 70 percent of the respondents held "the test in disregard of international public opinion . . . impermissible" only 26 percent felt uneasy about Japan's national security. A still smaller figure, 23 percent, thought that India's prestige would increase as a result of becoming a nuclear nation.[150]

One might editorialize to the extent that India's getting the bomb, in fact, took most of the glory and prestige away from developing such a capability. The advent of an Indian device perhaps demonstrated to the Japanese that development of the bomb was not solely the prerogative of a technologically advanced state but represented the results of a misdirected allocation of resources.

While official Japan found nothing good in the Indian test, Vice-Foreign Minister Fumihiko Togo made some very pertinent observations relating the test to the drive to ratify the NPT in Japan. Speaking before the Japan National Press Club, he noted that the test revealed "absolutely no positive factors" in relation to Japan's ratification of the NPT and implied that this event would increase difficulties with the right wing of the LDP.[151] He noted that there was "nothing in the contents of the treaty that would prevent Japan from ratifying it. It's just a matter of finishing the domestic preparations and we will have to proceed with this a bit more."[152]

The "domestic preparations" referred to by the vice-minister, in the main, concerned building the necessary consensus within the LDP and government to allow for ratification. In the fall of 1973 preliminary agreement had been realized between Japan and the IAEA for an inspection system meeting Japanese requirements for a program the equal of the Euratom accord; measures, at that time, were initiated to ratify the pact in the 1974 Diet. However, these plans ran into the determined opposition of Kinji

Moriyama, director general of the Science and Technology Agency, and the attempt was temporarily shelved.[153]   It was plain that although there was unhappiness over the Indian situation in Japan the matter of "finishing the domestic preparations" would be a rather formidable task.

By early June Japan's official displeasure toward India was translated into economic terms when the Tanaka government announced that aid to India provided to the aid-India consortium would not be increased. (It had been customary to increase the aid provided on a yearly basis.)[154] Further, soon thereafter, the Japanese government indicated it would not provide aid to India under the United Nations plan to assist developing countries counteract the affects of the oil crisis.[155]

As Japan was implementing its policy to indicate its disdain for Indian nuclear policy, other fast-breaking developments seemed to inundate the beleaguered Foreign Office. On June 14, 1974, it was announced from Cairo that President Nixon had agreed to provide Egypt with nuclear reactors and uranium.[156] Several days later a similar pledge of assistance for nuclear power was made to Israel.[157] And on June 17, China and France conducted atmospheric nuclear tests.[158]

Taken individually, all events could be explained away by an astute ministry, but coming as they did only a month after the Indian development, it appeared that truly a "chaotic nuclear age" had arrived.[159] Proponents of rapid ratification of the NPT in Japan were placed, once again, on the defensive.

Prime Minister Tanaka, on the stump for an LDP candidate in Osaka, reaffirmed his government's position saying,

> Japan, the sole victim nation in the world, will
> firmly maintain the three non-nuclear principles
> that it will not manufacture, hold, or permit
> nuclear weapons to be brought in. Japan opposes
> all kinds of nuclear tests by any nation. . . .
> We, needless to say, oppose the Chinese nuclear
> tests as well; and the offer of nuclear [energy]
> to Egypt and Israel should be confined to peace-
> ful utilization, to the last.[160]

It was reported in the press that the Foreign Ministry had looked at this series of events with some degree of dismay, fearing that the nuclear stability of the world was threatened; potential nuclear powers were seen as viewing the events of May-June as a "political excuse" to develop nuclear weapons and speed proliferation.[161]

Calls for a clarification of Japan's nuclear policy were made, underlining the lethargic pace of Japan's attempts to ratify the NPT. Special attention was placed on the fact that since Japan had not ratified the NPT, she would not be able to participate in the May 1975 conference of NPT member nations to reexamine progress in the field of nonproliferation.[162]

The Foreign Ministry was so concerned with the aid promised Israel that it queried the United States for the reasoning involved in providing fissionable materials and advanced nuclear technology to a state that had not signed the NPT. The U.S. government answered that strict bilateral controls would be applied by the United States, which would limit Israeli uses to peaceful purposes.[163]

While such assurances were greeted in some circles as adequate, the drive for Japan's ratification of the treaty by May of 1975 was seen to have received a severe setback by late June, and the Foreign Ministry, once hoping for a May 1975 ratification, was reported as seeing sometime after the summer of 1975 as a more realistic target date.[164]

However, in an interview published on June 28, 1974 the delegate to the IAEA and ambassador to Austria, Naraichi Fujiyama, revealed some significant information concerning the internal bureaucratic situation in Japan. Indicating that he had talked with Science and Technology Director General Moriyama on June 25, he stated that opposition from that source had lessened to the point that Moriyama was "not so strongly opposed." Fujiyama was not too optimistic in his comments and when asked a direct question as to why ratification was proceeding so slowly said,

> It is that there are objections within both the Ruling Party and the Opposition Parties and that a national consensus can hardly be obtained.[165]

This rather pessimistic outlook was moderated somewhat a week later when the Foreign Ministry reaffirmed that it would continue to seek "early ratification" of the NPT. The basic theoretical arguments to win consensus in the government and nation were as follows:

> 1. The Indian blast and related nuclear events do not essentially change the existing nuclear balance.
> 2. The nature of the NPT remains unchanged as long as the U.S. and Soviet nuclear deterrents exist.

3.   Japan's chances for a stable nuclear fuel supply would be better if the pact were ratified.[166]

This position was reaffirmed on the 17th by Toshio Kimura, newly appointed foreign minister, shortly after his attestation.[167] He indicated that Prime Minister Tanaka would attempt to create consensus within the LDP and that the government would introduce the issue into the next regular session of the Diet.[168]

The Japanese position on the NPT was buttressed further on the 20th, when the Foreign Ministry announced that Japan would tie nuclear assistance for power generation to participation in the NPT.[169] As a number of countries have approached Japan on this matter, it appeared that finally an economic determinant was being introduced into the problem.

It was held that any such assistance to other nations would be inspected by Japan, but unless Japan were a true member of the NPT, it could not justify inspecting other countries' use of Japanese technology.[170]

In this late July development it was reported that a negotiation delegation could be sent to IAEA headquarters in Vienna, perhaps by September, to begin final preparation for a draft safeguards agreement.[171]

With such positive developments on the bureaucratic scene, the remaining hurdle for the government remained the Soshinkai/Seirankai factional opposition to ratification. The Foreign Ministry surely advanced the linkage between nuclear technical assistance and the NPT to bolster its arsenal for the coming last-ditch stand of these opponents to ratification.

On July 29 it was announced in the Sankei Shimbun that Foreign Minister Kimura had ordered his subordinates to "conduct full-dress negotiations" with the IAEA and to begin "co-ordination within the Government immediately."[172] It was obvious that the task of consensus building would begin again in earnest aimed at Diet action in the 1975 session.

Within the government the Science and Technology Agency was seen as the target of most of the consensus efforts due to earlier opposition of its director to ratification moves. The attitude of this agency is extremely important when it is remembered that, in all probability, it will be charged with the task of carrying out safeguards inspections in line with any IAEA agreement, and it evidently had the power to block ratification attempts in the 1974 Diet. While it was hoped by some that attitudes were becoming more flexible in the agency, at least one observer noted that, within the government, the attitude of calling for caution toward treaty ratification had begun to prevail.[173]

The basic disquiet over France and China, which was reflected in the government of Japan's statement in 1970, remains today and has been augmented by developments in India, Egypt, and Israel. This leads to the conclusion that completion of a safeguards agreement on a basis of equality with Euratom may not necessarily speed the movement toward ratification on the part of Japan.

Basically, the question is more closely related to national security interests on Japan's part than technical considerations concerning the manner, frequency, form, or accuracy of inspections of nuclear materials. The LDP position, concerning the NPT, seems closer to that of the industrial lobby, which desires long-term access to uranium supplies, than to the Soshinkai slogan of "Do not close a way to nuclear armament in the future." It would appear that the movement toward ratification will peak prior to the spring of 1975; however, it is not a popular issue, and very little, if any, political capital is to be gained by resolute action to achieve ratification. With one eye on the relatively weak position of Prime Minister Takeo Miki since the factional difficulties of late 1974, it must be said candidly that more important priorities might be seen for the LDP than early ratification of the NPT.

If, however, the LDP decides to keep its option open, a great deal of subsequent policy must take into consideration the action of the political opposition and its attitude toward, not only the NPT, but the nuclear question in general.

THE POLITICAL PARTIES IN OPPOSITION

In essence, when the subject is nuclear weapons, and not the Security Treaty, the opposition parties--namely the Japan Socialist Party, Japan Communist Party, Komeito, and Democratic Socialist Party--do not oppose the policy of the LDP, as such. They all agree: No nuclear weapons for Japan! Their function, in respect to this question, is usually one of ensuring that the LDP faithfully executes its declared policy and prodding the LDP into negotiating positions that are somewhat more explicit than might otherwise be the case.

While the ruling LDP and opposition parties do currently agree on the Three Non-Nuclear Principles for Japan,
a very brief examination of the opposition parties' overall defense policies is warranted to highlight the differences in defense philosophy. It will be useful, therefore,
to review the parties' defense platforms as stated during
the December 1972 Diet elections as well as their historic
postures regarding this always volatile subject.

The Japan Socialist Party (JSP)

The JSP has been a steadfast advocate of "unarmed
neutrality" since the seventh convention of the Socialist
Party in 1951, when opposition to any rearmament proposals
was added as a fourth principle of peace to the three that
had been advanced since the Katayama government of 1947.[174]
The other three were that "Japan should (1) conclude one
peace treaty with all its former enemies, (2) maintain neutrality, and (3) neither conclude military pacts with any
one country, nor give military bases in Japan to any foreign country."[175]
The party public pledge for the election of December
1972 reflected these very early espoused principles:

We will abrogate the Security Treaty, and while
promoting diplomacy of non-militarization, peace,
and neutrality, we will conclude a treaty of nonaggression and friendship between Japan and China,
Japan and the Soviet Union, and with unified
Korea, and establish a structure for guaranteeing
lasting peace for all Asia. We will oppose the
Fourth Defense Plan and switch the SDF to a Peaceful Land Construction Force, with the people's
support.[176]

Since the election, the policy of "unarmed neutrality"
was dealt a very severe blow from an unexpected source.
During a recent visit to the People's Republic of China by
a group of ex-Imperial Army and Navy officers an opportunity
occurred for them to meet Chou En-lai. All in the tour
were socialists, and members of the Sino-Japanese Friendly
Ex-Soldiers Association. Chou En-lai reportedly said to
their leader,

After the end of WW II conventional wars have constantly occurred, for example the Chinese civil

war, the Korean war, conflicts in Indochina, Pal-
estine, etc.; however, there has been no nuclear
war. That is, "unarmed neutrality" cannot be realized; the Socialist Party has insisted that
Japan should not possess armed forces, but they
probably have some difficulty in getting the
people's support; it is natural that Japan has
self-defense power in order to establish independence, peace, democaracy and neutrality.[177]

It remains to be seen how the pro-China JSP will react to
this indirect lecture, but its basic content is very similar to the policies advocated by the LDP and DSP for years.

The Komeito

The Komeito has been active in elections for the House
of Representatives since 1967. In that year, 25 members
of that party were elected on a platform that advocated
world peace through pacifism and world racialism (on the
order of the one-world concept). It outlined as its objectives the achievement of total disarmament, total abolition of nuclear weapons, strengthening of the United Nations, and peace maintenance by a UN police force. It also
advocated an omnidirectional foreign policy and a "scaling-
down" of the Japanese-U.S. Security Treaty.[178]

In 1969 in preparation for the elections held in that
year, the Komeito issued a policy statement, which reflected
the party philosophy in its title "Toward the Realization
of World Peace Through Middle-of-the Roadism." The party's
attitude toward nuclear weapons was made clear: It was to
repudiate the possession, experimentation, and manufacture
of nuclear weapons.[179]

A series of traumatic events occurred in early 1970
in the wake of Sokagakkai and Komeito efforts to suppress
the publication of a series of books and articles highly
critical of the former.[180] The JCP, acting as defender
of the free press, brought the undemocratic practices to
light shortly after the Sokagakkai and Komeito announced
that they would officially separate.[181]

Since the separation of the two groups, the Komeito
has gradually increased its renovationist stance and was
reported in February 1973 to be considering seriously "immediate abrogation" of the Japanese-U.S. Security Treaty
as part of its defense policy.[182] The party pledge for
the 1972 election was as follows:

We will defend the peace Constitution and promote
the peace and neutralization of Asia with autonomous, equal-distance, neutral diplomacy. For this
purpose, we will promote the following: (1) establishment of lasting peace between Japan and
China, (2) reversion of the northern territory,
and conclusion of a Japan-Soviet peace treaty,
(3) promotion of Japan-Korea friendship, (4) increase in the Government's development aid to the
developing nations, (5) blocking of the Fourth Defense Plan, and (6) removal of the US military
bases, and early dissolution of the Japan-US Security Treaty structure.[183]

The Democratic Socialist Party

The DSP was founded on January 24, 1960 under the
leadership of Suehiro Nishio. In the initial platform, it
advocated internationally inspected disarmament but realized that several obstacles had to be overcome for that
to be possible and indicated that it approved of "more appropriate measures for our own security."[184] When it was
formed, Party Chairman Nishio stated his hope that the new
party would be in power within five years.[185]

At the 1962 Party Conference, it was decided that the
DSP would encourage the completion of an agreement to pro-
hibit nuclear tests; oppose nuclear weapons for West Germany, China, and others because nuclear proliferation was
considered a threat to the peace of the world; and promote
talks in the United Nations to achieve a relaxation of
tension and disarmament.[186] The party advocated a policy
of "minimum measures in order to defend the nation," which
included in its framework a denial of the possession of
nuclear weapons. The DSP held that even though the early
1960s appeared as an age of the spread of atomic and hydrogen bombs, this growth of weapons was based on a mis-
understanding of reality. The party noted that all disputes were being fought with conventional weapons and offered as examples the then current strife in Africa,
South Vietnam, and Algeria to strengthen its case.[187]

Ten years later, in March 1972, the party issued a
paper entitled "Establishment of a New Peace Order--Strat-
egy Toward Reduction of Tension in an Era of Multipolarity."
The "New Peace Order" was composed of six points, which
dealt with Japan and her role in the new multipolar international system, the adjustment of relations with the United

States to reflect the multipolar world, the realization of diplomatic relations with China, maintenance of peace on the Korean Peninsula, cooperation between Japan and the USSR, and new programs of economic cooperation.[188] In addressing the adjustment of relations with the United States, two principal problems were considered: Interestingly enough Part II was the "Adjustment of the Economic Situation," and Part I dealt with "A New System of Security Guarantee."[189] (The order indicated something about priorities.)

Regarding Part II and the security treaty, the DSP maintained that the U.S.-Japanese system was based on the strategy of the East-West confrontation, and it was not a progressive item of the "age of multipolarity." It was seen as a contradiction of the general trend toward a "New Peace Order," and it acted as a hindrance in the friendly relations of the United States and Japan. The policy statement called for the withdrawal of U.S. troops and bases and stated "we demand a new security guarantee that can create a new order of peace to correspond with the multipolar age."[190]

Earlier in the report, the DSP had reaffirmed its desire for Japan "to maintain its special character as a non-nuclear, peace nation in the era of the 1970's."[191]

The DSP public pledge for the 1972 election reflected its continuing pragmatic approach:

> We will promote peaceful diplomacy of autonomy and co-existence and contribute to the forming of a new, peaceful order in Asia. Especially, we will strive (1) to realize a Security Treaty without military bases and stationing of forces, by revising the Security Treaty, (2) to oppose the Fourth Defense Plan and form a national consensus on civilian control and defense, and (3) to establish an Indo-China reconstruction fund.[192]

The Japan Communist Party (JCP)

In the first published statement of the JCP in _Akahata_ after the reestablishment of the party in 1945, the theme "to eliminate militarism" was apparent.[193] However, eliminating militarism and advocating "unarmed neutrality" are two different things. In a more recent policy statement of the JCP, the subject of self-defense is dealt with in relation to the security treaty.

Our proposal for abrogation of the Security Treaty
and dissolution of the Self-Defense Forces is not
because we deny the right of self-defense [to Ja-
pan] but because American imperialism aims at invading Japan infringing on her sovereignty . . .
the Self-Defense Forces are an army that serves
the U.S. and oppresses the Japanese people. . . .
Japan . . . like any other Sovereignty [has] a
complete right to take . . . necessary and appropriate measure(s) to maintain the political
independence that she has won.[194]

As specific aspects of its policy the JCP advocates abrogation of the Security Treaty, opposition to nuclear weapons, and dissolution of the SDF.[195]
    In the 1972 elections the JCP policy pledge was as
follows:

We will have the American war of aggression against
Vietnam stopped and have the Tanaka Cabinet's cooperation discontinued. We will eliminate the
Japan-U.S. military alliance and win the peace
and neutralization of Japan. Following the restoration of Japan-China diplomatic relations,
[there will be] normalization of diplomatic relations with Vietnam and Korea [and] opposition to
the Fourth Defense Plan and dissolution of the SDF,
which is unconstitutional and subordinate to the
U.S. Self-defense for the future shall be decided
by the collective will of the people.[196]

After this review of the various philosophies of the
opposition parties, it would be beneficial to cite several
examples of their activities in the recent past to illustrate their potential and actual effect on the LDP and
public opinion on the nuclear question. As has been noted
previously, when the nuclear question is concerned, the
opposition parties have a significant watchdog function.
    In mid-November 1971, a JSP Representative, Tanosuke
Narazaki, charged in a meeting of the Special Committee on
the Okinawa Return Agreement that he had suspicions that
nuclear weapons were being stored at Iwakuni Air Base.
The base, a facility of the U.S. Marine Corps in Yamaguchi
Prefecture, had been visited by an investigatory group of
the JSP called the "Military Project Team." Narazaki noted
in his accusation that six ammunition warehouses at that
base were of suspicious nature, very similar to the facili-

ties reported to house nuclear weapons in Okinawa. Maps, photographs, and related documents were presented.[197]

Foreign Minister Takeo Fukuda replied that no nuclear weapons were "at any U.S. bases in Japan," and this was repeated specifically covering Iwakuni, but denials by both the Japanese government and U.S. representatives did not placate the Socialist organization, which had begun to mobilize at the Yamaguchi headquarters. Anti-nuclear weapons rallies followed, with about 2,800 persons participating.

Demonstrating that the Japanese government was not taking the issue lightly, Major General Kimio Ito of the Japanese Defense Agency (JDA) was sent to investigate. In an unprecedented move, the U.S. commander invited the general to tour the inside of the suspect facility. The general found only conventional torpedoes and depth charges.[198]

Narazaki noted in a reply on November 28, that an investigation by the JDA meant nothing, as it was a "one-sided vindication." He indicated that he would continue to probe into this and related questions.[199]

To catalog all incidents of this kind would be beyond the scope of this book, but further brief examples of the never-ending pursuit of U.S. and LDP collusion are warranted. The Komeito, after the above event, formed a Non-Nuclear Investigation Headquarters on November 30, 1971 to investigate the presence of nuclear weapons in Japan.[200] It rapidly produced the desired controversy when Komeito Councilor Akira Kuroyanagi charged that both nuclear weapons and poison gas were stored at Atsugi Air Base (Kanagawa Prefecture) and substantiated his claim by submitting pictures of grazing goats in a barbed wire enclosure. (The goats, of course, were seen as a crude system to warn of gas leaks.) The U.S. Navy replied to the charge by saying that the goats were there to eat grass. Kuroyanagi was not deterred; neither was the Komeito, which listed this event as one of its major successes of 1971.[201]

The Non-Nuclear Investigation Headquarters of Komeito actually checked 26 U.S. bases and ammunition depots. It requested that Yokota Air Base be checked further because of "suspicion that nuclear weapons might be stored" there, and Yokosuka might be used for gas and nuclear weapons.[202] These matters were all taken up by the Diet and received considerable coverage in the mass media.

On March 1, 1972, the 18th anniversary of the Bikini H-bomb tests, the JCP-sponsored Gensuikyo (Japan Council Against Atomic and Hydrogen Bombs) held a rally to commemorate that event. At the rally an individual identified as a former U.S. Air Force sergeant, Al Hubbard, announced that he had participated while stationed at Tachikawa (1963-65) in bringing atomic bombs into Japan.[203] His testimony was immediately denied by the U.S. Embassy as well as the U.S. Forces-Japan, but that did not reduce the magnitude of the repercussions. Hubbard was questioned at length, and several significant inconsistencies were revealed in his story, but he did not reduce his adamantly held claim. He left Japan two weeks later on March 14 after having talked to several Diet member groups.[204] All in all, the JCP and Gensuikyo had noticeably upset the domestic political scene.

One final example will serve to illustrate the kind of activities opposition parties engage in regarding the nuclear issue. This last incident was the result (once again) of JSP member Yanosuke Narazaki releasing what was reported to be a secret U.S. Navy telegram concerning the creation of a U.S.-Japanese bilateral nuclear force.[205] The release, as might be expected, precipitated a storm of criticism and threatened the "tranquility" of the Diet session. By the next day, denials were streaming in from U.S. Defense Department sources, U.S. diplomatic sources, and the Japan Defense Agency, but rumors abounded that this was the issue that the opposition parties would use to unseat the Sato cabinet.[206] Immediately, the JSP, Komeito, and DSP consulted on joint strategy for the issue. The release of the telegram came about one month prior to the scheduled return of Okinawa to Japan, and these three opposition parties agreed that the bilateral nuclear force must be related to a secret U.S.-Japanese deal for return of the islands and dediced to force the Sato cabinet to resign.[207]

The U.S. Embassy held that the telegram was a forgery,[208] but Narazaki only repeated his earlier assertion that the "SDF is already taking an emergency nuclearization set up."[209] Since the actual telegram in question only directed the resumption of talks, the media began to speculate as to what kind of bilateral force was envisaged. The Asahi admitted it did not know but stated that it was "probably a plan to have the MSDF [Maritime Self-Defense Force] board merchant ships loaded with Polaris missiles or have them board U.S. polaris submarines."[210]

The exeuctive board of the LDP met to consider the telegram and issued a very concise statement:

This kind of problem produces very great effects on the people, such as uneasiness. If the contents of the telegram are genuine, the Government should immediately retire . . . if they are not genuine, Mr. Narazaki should take the responsibility for it.[211]

As time progressed, it became apparent that it was a case of forgery, but Narazaki refused to bend, replying, "If nuclear armament comes to sprout even a little, it is our duty to wipe it out. I have taken up the problem from that position."[212]

The issue ended with Narazaki nervously hurrying out of the Lower House Foreign Affairs Committee to make an appointment after being asked pointedly to confirm the authenticity of the telegram.[213]

These four examples of the role of the opposition parties in performing the watchdog function may have left the impression that their eternal vigilance is always in vain. Such is not the case. In 1965 the resourcefulness of the JSP led to the disclosure of the "Three Arrows Study," a contingency plan dealing with the defense of Korea, which had been written by senior Ground, Air, and Maritime Self-Defense officers.[214] It provided for the overseas deployment of Japanese forces and assumed that nuclear weapons would be introduced into Japan, among other things.

Another success was registered in February 1972 when alert interpellation by JSP, Komeito, and DSP Diet members caught Prime Minister Sato and his Finance minister, Mizuta, in a very compromising situation over the relationship between the 1972 draft budget and the Fourth Defense Build-Up Plan.

Such victories more than compensate for the numerous false alarms and demonstrate clearly that opposition parties do, in fact, exercise a very real restraining influence on the party in power.

THE BUSINESS COMMUNITY AND THE
NUCLEAR OPTION: THE ATOMIC INDUSTRIES GROUP

No commentary on the domestic political environment and Japan's nuclear option would be complete without mention of the position of business and industry with regard to this question. It has been established in the works of Thayer, Fukui, Langer, and others that there is a direct relationship and close interaction between government, party, and business. It can be assumed that the attitude of business toward the nuclear option could play a very substantial role in the course of future policy decisions.

First, however, it would appear useful to establish within the Japanese business community generally the particular importance of those industries closely involved in the nuclear question and those who would, most likely, become active lobbyists, either for or against the option, because of inherent parochial interests.

There are five consortia in Japan concerned with the production of equipment for the construction and operation of nuclear power reactors. These are the Mitsubishi Atomic Power Industries, consisting of approximately 25 Mitsubishi-related firms; the Tokyo Atomic Industrial Consortium of 27 Hitachi-Fuyokoi Group concerns; Sumitomo Atomic Energy Industries, Ltd. with 37 Sumitomo firms; Nippon Atomic Industry Group Company, Ltd. of 36 Mitsui firms, including Toshiba; and the Daiichi Atomic Power Industry Group made up of 22 Furukawa and Kawasaki companies including Fuji Electric Machinery.[215]

The financial and personnel status of the atomic power industries and related enterprises can be seen in this fiscal year 1970 report.

> Total expenditure by private industry: Y172,300 million
> Expenditure by electric power utilities: Y107,900 million
> Expenditure by mining and manufacturing industries: Y63,300 million
> Expenditure by trading firms: Y1,101 million
> Sales of mining and manufacturing industry: Y54,800 million
> Number of personnel engaged exclusively in nuclear business of mining and manufacturing and of electric utilities: 14,857 persons.[216]

Of the personnel engaged in atomic-related enterprises, 6,409 were technical specialists, of which 4,822 were mining and manufacturing specialists and 1,587 were specialists in electric power utilities.[217]

If the total figure of sales and expenditures is compared with the fiscal year 1970 gross national product, the relative financial impact of the industry can be indicated. In fiscal year 1970 the Japanese nuclear industry accounted for approximately 0.3 percent of the GNP, a figure 0.5 percent lower than that allocated for defense expenditures in the same year.[218]

The political power of this industry is not revealed adequately through such comparative figures since the atomic industry is intertwined with the nine electric power companies of Japan and, of course, the major business groups of Mitsubishi, Mitsui, and so on. Moreover, future power generation tables are posited on the availability of greatly increased nuclear generating capacities. By 1980, for example, the Central Electric Power Council has programmed a total of 74 nuclear plants for operation or some phase of construction. Such a massive influx of nuclear power facilities will mean that 25 percent of all electric power output will be nuclear based by 1980.[219]

Of further political significance is the fact that the prime minister sits as chairman on the Electric Power Resources Coordination Council, a government body that functions as coordinator of activities of the various ministries involved in programs for development of electric generating capacity.[220] Through the Japan Council of Atomic Energy, as well as the Japan Atomic Industrial Forum, the industry can coordinate its policy and publicize it.

As mentioned previously in this study, the Japan Council of Atomic Energy Industry and the Japan Atomic Industrial Forum (JAIF) have indicated a positive attitude toward ratification of the NPT. In April 1972, the senior managing director of the JAIF, Seinosuke Hashimoto, stated that

> industrialists have been making detailed investigations . . . and after studying methods to permit nuclear proliferation, have decided to support the signing of the treaty on condition that it does not impair the nature and the application of international safeguards, nor obstruct the peaceful application of atomic energy, and that all parties to the treaty are assured of equal rights.[221]

Speaking as he did in 1972, it is obvious that Hashimoto was referring to ratification when he inadvertently said "signing."

Thus, while the nuclear power industry has gone on record, on a number of occasions, favoring ratification, and even "an earlier ratification" of the NPT and has with its policy indicated its position with respect to nuclear weapons, it might be useful to recall some of the positions taken by representatives of other sectors of Japanese business and industry toward the nuclear question.

In October 1969, Takeshi Sakurada, one-time head of Nikkeiren (Japan Federation of Employers) stated in a speech that Japan was only one-half a nation, as only in a state possessing an independent defense potential "can full sovereignty be achieved." The Sakurada Statement (as it came to be known) also called for the revision of Article IX of the so-called peace constitution.[222] While not an outright advocacy of nuclear armament the proposal carried a very broad connotation (if it is assumed nuclear weapons are required to produce an independent defense potential). The fact that it came from one of the "Zaikai Shitenno," or four emperors of the Zaikai, made it a very noteworthy comment indeed.[223] Sakurada, by virtue of his position at the airy heights of Japanese industrial circles, had frequent occasion to make his opinions known.

In June 1971, another member of the Zaikai, Mitsubishi Heavy Industries Board Chairman Fumihiko Kono commented on the nuclear question directly saying, "It is not necessary for Japan at all to arm itself with nuclear weapons. American nuclear weapons are good enough." Kono made the remarks as he was becoming chairman of the Keidanren (Federation of Economic Organizations) Defense Production Committee on June 29, 1971. Kono indicated that Japan should concentrate on being "prepared for local wars with nations nearby," as that was "good enough."[224]

The chairmanship of the Defense Production Committee of the Keidanren placed Kono in the position of being a recognized spokesman for the entire defense industry. Prior to that time, he spoke for Mitsubishi as one-time president, then board chairman.[225] Mitsubishi Heavy Industries interestingly enough has garnered a major portion of defense contracts since 1965. In fiscal year 1969 it captured 31 percent of the total defense procurement for a defense contract income in excess of 70 billion yen, but still only 10 percent of Mitsubishi's total business.[226]

Kono, besides the positions mentioned, was also a vice-president of Keidanren and served on the prestigious Sanken (Industrial Problems Study Council) along with Takeshi Sakurada and 22 other top officials of Japanese industrial circles.[227] The Sanken has been called "the supreme command of Zaikai, the largest and strongest pressure group in Japan."[228]

More recently, January 1972, Kono spoke out again regarding the nuclear issue in connection with his plan to reduce the economic burdens of the United States vis-à-vis defense costs in Japan. Kono noted that Japan could help reduce U.S. expenditures by the "(1) purchase of U.S.-made weapons; (2) purchase of medium-term bonds; (3) the shifting of economic co-operation."[229] In reference to the nuclear question, he opined, "as for Japan which is under the U.S. nuclear 'umbrella,' is it not all right to think about paying fees for the umbrella in the future?"[230]

He indicated that he was speaking from his own personal view that Japan could "pay 200 to 300 million dollars a year as a fee" but he feared that such a payment would be thought to contravene the "non-possession of nuclear weapons pledge of the government."[231]

While the Kono proposal was dismissed two days later by the director general of the Defense Agency, Masumi Esaki, in a brisk "Japan is co-operating thoroughly with the U.S., and there is no need of sharing,"[232] the idea was not limited to Kono. This idea gained a new and wider acceptance after the publication of then President Nixon's foreign policy report of May 1973, which indirectly (according to Japanese observers) referred to the "free ride" Japan has had with regard to security.[233] In fact, this concept of a "charge for the nuclear umbrella" was to be discussed at a June U.S.-Japanese businessmen's conference.[234]

Another report stated, "there has been an opinion similar . . . even within financial circles. But, the general situation is that, as a 'national consensus,' the standpoint of adhering to the three non-nuclear principles will be maintained, to the last."[235]

Realistically, this is the only public stance responsible businessmen can take in Japan at this time. Japanese industrialists, possibly better than most political observers, must realize the current technical limitations on Japan and her long-term (25 to 30 years) dependence on outside sources before a self-sufficient nuclear status could be realized. Any hasty moves toward a nuclear program without a nuclear-weapons state as a patron could bring economic disaster to the island nation's nuclear industry and cause other grave political and economic repercussions.[236] Realizing this, the Japanese atomic power industry will concentrate on improving overall nuclear technical competence with advanced programs for centrifugal enrichment and the development of advanced reactors, especially commercially successful fast breeder reactors.

While the power to lobby intensively for rapid ratification of the NPT is at the disposal of Japan's industrial leaders, there is currently little to indicate any large-scale mobilization of resources toward that end. Conversely, there is nothing at all to indicate a desire to build a "Mitsubishi bomb" on the part of Japanese indus-

trial circles. Admitting the close and continuous intercourse that exists between business, party, and government,
there is no reason to expect any movement toward either
policy pole until (1) the international political/economic
situation becomes more stable and admits to some long-
range interpretation and (2) bilateral safeguard negotiations between Japan and the IAEA run their course. However, with every year the time lag between project initiation and demonstrable capability becomes less.

PUBLIC OPINION AND THE NUCLEAR OPTION

It is held by some Japanese political critics that
"nuclear allergy"--the keenly felt aversion to nuclear
weapons and implements for their delivery--dates from the
moment of the U.S. attacks on Hiroshima and Nagasaki in
the waning days of World War II. They argue that the natural, indignant reaction of the Japanese was suppressed
during the period of the U.S. occupation of Japan. Other
Japanese analysts insist that the "nuclear allergy" was
artificially created by the political left and is nothing
but a product of the cold war. They argue that, as it was
created by propaganda, skillful manipulation of the mass
media could bring about its elimination.[237]

In either case, there is agreement that a "nuclear
allergy" does in fact exist. This term, so often used by
the Japanese, was not of Japanese origin. It was first
attributed to Secretary of State John Foster Dulles who
reportedly said in 1954, "The Japanese have caught a nuclear allergy."[238] It is also from 1954 that the great
Japanese opposition to nuclear weapons manifested itself.
The cause célèbre was the Fukuryo Maru Incident, when a
fishing boat received high levels of fallout from the
Bikini H-bomb test of March 1, 1954. When news was released, a massive reaction developed throughout Japan. In
the words of the left-dominated Gensuikyo (Japan Council
for the Prohibition of Atomic and Hydrogen Bombs), "a chain
reaction of fear--then hysteria--swept the islands when it
was announced that the fishing boat, Number 5 Lucky Dragon
[Fukuryo Maru], had been caught in the atomic fallout and
that the fisherman named Kuboyama had died from radiation."[239] Japanese anger did not subside when Dulles
called the fishermen spies and their sickness "blood hepa-
titis."[240] Millions of Japanese--estimated at anywhere
from 23 million to 40 million--signed petitions urging
abolition of all atomic bombs.[241]

The initial outcry did seem genuine and at first was not associated with any particular political party. The reaction probably contained a strain of incipient nationalism and was thus all the more vocal. In the book Japanese Opinion Polls with Socio-Political Significance,[242] some of the antinuclear feeling during that era is apparent.

In an Asahi poll of May 10, 1954, a total of 2,498 individuals were asked if they supported the attitude of Foreign Minister Okazaki, who stressed cooperation with the U.S. H-bomb tests in order to defend the security of liberal democratic countries. Agreement was obtained from only 11 percent of those asked, while 55 percent replied in a negative manner.[243]

More than a year later, in a survey conducted by the Yoron Kagaku Kyokai (Scientific Public Opinion Association), respondents were asked, "What do you think about the H-bomb testing?" Eighty-two percent replied that the government should request its discontinuation, and 12 percent replied "it is inevitable."[244] This extremely high negative opinion came after the issue had been attracting nationwide attention for over a year. A poll in July 1957 reflected the same high degree of opposition. When asked "Do you think every kind of A and H bomb test should be prohibited?" some 87 percent of the respondents felt they should be, and only 5 percent thought they should not be limited.[245]

Thus, by the 1955-56 period, the Japanese attitude toward nuclear weapons had been recorded in several newspaper polls and by other opinion analysis groups. As to the question of public reaction to the 1945 events, information is available but rather suspect in nature. In 1970, a poll was conducted by the Mainichi in an effort to shed some light on this matter. This poll, taken 25 years after the event, must be viewed with some obvious reservations. The results of the poll are found in Table 2.1.

While it is interesting to note the "generation gap" in the last response of "A" and "B," of greater significance is the percentage who felt atom bombs should not be used "for any reason whatsoever." This kind of sentiment is not limited to the man in the street but can be seen today, based on far more reasoned analysis, even in the Defense Agency, where Chief of the Defense Bureau of the Defense Agency Kubo stated,

Even if we receive a nuclear attack some day . . . we should surrender to such a foe. What is

92

TABLE 2.1

Feeling Toward Use of A-Bomb, 1970
(percent)

Question A: "When I got to know the calamities caused by
the dropping of A-Bombs, my impression was
. . . (plural answers permitted)"

	Adults (over 30)	Youth (16-19)
This is war	32	50
Astonishment at immense destructive power	45	30
Misery	29	35
Indignation against the country that dropped them	36	28
Indignation against the Japanese government, which invited this	19	22
No more war, never	52	39

Question B: "About the dropping of A-Bombs, I think it
was . . . "

	Adults (over 20)	Youth (16-19)
Natural in warfare	8	6
Unavoidable for the United States	5	6
Acceptable as leading to end of war	3	5
Wrong in using at that stage	2	4
Too great a loss for Japan	14	17
Should not be done for any reason whatsoever	61	56

Source: Mainichi, August 3, 1970. Reprinted by permission.

93

important is not how to win but how to settle a
war. Defeat with many people alive is . . . more
valuable than victory without a living creature
left.[246]

Kubo has stated his view in the Diet that nuclear weapons do not offer a viable option for Japan in a military
sense, and he, therefore, opposes them for the JSDF. As
might be expected, this attitude is not universally shared
among the officers of the defense forces. Reportedly, a
few younger officers, especially in the Air Self-Defense
Force, would prefer to see the most modern weapons possible
in their arms inventories. (I must admit frankly that I
have yet to meet an officer who says that Japan should have
nuclear weapons. This comment is based on conversations
with senior JDF officer personnel who have indicated that
this is an attitude among a _few_ personnel.)
    Other indicators of mass opposition on the part of
the public to nuclear weapons can be seen in the following
polls concerning Japanese reactions to the controversy that
surrounded the return of Okinawa, the growing consciousness
of a Chinese nuclear capability, and the non-nuclear policy
of the Sato government.
    The Yomiuri Shimbun conducted a poll in 1968 that
directly asked the respondents to indicate their attitude
toward the return of Okinawa with nuclear bases. In the
results, released on April 22, 1968 only 3 percent favored
this course; 66 percent opposed; 20 percent thought it
inevitable; and 11 percent gave "don't know" answers.
Thus, only 3 percent of the total respondents actually
favored the continuation of nuclear bases on the main Ryukyu
island, but at least 23 percent were prepared to acquiesce.[247]
    In a two-part survey that was conducted during the
last half of March and the early part of April 1968, the
Yomiuri asked the following question: "The Sato Cabinet
has made clear its basic policy in relation to nuclear
weapons and atomic bombs, etc., saying 'Japan will not
possess, not allow introduction of, and not produce nuclear
weapons.' Do you agree or disagree with this policy?"
Replies are reflected in Table 2.2.
    In December 1968, the Asahi asked the question "Should
Japan have nuclear armament?" Answers were grouped by
"right now," "sooner or later," or "should not." In this
1968 poll 21 percent of the respondents indicated that
Japan should have nuclear weapons and 66 percent answered
in the negative.[248]

TABLE 2.2

Sato Cabinet Policy Toward Nuclear Wespons, 1968
(percent)

	March	April
Agree	72	78
Disagree	10	8
Does not make any difference	8	7
Some other opinion	2	1
I do not know	6	5
No answer	2	1

Source: Yomiuri, April 22, 1968. Reprinted by permission.

In a two-part survey conducted by the Mainichi on the 12th and 29th of May in 1969, the results shown in Table 2.3 were obtained from the same basic questions.

The average answer for "right now" was 2 percent; "in the future," 16 percent; "sooner or later," 27 percent--which produced a total average of 45 percent of the respondents who indicated Japan should have nuclear armaments. In this poll, 46 percent were opposed.[249]

The Mainichi survey further indicated that graduates of college were less inclined to think that Japan should have nuclear weapons than the noncollege graduates (see Table 2.4).

In December 1969, the Yomiuri Shimbun questioned some 2,357 people and received answers from 78.6 percent. The question of interest to this survey concerned the possible reintroduction of nuclear weapons into Okinawa after that island had been returned to Japan. The respondents were asked if the government of Japan should refuse the entry or permit the entry of such weapons if asked by the United States. Seventy percent replied that entry should be denied, 10 percent recommended permission be granted, and almost 20 percent were undecided or had no answer. Again, more than 70 percent of the respondents had indicated an antinuclear policy, while only 10 percent called for a policy to permit the introduction of nuclear weapons.[250]

In a national poll conducted by the Yomiuri among 3,000 men and women and released on May 31, 1970, the subject of militarization was examined at great length.

95

TABLE 2.3

Reaction to Nuclear Armament by Age Group
Question: "Should Japan Have Nuclear Weapons?"

Age Group	Right Now	Near Future	Sooner or Later	Total	Should Not
20s	2	17	25	44	51
30s	2	15	25	42	51
40s	3	16	28	47	47
50s	2	18	32	42	40
Over 60	3	17	30	50	36

Source: Mainichi, May 12 and 29, 1969. Reprinted by permission.

TABLE 2.4

Reaction to Nuclear Armament by Students
Question: "Should Japan Have Nuclear Arms?"

	Now	Soon	Sooner or Later	Total	No
Graduates of middle school	2	18	28	48	43
High school	1	16	29	46	48
College or university	3	14	21	38	58

Source: Mainichi, May 12 and 29, 1969. Reprinted by permission.

To the obvious question "Has militarism revived in Japan?" 22.6 percent replied that they thought it had, and 50.5 percent thought it had not. Table 2.5 gives results on the question of primary concern to this book, "Do you desire nuclear weapons for Japan?"

This poll also revealed a very interesting trend with respect to Sino-Japanese relations. Two Yomiuri polls in 1968 had indicated that respondents were quite anxious over the Chinese "threat." This was demonstrated when 35 percent expressed a "strong" feeling of threat from China; in an April 1969 Mainichi poll the figure increased to 43 percent of respondents strongly fearing their neighbor. The figure reached its high in the Mainichi poll of March 1970, when a high degree of fear was indicated by 46 percent of those responding. Only two months later, in May 1970, this expressed fear dropped suddenly to 18.6 percent.[251]

The Yomiuri also conducted a rather extensive survey of Tokyo University students and compared the results with the attitudes as found from the survey immediately above. The respondents numbered only 490 and were primarily sophomores (90 percent). Only 0.6 percent were freshmen, 9 percent were juniors, and 0.4 percent were seniors. The survey was far-ranging, touching on future possible defense options for Japan, and took place during a sit-in to protest automatic extension of the U.S.-Japanese Security Treaty. The students were asked to give their reaction to the idea of Japan's having nuclear weapons. Table 2.6 compares student answers with opinions obtained from respondents in the public at large.

TABLE 2.5

Public Reaction to Nuclear Armament
Question: "Do You Desire Nuclear Arms?"

Response	Percent
Highly desirable	2.5
Rather desirable	5.2
Either way	12.1
Rather undesirable	22.3
Extremely undesirable	45.3
Do not know	12.6

Source: Yomiuri, May 31, 1970. Reprinted by permission.

TABLE 2.6

Comparison of Students' and General Public's Reactions to
Nuclear Armament
Question: "Are Nuclear Arms Desirable for Japan?"
(percent)

	Students	Public
Highly desirable	4.1	2.5
Rather desirable	2.7	5.2
Either way	5.3	12.1
Rather undesirable	9.8	22.3
Extremely undesirable	76.3	45.3
Do not know	1.8	12.6

Source: Yomiuri, June 19, 1970. Reprinted by permission.

If it is remembered that the student respondents were taking part in an antisecurity treaty demonstration at the time of their interviews, the answers are very interesting.

From October 2, 1971, for three days, the Yomiuri conducted a survey that contacted 3,700 adults. Answers were obtained from 2,965 persons--a recovery rate of 80.1 percent. This survey covered a broad range of international and domestic subjects but did not inquire as to the nuclear question. However, the question of militarism was covered in the inquiry and revealed that 49.8 percent of the respondents thought that militarism had revived or was in the process of reviving.[252] Another question was asked that related to the respondents' faith in the U.S. commitment to defend Japan. The answers showed that of those surveyed, only 29.6 percent thought the United States "will defend Japan" in an emergency; 38.2 percent replied the United States would not help, and 32.2 percent were undecided.[253]

A Mainichi survey of May 3, 1972 asked, "Do you think or do not think that Japan should have nuclear armaments?" There were 3,015 voters chosen, and a recovery rate of 74 percent was realized. The answers in this poll showed the party preferences of the respondents and is particularly valuable from that respect (see Table 2.7).

The last survey to be introduced, as an example of public opinion on the nuclear question, is the Sankei Shim-

TABLE 2.7

Reaction to Nuclear Armament by Political Parties
Question: "Should Japan Have Nuclear Arms?"
(percent)

Reaction	Total	LDP	JSP	Komeito	DSP	JCP	None
Should arm itself with nuclear armament immediately	2	3	2	4	4	1	1
Should arm itself with nuclear armaments in the near future	11	16	10	11	6	3	8
Should do so sometime or other	22	31	19	13	28	12	17
Should absolutely not arm itself with nuclear weapons	58	45	65	68	61	80	67
Do not know	7	5	4	4	1	4	7

Source: Mainichi, May 3, 1972. Reprinted by permission.

bun "Survey of 1,000 Persons." The results of this survey appeared on November 25, 1972 and, as such, are the latest figures available. However, the sample was smaller than the other nationwide polls that have been introduced in this study. The poll queried its respondents about the "possibility of nuclear armaments 10 years from now." Those indicating that Japan would have such weapons numbered 42 percent, which was down from the 1971 Sankei survey, which registered 43.9 percent.[254]

It would appear, from an assessment of the polls available to this researcher, that two specific types of questions concerning nuclear weapons have been asked. One question has been quite delimited, asking the respondent only about the desirability of nuclear weapons for Japan or for his opinion on the Three Non-Nuclear Principles.

99

In polls of this kind the response has been fairly consistent, and negative answers over 60 percent of those who answered have been registered. This question allows the respondent a "moral option," and the depth of the nuclear allergy shows through.

The second type of question, however, introduces latent policy considerations when the question is "Should Japan have nuclear weapons?" The Chinese nuclear threat, which caused a "strong feeling of threat" for 46 percent of the Japanese questioned in the Mainichi poll of March 27, 1970, had registered a level of "some feeling of threat" on the part of 78 percent of the respondents, a figure identical to the previous year and 6 percent higher than a Yomiuri poll of 1968. Thus, when the respondents were asked if Japan should have nuclear weapons, it is possible that the context of international politics is introduced and the Japanese who were questioned, therefore, answered in a more nationalistic manner. This produced affirmative answers to a much higher degree, and reached a high of 45 percent in the Mainichi poll of May 1969. By May 1972, when the Northeast Asian environment had changed drastically with the Sino-U.S. rapprochement and increasing overtures for normalization of Sino-Japanese relations, the percentage of respondents answering that Japan should have nuclear weapons had dropped to 35 percent.

In the latest poll available, for this analysis, those indicating that Japan would have nuclear weapons increased to 42 percent. This particular increase indicates one of several possibilities: (1) a difference between the words rendering "would" and "should" (the use of "would" might indicate an acceptance of inevitability on the part of the respondents, but not necessarily personal approval); (2) that the last poll available, since it was approximately one-third the size of other polls used, might show trends when compared against itself, but might have a built-in error factor different from the other polls; (3) that attitudes have changed in light of the "Nixon shocks," Sino-U.S. rapprochement, and a growing awareness of the gradual withdrawal of U.S. forces from Asia.

In summary, it appears that the basic dislike of nuclear weapons has not appreciably lessened in almost two decades during the period of this review, but there has been a growing pragmatism and awareness of a changing Japanese role in the international system. The growing nationalistic pragmatism seems to have overcome moral disgust and has led an increasing number of respondents to record that "Japan should have nuclear weapons." This attitude was especially high during the period of perceived Chinese threat, dipped, and then registered a slight increase. This latter period has been accompanied by greater Japanese-U.S. economic competition.

The one conclusion to be drawn from this overview of public opinion polls is that, in the face of what is considered an extreme threat to the Japanese state (based on the reactions reflected in the 1967, 1968, and 1969 polls in response to the incipient Chinese nuclear threat), the government of Japan probably could advocate a nuclear rearmament program of some description and receive the support of a considerable portion of the population if the perception of external threat was high. Whether that portion would be enough to effect a revision of the constitution is an interesting point, and whether the constitution would need revision under those circumstances is another.

SUMMARY: THE DOMESTIC POLITICAL FACTORS

Currently those who advocate outwardly the development of nuclear weapons for Japan are extremely few in number; however, those who are in positions of responsibility seem to be reluctant to close the door completely to Japan's nuclear option. There are some (members of the Soshinkai of the LDP) who advocate that "a free hand as to atomic energy should not be restricted forever";[255] and they were strong enough in the spring of 1972 to halt any forward movement toward ratification of the NPT that existed at the time. Since then, the "stalled" situation has been reiterated by MITI's Nakasone, in July 1972, and by a "government source" in January 1973. The author's own interview program in February 1973 provided additional data to indicate that only technical talks on safeguards were possible then, and that no "real" progress, in the political sense, could be recorded during 1973. The next year was the year of opposition from the Science and Technology Agency and of the developments in India, Egypt, and Israel. The summer of 1975 is now seen as the earliest that ratification can be accomplished.

While progress toward NPT ratification is miniscule, public opinion and the political opponents of the LDP--the JSP, JCP, Komeito, and DSP--remain genuinely opposed to any overt moves toward a nuclear weapons program; however, it is possible that the advocacy of a nuclear arms program by the government of Japan might be tolerated by the general public if the international situation altered so drastically so as to present an imminent danger to the continued existence of the Japanese state.

In a "normal" political environment, which is highly critical of any moves toward nuclear weapons, Japanese policy-makers and the LDP, from a strategic defense policy viewpoint, have to face the reality of not being able to develop, test, and store nuclear weapons prior to a dis-advantageous deterioration of the international system. Thus, in order to pursue the "crash program" option, the only one available under normal political conditions, the government of Japan and the Liberal Democratic Party will have to follow a policy of parallel and ancillary develop-ment of all the technological capabilities needed to pro-duce and deliver nuclear weapons, so the time lag from program initiation to effective deterrent force will be as short as possible.

Whether or not this has been the case will be examined in the following two chapters, which will review the status of Japan's nuclear power program and programs that are re-lated to advanced systems that could contribute to the de-livery of nuclear warheads.

NOTES

1. Hugh Borton, Japan's Modern Century (New York: Ronald Press, 1970), p. 572.

2. UN Arms Limitation Office, Foreign Ministry of Japan, Kakuheiki Kakusan no Sengai Ryoku (Tokyo: Foreign Ministry of Japan, 1972), p. 42.

3. Ibid., p. 43.

4. Defense Agency of Japan, The Defense of Japan (Tokyo: Defense Agency of Japan, 1970), p. 40.

5. Yomiuri, March 15, 1973, U.S. Embassy translation.

6. The word senjutsu was used, which is normally translated as "tactics"; however, the word can, depending on the context, also be rendered as "strategic." Yomiuri, March 15, 1973. Comment based on the appended remarks of the translator of the U.S. Embassy Translation Service.

7. Tokyo Shimbun, March 18, 1973, U.S. Embassy trans-lation.

8. Ibid.

9. Asahi, March 21, 1973, U.S. Embassy translation.

10. Ibid.

11. Ibid.

12. Borton, op. cit., p. 586.

13. Yomiuri, June 21, 1971, U.S. Embassy translation.

14. Government of Japan, The Atomic Energy Basic Law No. 186 (Tokyo: Government of Japan, 1955), pp. 1-2 (held by author).

15. UN Arms Limitation Office, Kakuheiki Kakusan, p. 118.

16. Ibid.

17. Ibid.

18. Ibid., p. 119.

19. Asahi Evening News, March 14, 1972.

20. Atoms in Japan, July 1972, p. 14.

21. Edwin O. Reischauer, Japan: The Story of a Nation (New York: Alfred A. Knopf, 1970), p. 273.

22. Donald C. Hellmann, Japanese Domestic Politics and Foreign Policy (Los Angeles: University of California Press, 1969); Haruhiro Fukui, Party in Power (Los Angeles: University of California Press, 1970); and Nathaniel B. Thayer, How the Conservatives Rule Japan (Princeton, N.J.: Princeton University Press, 1969).

23. Sankei, December 12, 1972, U.S. Embassy translation.

24. Mainichi, June 21, 1972, U.S. Embassy translation. Although Tanaka and Fukuda did engage in a bitterly fought contest for party leadership, there are indications of a possible rapprochement between the two, which even goes so far as to contemplate a Katsura-Saionji-style long-term alternation of the office of prime minister. Whether or not this kind of "deal" would really interest the 67-year-old Fukuda is speculative indeed; after the events of July 1974, this kind of long-range cooperation would seem to be out of the question.

25. Yomiuri, June 8, 1972, U.S. Embassy translation.

26. Mainichi, June 21, 1972, U.S. Embassy translation. Note: This figure of 855 million yen represents only reported contributions and was arrived at by combining the Tanaka and Hashimoto contributions. By virtue of being the faction of the prime minister, it will have attracted a significant increase in 1972-73, in relative terms.

27. Mainichi, June 21, 1972, U.S. Embassy translation.

28. Asahi, December 12, 1972, U.S. Embassy translation.

29. Paul F. Langer, Japanese National Security Policy--Domestic Determinants (Santa Monica, Calif.: RAND Corporation, 1972), p. 24. Note: The Sato faction has now divided into the Tanaka and Fukuda factions, with the larger number, especially younger members, going to the Tanaka faction (Yomiuri, June 8, 1972).

30. Interview in Japan, February 1973.

31. _Asahi_, November 20, 1971. The Yasukuni Shrine Bill called for the nationalization of that particular shrine and was objected to by the Christians as giving new life to a state-church system.

32. Ibid.

33. Ibid., September 4, 1972.

34. Langer, op. cit., p. 25.

35. _Mainichi Daily News_, November 13, 1970.

36. _Sankei_, December 12, 1972, U.S. Embassy translation.

37. Thayer, op. cit., p. 46.

38. _Mainichi Daily News_, October 9, 1970.

39. Thayer, op. cit., pp. 323-32.

40. See especially Langer, op. cit., for this point of view.

41. Stockholm International Peace Research Institute, _SIPRI Yearbook of World Armaments and Disarmament 1969/1970_ (New York: Humanities Press, 1970), pp. 462-63. Within the LDP, the Foreign Affairs Research Council (chairman, Aichi Kiichi) established a Nuclear Nonproliferation Treaty Committee to study this matter on March 2, 1972. Sasaki Yoshitake was appointed chairman of that committee.

42. UN Arms Control Group, Foreign Ministry of Japan, "Statement by Ambassador Tanaka at the Conference on the Committee on Disarmament of August 17, 1971" (Tokyo: Foreign Office, 1971), and ibid., at the meeting of the CCD on July 6, 1971.

43. UN Arms Control Group, July 6, 1971.

44. UN Arms Control Group, August 17, statement.

45. UN Arms Control Group, March 28, 1972, statement of Ambassador Nishibori.

46. Ibid.

47. Langer, op. cit., p. 22.

48. See especially Thayer, op. cit., pp. 210-11.

49. Ibid.

50. _Mainichi_, April 2, 1972, U.S. Embassy translation.

51. Ibid.

52. Langer, op. cit., p. 33.

53. Ibid., p. 31; and World Policy Research Institute, _Japan's Defense and Security_ (Tokyo: World Research Institute, 1968).

54. Langer, op. cit., p. 33.

55. Ibid., p. 34.

56. National Defense College, "Shin Anpo Joyaku-no Ron Ten" (LDP, April 1960), _Kakuto no AnpoSeisaku_, 1973, pp. 13-14.

57. National Defense College, "Anzen Hosho ni Kansuru Chosa Kai" (LDP, July 1963), Kakuto no AnpoSeisaku, pp. 110-11.

58. Ibid.

59. Walter C. Clemens, Jr., The Arms Race and Sino-Soviet Relations (Stanford, Calif.: Hoover Institution on War, Revolution and Peace, Stanford University, 1968), p. 86.

60. National Defense College, "Soren no Seisaku oyobi Chukyo no Kaku Jikkenga Wagakuni no Anzen Hosho ni Oyobosu Eikyo Narabi ni kore ni Taisuru Wagakuni no Torubeki Hosaku" (LDP, November 1964), Kakuto no AnpoSeisaku, p. 119.

61. Ibid.

62. Ibid., p. 123.

63. Ibid., p. 125.

64. Ibid., p. 125.

65. National Defense College, "Kyokuto Josei to Waga-kuni no AnzenHosho" (LDP, May 1965), p. 126.

66. Ibid.

67. Ibid., p. 130.

68. National Defense College, "Kyokuto to Wagakuni no AnzenHosho Taiasku" (LDP, May 1965), Kakuto no AnpoSeisaku, p. 146.

69. Ibid.

70. Ibid.

71. Ibid.

72. National Defense College, "Wagakuni no Anzen Hosho ni Kansuru Chukan Hokoku" (LDP, June 1966), Kakuto no Anpo-Seisaku, p. 157.

73. Ibid.

74. World Policy Research Institute, op. cit., pp. 6-7.

75. Ibid., p. 6.

76. National Defense College, "Wagakuni no Anzen Hosho ni Kansuru Chukan Hokoku," p. 157.

77. Ibid.

78. Ibid.

79. World Policy Research Institute, op. cit., p. 6.

80. Ibid.

81. National Security Research Council, Nihon no Anzenhosho, 1970 e no Tembo (Tokyo: Asagumo Sha, 1968), pp. 293-342. While not an official organ of the LDP, this research organization can be considered a semiofficial body. It is not party or government but is subject to overlapping membership.

82. Ibid.

83. Ibid., pp. 327-28 and 301-02.

84. National Defense College, "Anpo Seisaku no Ronten" (LDP, April 1969), <u>Kakuto no AnpoSeisaku</u>, p. 37.

85. National Defense College, "Nichibei Anpojoyaku no keizoku ni Kansuru Toseimei" (LDP, July 1970), p. 6.

86. <u>Tokyo Shimbun</u>, November 14, 1972, U.S. Embassy translation.

87. Ibid., October 15, 1972, U.S. Embassy translation.

88. <u>Shokun</u>, October 1970.

89. Osamu Kaihara, <u>Nihon Retto Shubitairon</u> (Tokyo: Asagumo Sha, 1972), pp. 327-29.

90. Interview in Japan, February 1973 (not with Genda). See also Michael Hughes, "Japan's Air Power Options" (Medford, Mass.: Ph.D. dissertation, Tufts University), p. 64.

91. Langer, op. cit., p. 26.

92. John K. Emmerson, <u>Arms, Yen and Power: The Japanese Dilemma</u> (Tokyo: Charles E. Tuttle, 1972), p. 129.

93. Ibid., p. 339.

94. <u>Mainichi</u>, December 10, 1971, U.S. Embassy translation. The statement was made by Yasui Yoshinori, JSP Hokkaido, 2nd District, during interpellation on December 10, 1971.

95. Ibid.

96. Emmerson, op. cit., p. 339.

97. Ibid., p. 351.

98. Kaiharu, <u>Nihon Retto Shubitairon</u>, pp. 325-27.

99. Ibid., p. 323.

100. Ibid., pp. 322-24.

101. Ibid., pp. 326-27.

102. <u>Yomirui</u>, February 16, 1973, U.S. Embassy translation.

103. Ibid.

104. <u>Asahi</u>, February 6, 1972; and <u>Nihon Keizai</u>, February 8, 1972, U.S. Embassy translations.

105. <u>Tokyo Shimbun</u>, February 9, 1972, U.S. Embassy translation.

106. <u>Asahi</u>, February 22, 1972, U.S. Embassy translation.

107. <u>Yomiuri</u>, February 10, 1972, U.S. Embassy translation.

108. <u>Tokyo Shimbun</u>, May 2, 1972, U.S. Embassy translation; and <u>Asahi</u>, October 10, 1972, U.S. Embassy translation.

109. Interview in Japan, February 1973.

110. <u>Asahi</u>, October 19, 1972, U.S. Embassy translation.

111. <u>Atoms in Japan</u>, July 1972, p. 53.

112. Ibid., p. 55.

113. Ibid., p. 53.

114. Japan, Ministry of Foreign Affairs, <u>Kakuheiki Kakusan no Senzai Ryoku</u> (Tokyo: Arms Limitation Office, July 1972), p. 116. Translation by the author.

115. Ibid.

116. Stockholm International Peace Research Institute, <u>The Near-Nuclear Countries and the NPT</u> (New York: Humanities Press, 1972), p. 112.

117. <u>Tokyo Shimbun</u>, December 11, 1971, U.S. Embassy translation.

118. Ibid., January 7, 1972, U.S. Embassy translation.

119. <u>Yomiuri</u>, March 3, 1972, U.S. Embassy translation.

120. <u>Japan Atomic Industrial Forum (JAIF) Weekly</u>, March 16, 1972.

121. <u>Mainichi</u>, March 9, 1972, U.S. Embassy translation.

122. <u>Tokyo Shimbun</u>, March 15, 1972, U.S. Embassy translation.

123. <u>Atoms in Japan</u>, May 1972, p. 3.

124. Ibid., pp. 5-6. Safeguards--"A device by which control is exercised on all forms of peaceful nuclear activities in order to ensure that no disguised production of nuclear weapons can take place." Ryukichi Imai, "Nuclear Safeguards," <u>Adelphi Papers #86</u>, March 1972, p. 1.

125. <u>Atoms in Japan</u>, May 1972, p. 6.

126. Ibid.

127. Ibid., p. 3.

128. <u>JAIF Weekly</u>, June 8, 1972.

129. <u>Atoms in Japan</u>, July 1972, p. 14.

130. <u>Mainichi</u>, June 4, 1973, U.S. Embassy translation.

131. <u>Sankei</u>, June 7, 1973, U.S. Embassy translation.

132. <u>Tokyo Shimbun</u>, January 5, 1973, U.S. Embassy translation.

133. <u>Tokyo Shimbun</u>, January 5, 1973; and <u>Asahi</u>, January 6, 1973, U.S. Embassy translations.

134. See <u>Atoms in Japan</u>, August 1972, pp. 29-43 for problems related to local opposition to many proposed nuclear power plants. Data on the decline in "spirit" of the atomic industry lobby came from a very high Foreign Office source, February 1973.

135. Hisao Iwashima, "Japan's Defense Dilemma," p. 4. Unpublished paper, National Defense College, Tokyo, Japan, March 14, 1973.

136. <u>Sankei</u>, June 28, 1974, U.S. Embassy translation.

137. <u>Mainichi</u>, June 4, 1973, U.S. Embassy translation.

138. Ibid.

139. <u>Nihon Keizai</u>, June 18, 1973.

140. <u>Asahi</u>, May 19, 1974.

141. <u>Yomiuri</u>, May 19, 1974.

142. Ibid.
143. Japan Times, May 19, 1974.
144. Ibid.
145. Ibid.
146. Washington Post, May 21, 1974.
147. Foreign Broadcast Information Service (FBIS), May 23, 1974.
148. Ibid.
149. Washington Post, May 26, 1974.
150. Sankei, May 23, 1974.
151. Los Angeles Times, May 25, 1974.
152. Ibid.
153. Washington Post, May 26, 1974.
154. Nihon Keizai, June 11, 1974.
155. FBIS, June 14, 1974.
156. New York Times, June 15, 1974.
157. Mainichi, June 19, 1974.
158. Sankei, June 18, 1974.
159. Ibid., June 19, 1974.
160. Tokyo Shimbun, June 19, 1974, U.S. Embassy translation.
161. Sankei, June 18, 1974, U.S. Embassy translation.
162. Yomiuri, June 18, 1974, U.S. Embassy translation.
163. Asahi, June 24, 1974.
164. Ibid.
165. Mainichi, June 28, 1974, U.S. Embassy translation.
166. Asahi Evening News, July 1, 1974.
167. Ibid., July 18, 1974.
168. Yomiuri, July 18, 1974.
169. Ibid., July 21, 1974.
170. Ibid.
171. Ibid.
172. Sankei, July 29, 1974, U.S. Embassy translation.
173. Yomiuri, August 11, 1974.
174. Allan B. Cole and others, Socialist Parties in Postwar Japan (New Haven, Conn.: Yale University Press, 1966), p. 34.
175. Ibid., p. 33.
176. Tokyo Shimbun, November 14, 1972, U.S. Embassy translation.
177. Iwashima, op. cit., p. 2. Data source was Nicchu-Yukokyugunjin Kai, no. 151 (February 1973).
178. World Policy Research Institute, op. cit., pp. 42-47.
179. National Defense College, "Chudoshugi ni yoru Seikaiheiwa Jitsugen e no Michi" (Komeito, March 1969), Kakuto no Anposeisaku, p. 89.

180. Mainichi Daily News, February 17, 1970.

181. Ibid., February 3, 1970.

182. Tokyo Shimbun, June 15, 1972, U.S. Embassy translation. Also see the latter part of this chapter dealing with the Komeito antinuclear activities.

183. Ibid., November 14, 1972.

184. Cole, op. cit., p. 75.

185. Mainichi Daily News, April 17, 1970.

186. National Defense College, "Showa Sanjunananendo Totaikai Kettei no Gaikoseisaku--Wagakuni no Anzen to Heiwa no tami ni" (DCP, April 1962), Kakuto no AnpoSeisaku, p. 28.

187. Ibid., p. 35.

188. National Defense College, "1972 nen do Undo Hoshinan," Kakuto no Anposeisaku (DSP, March 1972), pp. 10-15.

189. Ibid.

190. Ibid., pp. 12-13.

191. Ibid., p. 11.

192. Tokyo Shimbun, November 14, 1972.

193. Akahata, no. 1 (October 20, 1945), as quoted in Robert A. Scalapino, The Japanese Communist Movement: 1920-1965 (Santa Monica, Calif.: RAND, 1966), p. 79.

194. World Policy Research Institute, op. cit., p. 50.

195. Ibid., p. 51.

196. Tokyo Shimbun, November 14, 1972, U.S. Embassy translation.

197. Asahi, November 17, 1971, U.S. Embassy translation.

198. Ibid., November 25, 1971.

199. Yomiuri, November 29, 1971, U.S. Embassy translation.

200. Komeito, The 10th National Convention (Tokyo: Komeito, June 1972), p. 82.

201. Ibid.; and Asahi, December 8, 1971, U.S. Embassy translation.

202. Komeito, op. cit., p. 82.

203. Nihon Keizai, March 2, 1971, U.S. Embassy translation.

204. Asahi, March 14, 1972, U.S. Embassy translation.

205. Sankei, April 13, 1972; Sankei, April 14, 1972; and Yomiuri, April 14, 1972--all U.S. Embassy translations.

206. Nihon Keizei, April 14, 1972, U.S. Embassy translation.

207. Ibid.

208. Yomiuri, April 14, 1972, U.S. Embassy translation.

209. Tokyo Shimbun, April 14, 1972, U.S. Embassy translation.

210. <u>Asahi</u>, April 13, 1972, U.S. Embassy translation.
211. <u>Mainichi</u>, April 14, 1972, U.S. Embassy translation.
212. <u>Asahi</u>, April 27, 1972, U.S. Embassy translation.
213. <u>Yomiuri</u>, May 18, 1972, U.S. Embassy translation.
214. Thomas Marle Brendle, "Japan's Ground Self-Defense Force, 1950-1970; Problems Encountered in Developing and Managing an All Volunteer Army," Ph.D. Dissertation, Fletcher School of Law and Diplomacy, Tufts University, Medford, Mass., 1971.
215. <u>Mainichi Daily News</u>, April 21, 1972; and <u>Atoms in Japan</u>, June 1972, p. 29.
216. <u>Atoms in Japan</u>, December 1971, p. 10; and ibid., April 1972, p. 21.
217. Ibid.
218. Japan, Budget Bureau, Ministry of Finance, <u>The Budget in Brief</u> (Tokyo: Ministry of Finance, 1971), pp. 38 and 64.
219. <u>Atoms in Japan</u>, May 1972, p. 10, and May 1971, p. 6.
220. John E. Endicott, "Japan's Nuclear Option," unpublished MALD Thesis, Fletcher School of Law and Diplomacy, Tufts University, September 14, 1972, p. 44.
221. <u>Atoms in Japan</u>, April 1972, p. 20.
222. <u>Yomiuri</u>, October 18, 1969.
223. <u>Mainichi Daily News</u>, January 21, 1971.
224. <u>Yomiuri</u>, June 30, 1971, U.S. Embassy translation.
225. <u>Mainichi Daily News</u>, November 17, 1970.
226. Langer, op. cit., pp. 66-67.
227. <u>Mainichi Daily News</u>, November 17, 1970; and ibid., January 26, 1971.
228. Ibid., January 26, 1971.
229. <u>Nihon Keizai</u>, January 14, 1972, U.S. Embassy translation.
230. Ibid.
231. Ibid.
232. <u>Mainichi</u>, January 16, 1972, U.S. Embassy translation.
233. Sankei, June 17, 1973, U.S. Embassy translation.
234. Ibid.
235. <u>Nihon Keizai</u>, January 14, 1972, U.S. Embassy translation.
236. For more on this subject, see Chapter 3 of this study.
237. Takeshi Muramatsu, "Japan's Choice" (unpublished paper, Tokyo, 1971), pp. 16-17.

238. Seinosuke Hashimoto, _Nihon no Genshiryoku, 15 nen no Ayumi_ (Tokyo: Japan Industrial Forum, 1971), p. 19.

239. Jijimondai Kenkyujo, _Gensuikyo_ (Tokyo: Jijimondai Kenkyujo, 1961), pp. 1-2. (This publication is in English.)

240. Hashimoto, op. cit., p. 19.

241. _Gensuikyo_ claims 23 million (p. 4), according to the above referenced Jijimondai publication, while 40 million is the figure cited in J. A. A. Stockwin, _The Japanese Socialist Party and Neutralism_ (Victoria: Melbourne University Press, 1968), p. 88.

242. Allan B. Cole and Naomichi Nakanishi, eds., _Japanese Opinion Polls with Socio-Political Significance 1947-1957_ (Medford, Mass.: Fletcher School of Law and Diplomacy, undated), pp. 704, 721, and 763.

243. Ibid., p. 704.

244. Ibid., p. 72.

245. Ibid., p. 763.

246. _Mainichi Daily News_, May 27, 1972. In an interview on February 15, 1973, Kubo mentioned that, on occasion (the above article, for example), "strategic accommodation" is incorrectly translated as "surrender"--the basic difference was not pointed out at the time.

247. _Yomiuri_, April 22, 1968. (Newspapers in this section are the author's translations, unless otherwise noted.)

248. _Asahi_, December 1968.

249. _Mainichi_, May 12 and 29, 1969.

250. _Yomiuri_, December 11, 1969.

251. Prime Minister's Office, "Kokumin no Boeiishiki," _Chosa Geppo_, February 1972, p. 66. An analysis of events between Japan and China that led to this dramatic shift could be the subject of a detailed study in itself. However, several milestone events do stand out that help in explaining the sudden relaxation of anxiety on the part of respondents. First, the turmoil of the Cultural Revolution was winding down. The Red Guard fury had all but passed, and it will be recalled that in August 1970 Mao ordered the Red Guard back into the disciplined Communist Youth League. That fire had burned itself out. (See the _Mainichi Daily News_, August 22, 1970.) The above point would not be enough to explain the sudden change without several other key developments:

1. In a low-key announcement in mid-February 1970, Prime Minister Sato stated in the Diet that he intended to "establish ambassadorial-level contacts with mainland China." (_Mainichi Daily News_, February 18, 1970.)

2. On March 5, the Memorandum Trade Mission left for China headed by Yoshimi Furui. (<u>Daily Yomiuri</u>, March 6, 1970.)

3. On March 12, evidently through the good offices of the memo mission and Furui, Aiichiro Fujiyama was invited to China.

4. Fujiyama visited China for approximately one month and on his return (April 23) called for recognition of Peking. (<u>Mainichi Daily News</u>, April 24, 1970.)

5. On May 8, Sato announced that the government of Japan "was prepared to enter into government-to-government contracts with China to promote mutual understanding." (<u>Mainichi Daily News</u>, May 9, 1970.)

6. An inordinate amount of news of China appeared in the newspapers concerning the prospects for renewed relations. In summary, the attitudes reflected in the poll correspond remarkedly to certain key events during the March-May period.

252. <u>Yomiuri</u>, October 19, 1971.
253. Ibid.
254. <u>Sankei</u>, November 25, 1972, U.S. Embassy translation.
255. Ibid., February 14, 1972.

ITS DEVELOPMENT AND CURRENT STATUS

Any complete understanding of Japan's nuclear option must include a brief introduction into the mechanism that has made such an option possible. The civilian or peaceful nuclear program must be turned to, for it is from this base that, so to speak, swords could be made from plowshares.

The Japan Atomic Energy Commission (JAEC) was established under provisions of the Law for Establishment of the Atomic Energy Commission of December 19, 1955. Incorporated into Article 2 of this act was the proviso that the development and utilization of nuclear energy "be limited to peaceful purposes and performed independently under democratic management." The law further required that the data resulting from the development programs "be made public to contribute to international cooperation."[1]

The JAEC, actually set up in January 1956 as a part of the Prime Minister's Office, was assigned the task of planning and executing the atomic energy program, subject, of course, to the Prime Minister's concurrence. Other organizations were created in rapid succession to prosecute, in various capacities, the provisions of the Atomic Energy Law. The following groups were subsequently established: the Radiation Council (1956), to discuss standards to prevent radiation hazard; the Japan Atomic Energy Research Institute (1956), a joint government/industry endeavor for atomic research; the Japan Atomic Industrial Forum (1956), an industrial body to promote peaceful uses of atomic energy; the Power Reactor and Nuclear Fuel Development Corporation (PNC, 1957), a development corporation to advance power reactor and fuel capabilities; the National Institute for Radiological Sciences (1957), set up as part of the Science and Technology Agency to do research into the problems of radiation hazards; and most recently, in 1963, the Japan Nuclear Ship Development Agency, established to oversee the building of nuclear-powered ships.[2]

This rather elaborate business and governmental structure was further strengthened by the creation of the five nuclear consortia consisting of Mitsubishi Atomic Power Industries, Inc.; the Tokyo Atomic Industrial Consortium; Nippon Atomic Industry Group Company, Ltd.; Sumitomo Atomic Energy Industries, Ltd.; and the First Atomic Power Industry Group.[3] Various universities and private research laboratories reinforce this general structure, giving it a wide base.

The early Japanese program was affected by the general euphoria common to all those who participated in the various early peaceful application programs. High hopes for rapid progress ran into the cold realities of the technical difficulties, and what was called the "era of slow-down" was entered.[4] However, by 1967 and the long-range program of that year (replacing a 1961 plan), it was clear that development difficulties had been generally overcome and a new era of more substantial progress had begun.[5] The renewed confidence was based on several factors: During the period November 1961 through March 1965, no less than eight research reactors went critical (including the first Japanese-made research reactor in 1962) providing considerable empirical knowledge as well as theory;[6] the United States had succeeded (1966) in bringing nuclear reactors into economic competition with conventional methods; and by 1967 more than 10,000 "technical experts" in Japan had been trained.[7]

Political and economic experiences during the period of the "slow-down" and subsequent events also had a significant bearing on the Japanese persistent interest in the potentialities of nuclear power. Particularly critical was the 1956 Suez crisis and the stark realization of Japan's inordinate reliance on oil from the Middle East. An increasing dependence on oil generally, and on Middle East oil specifically, became even more pronounced as hydroelectric capacity neared its maximum obtainable levels. Between 1956 and 1964 the place of hydro-derived power declined from approximately 62 percent of total installed capacity to slightly more than 41 percent.[8]

In the face of increasing energy demands and the other cited forces, atomic power was turned to in the hope

that by reducing dependence on inported fossil fuels, the
actual cost of electric power could be stabilized or, in
fact, reduced. (Events of October-November 1973 confirmed
the necessity for Japan to seek diversification of fossil
fuel sources to lessen its dependence on the Middle East.)
Japan also sought the overall technical advance inherent
in a nuclear power program, which could be made available
to its industry. Nuclear power offered an answer to Japan's
electric power generation need through the fast breeder
reactor (FBR), which can reproduce its plutonium core
every 10 years, and nuclear research held out the possibility of actual energy self-sufficiency through fusion reactors in the 21st century.

In April 1972, the Central Electric Power Council* released its long-term plan, which stated the need for construction starts on 60 nuclear plants during the period
April 1971 through 1980. These plants will supply a total
of 66,880 megawatt hours (mwe). By the end of the period,
38 nuclear plants will be operational, providing some
32,900 mwe. Nuclear plants will thus be in operation or
under construction in 74 locations in Japan, with a total
capacity planned of 75,107 mwe.[9] (See Appendix A for the
complete list of planned nuclear power plants for 1971-80,
as well as a map, Appendix B, of power reactors in operation or under construction as of 1971.)

The forecast of 32,900 mwe generation capacity by
1980 compares adequately with the revised estimates published in 1967, which projected from 30,000 to 40,000 mwe
capacity by 1985.[10] Demand for electric power is expected
to increase so that by 1980 the estimated demand will be
810 billion to 880 billion kwh. Of significance is the
role expected to be played by the individual household
consumer. The per capita electric power consumption will
increase from its 1971 level of 2,700 kwh to 7,000-7,600
kwh by 1980 (the approximate level of U.S. per capita consumption in 1971).[11]

The construction and operation of nuclear power plants
while a significant achievement in itself must be supported
by a capability to satisfy the complex demands of the nuclear fuel cycle. Power generation is only a part of this
cycle and depends upon the initial phases of the cycle to
sustain power generation over a long time span.

---

*The Central Electric Power Council is a coordinating
group composed of the nine private power companies as well
as the Electric Power Development Company, which is semi-
governmental in nature.

THE NUCLEAR FUEL CYCLE

Does Japan have the capacity to meet the requirements of this cycle; can fuel be processed in Japan on a unilateral basis or only in concert with other powers? These questions will be addressed in this coming section.

The nuclear fuel cycle has been described as consisting of eight primary steps:

1. Mining and milling of uranium.
2. Refining of uranium and conversion to uranium hexafluoride.
3. Enrichment of the uranium in the isotope U-235.
4. Conversion of enriched uranium to fuel material.
5. Fabrication of reactor fuel elements.
6. Use of fuel elements in nuclear power plants.
7. Reprocessing of spent fuel.
8. Disposal of radioactive waste.[12]

Each step will be discussed as related to the Japanese nuclear experience.

Mining and Milling of Uranium

Only Canada, South Africa, Southwest Africa, and the United States have proven reserves of low-cost uranium. Low-cost ores are considered to be those that can be mined by more or less conventional means and contain approximately 0.1 percent of uranium.[13]

Japan, although an energy-intensive nation, has not, as yet, found sufficient natural uranium deposits to meet its requirements. It is estimated that Japan will need 7,000 tons of uranium a year by 1980; 13,000 tons a year by 1985;[14] and 21,000 by 1990; however, the confirmed U_3O_8 reserves are considered to be a scant 8,000 metric tons.[15] These reserves* can be exploited for less than $15 a pound, and 90 percent of the confirmed reserves are located in the Ningyo-toge and Tohno areas of Japan. These

*"Reserves of uranium and the production of concentrates are expressed in English short tons of uranium oxide (chemically U_3O_8)--one short ton being 910 kilograms" (U.S. Atomic Energy Commission, "Remarks by Clarence E. Larson," USAEC News Releases, August 9, 1972, p. 4).

sites are located north of Gifu City and north of Okayama (across on the Japan Sea Side) on the island of Honshu.[16]

In an effort to locate additional deposits, the PNC and the Geological Survey of Japan have conducted and continue to conduct extensive exploration activities composing airborne radrometric, automobile-borne radrometric, surface radiation, geochemical-prospecting, geophysical-prospecting, and radon-prospecting survey techniques. Over 100 sites have been found radioactive, but most were considered nonexploitable due to their geological structure.[17]

In January 1971 a very promising find was reported on the northern part of Okushiri Island, Hokkaido. Thirty locations were found with ore deposits of greater than 0.1 percent grade U_3O_8, and the site itself is thought to contain at least as much as the finds in the Tohno district, which numbered approximately 4,000 tons.[18]

With current anticipated reserves at approximately 13,000 tons (of which only 5,000 tons will have been developed by 1985), Japan obviously must rely on external sources for uranium. To date, the principal supplier has been the United States. By June 1971, some 50,000 short tons were available under short- and long-term contracts.[19] By May 1973, this figure had been increased to 60,000 short tons and involved agreements with the United States, Canada, the United Kingdom, South Africa, and France. An agreement for an additional 13,000 short tons was being sought with Australia in May 1972, after access to the Australian resource, estimated to be 140,000 short tons, had been gained by agreement in February 1972.[20]

Japan is also actively engaged in a program developing uranium resources overseas. Since 1966 overseas resource development has been conducted in the United States, Canada, South Australia, Somalia, Thailand, Malaysia, Niger, and countries of Central and South America.[21]

One factor, in effect, retarding the development of uranium resources is the depressed market due to a surplus. The price of uranium has gone down to $6 (U.S.) a pound as a result of overproduction in the 1950s and 1960s, with a concomitant lag in anticipated uranium consumption; however, exploitation of many areas possible at $10 to $15 (U.S.) a pound will possibly look more attractive as fuel oil reaches $14 or more a barrel.[22]

Refining

The conversion of uranium oxide (yellow cake) to uranium hexafluoride is the next process in a complete fuel cycle; it is accomplished locally in Japan at Ningyo-toge.[23] The Power Reactor and Nuclear Fuel Development Corporation is currently engaged in developing on an intermediate scale a complete refining process. It is anticipated that as the development of overseas resources becomes a reality, Japan will have to refine a "considerable quantity of uranium ore locally."[24]

Generally speaking, the technological base to meet the future increased demands inherent in the refining process is being prepared and offers no concrete obstacles to Japan's nuclear development.[25] In August 1972, it was announced that a pilot plant incorporating a new uranium production process had been completed at Ningyo-toge. This new process offers an advantage in that uranium is extracted as cholride then electrolytically reduced to uranous chloride and converted directly into uranium tetra-flouride. The former system was to produce yellow cake in a rough refining process, which was then further refined by a process called the "dry method" into uranium tetrafluoride. The yellow cake state is omitted in the new process of electrolytic reduction.[26] A capability to produce 100 tons of uranium hexafluoride annually will be sought by 1974. Total development costs were cited as being 166 million yen.[27]

Enriched Uranium Production

The process of increasing the concentration of U-235 atoms in uranium from the 0.7 percent found in its natural state to 2 to 3 percent necessary for light water reactors (or 93 percent for nuclear weapons) is most commonly accomplished by a process called gaseous diffusion. Currently, only five nations--the United States, the United Kingdom, France, the USSR, and the PRC--have performed this rather sophisticated phase of the fuel cycle. In essence, uranium hexafluoride gas is forced through a "barrier," which results in the lighter U-235 atoms diffusing at a faster rate than the U-238 atoms. This, in turn, provides a concentration of U-235.[28]

To date, the only large-scale commercial producer is the United States, which is currently overproducing in order to optimize the use of the three plants built at a total investment of $2.3 billion. (An additional $850 million will be invested to update the capacity and performance of these plants.) The overproduction has resulted in a large amount of "preproduced" uranium and has been offered to interested countries (Japan) at a fair commercial price.

As sufficient as the production capability seems at this date, by 1981 or 1982, the United States will not be able to meet its own domestic enriched uranium production needs and the demands of the rest of its present customers.[29] Indeed, by 1980, Ryukichi Imai of the Japan Atomic Power Company estimates that Japan's needs for enriched uranium will reach 5.3 million kilograms separative work units (SWU), or 5,830 tons SWU.[30] At a price of $38 a kilogram SWU, that represents a sizable market for the U.S. atomic industry. (By 1990, the Japanese demand will rise to 13.5 million kilograms SWU and by the year 2000 to 15.4 million kilograms SWU.)[31]

In recognition of the acute enrichment supply program facing the world in the decade of the 1980s and beyond, the United States in mid-July 1971 sent a letter to the European Community, Britain, Canada, Australia, and Japan, which indicated U.S. readiness "to enter into talks on the sharing of uranium enriched technology." The memo indicated that the United States was ready to make the technology available "on condition that arrangements are made with the United States on financial plans and the preservation of secrets."[32]

On October 28, 1971 it was announced that a "preparatory meeting on enrichment technology sharing, between the U.S.A. and Japan, Canada, and Australia" would be held in November 1971.[33] The announcement of the note and the preparatory meeting had such an impact on the Japanese that the Japan Atomic Energy Commission was required to cut its budget for independent development of a gaseous diffusion process to about $1.7 million, while the budget request of $4.2 million for development of a centrifuge process was unaffected. It was argued by the Japanese Ministry of Finance that the coming breakthrough in U.S. data-sharing would make both development programs unnecessary.[34]

Talks continue between the United States and Japan intermittently on this matter; while a breakthrough has not been reported progress had been made. In November 1972, talks were held in Washington between the U.S. Atomic Energy Commission and Japan Atomic Energy Commission representatives, which led to the formation of a working group to study a joint plant.[35] Indeed, the Japanese Uranium Enrichment Project Research Council has been conducting joint feasibility research with the American firms of Bechtel, Union Carbide, and Westinghouse to determine costs involved in constructing an enrichment plant somewhere in the United States (possibly Alabama). Initial results suggested that the sum of $2.75 billion would be required. The costs would be allocated as follows: a plant with 9,000 tons' SWU capacity, $1,650 million; electric power plant including reserve power of 3,175,000 kw, $990 million; total costs of research for these studies, approximately $6 million. These immediate research costs are being shared on a 50-50 basis between the Japanese and U.S. groups; the studies are due to be complete in December 1974.[36]

By August 1974, the prospects for this particular joint venture were becoming unclear at best. Due to problems in obtaining investment capital, and doubts about the commercial feasibility of the scheme, the U.S. companies, especially Union Carbide and Westinghouse, were considering nonparticipation.[37]

Although the above venture was looking uncertain, another proposal, advanced by General Electric Company and Exxon Corporation, was receiving positive reaction from the Japanese power industry. This particular plan is based on use of a centrifugal separation process with 20 percent of the capital provided by Japan. This level of participation would give Japan 20 percent of the output.[38]

Several other paths for uranium enrichment are open, such as turning to new suppliers such as the USSR, collaboration in a joint European scheme, or embarking on a program to achieve a limited domestic enrichment capability

The importation of enriched uranium from the Soviet Union has often been looked at as a possible source of diversified supplies, as it is estimated the existing Soviet capacity per year is between 9,000 and 12,000 tons SWU as compared with 17,000 tons SWU for the United States. As France (1971), West Germany (1972), Belgium (1973), and Italy (1974) have contracts to import enriched uranium, the Soviet alternative has been taken more seriously, especially since the price is reportedly lower than that of the U.S. product. In June 1973, a Japanese inspection mission headed by Doko Toshio and sponsored by the Japan Atomic Industrial Forum was invited to the USSR to review selected facilities.[39]

In July 1974, the Japanese government indicated that this alternative was being very attractively pressed by the Soviet Union. Inasmuch as the United States has informed Japan that it will not conclude any new supply agreements for the period after 1982, the Soviet offer to furnish supplies needed by 1990 is interesting indeed.

While the price is right, as well as the quality, Japan continues to follow a cautious position, as there is no bilateral atomic energy agreement between the two countries and the Soviets have not provided enough information to assure Japan of a stabilized supply.[40]

Some of the international ventures that Japan is watching closely, and may, indeed, finally choose to cooperate with include a British, West German, and Netherlands tripartite project to construct centrifugal enrichment plants by 1980 of 2,000-3,000 tons SWU per year,[41] and a French scheme to build with Japanese participation a Pacific Basin gaseous diffusion enrichment plant capable of 6,000-7,000 tons SWU yearly.[42] France also has a European project that includes Britain, West Germany, Belgium, and Italy to build a diffusion plant in Europe,[43] and Japan may be invited to join or France might propose to enter into a long-term contract with Japan to supply enriched uranium to Japan.[44]

Australia may provide as much as 50 percent of its natural uranium to Japan for enrichment.[45] Prospects for Canadian uranium have also caused some interest; the Japanese trading firm, Marubeni, bought 1 million shares, a 5 percent interest in the enterprise, in the Canadian company Brinco, which is contemplating the construction of a gas diffusion plant using U.S. Atomic Energy Commission (USAEC) technology.[46]

The JAEC responded favorably to an initial invitation for some kind of association with the tripartite group as some valuable technology might be forthcoming in centrifuge manufacture, and the JAEC hopes to resolve its policy by the end of 1974 with respect to the French and U.S. offers.[47]

On August 17, 1972 the Committee on Technological development for Uranium Enrichment reported, after a one year's study on the relative merits of gaseous and centrifugal enrichment methods, that the "centrifugal method of separation is more appropriate than gaseous diffusion for Japan to embark on uranium enrichment technology and begin production by 1985, and achieve competitiveness by world standards."[48]

One of the difficulties with secret technology for gaseous enrichment is its incompatibility with the "open, democratic and independent" program in Japan. The centrifugal system was seen in a favorable light as:

1. The technology gap between Japan and in Western countries on centrifugal separation has

narrowed and it is possible for Japan to use its
own technology in building a plant that is international by competitive [sic]

   2. The initial investment needed for centrifugal separation is comparatively high, but
this process requires only small quantity of electricity in production compared with that for
gaseous diffusion plant, and it will be possible
to increase facilities step by step [sic]

   3. Economic prospects are brighter than for
the gaseous diffusion method.[49]

   The above report of a committee of the JAEC went on
to recommend a budget for a pilot plant of $23 million--
almost five times the allocation for centrifuge R and D in
fiscal year 1972. The actual 1972 budget for R and D of
the centrifugal process was 1.452 billion yen, which on a
306 yen to the dollar basis, was $4.74 million. The bud-
get requested for fiscal year 1973 was 6.274 billion yen
but was reduced to 5.201 billion yen in the budgetary process. The amount of 5.201 billion yen at 265 yen to the
dollar is $19.62 million. Thus, the actual increase in
the government plan between fiscal year 1972 and fiscal
year 1973 amounted to almost four times the 1972 budget.[50]
   The Japan Atomic Energy Research Institute (JAERI)
was allotted 227 million yen for centrifugal development
in addition to the 5.201 billion yen given to the Power
Reactor and Nuclear Fuel Development Corporation. PNC
will test 13 cascades involving 180 centrifuges, develop
safety standards, and generally continue developmental activity on a national priority basis.[51]
   The committee reporting on enrichment policy did not
recommend the elimination of gaseous diffusion research to
insure that some information will be available if Japan is
asked to participate in a joint venture. While a budget
of approximately 500 million yen was advised for continued
gaseous diffusion research[52] and 450 million yen was actually requested,[53] no specific references have been made
concerning the actual amount allocated for research. One
item of 115 million yen was allocated to the Uranium Enrichment Committee of the Central Research Institute of
the Electric Power Industry for unspecified "research."
This could represent some funds that are allocated to
gaseous diffusion out does not seem to be the total
amount.[54]
   On June 1, 1972, the JAEC presented a revised Long-
Range Program on Development of Atomic Energy. In Chapter

2, Section 2, the commission established its general policy
concerning uranium enrichment.

> Japan must . . . see that supplies of enriched
> uranium are available from the United States for
> power plants that will be commissioned up till
> 1980, and the necessary R and D must be done by
> Japan itself to make sure that domestic production
> can supply the further needs beyond 1980, as well
> as Japan participating in international enrichment
> projects.[55]

The development of enrichment technology is currently
being furthered by the PNC and Japan Atomic Energy Research
Institute (JAERI) on both centrifuge and gaseous diffusion
processes.[56] Definite progress on the centrifugal method
has been reported. In January 1972 the Power Reactor and
Nuclear Fuel Development Corporation announced that 10
domestically built centrifugal machines would begin test
operations by April. High-speed drums that reportedly
can be operated for 1,000 consecutive hours at 300 meters
a second can turn out uranium enriched to 1.4 percent.
This enrichment level is not sufficient for the light water
reactors currently used in Japan, but when the cascade is
increased by adding more drums, a higher enrichment level
will be attained.[57]

Some Japanese advancement has also been reported in
developing gaseous diffusion techniques, especially in the
fields of barriers, hardware, and software. In July 1971
the Institute of Physical and Chemical Research opened its
diffusion device to the press. The experimental complex
was reported as consisting of six cascades in a high temperature room (10 x 3 x 3 meters). After the connection
of three additional cascades, experiments--conducted thus
far in argon gas--will be accomplished with uranium hexafluoride.[58]

The Institute of Physics and Chemistry Research has
been developing a gaseous diffusion process since 1967,
and data have been accumulated on "barriers, compressors,
diffusion cylinders, materials, analysis and control."[59]

While Japan is now quite dependent on the United
States for its supplies of slightly enriched uranium, the
policy of the government of Japan seems clearly to be one
of reducing such dependence by realizing some kind of
capability by the 1980s (most likely in the centrifugal
process) and possibly participating in a foreign plant,
either bilaterally with the United States or France or mul-
tilaterally as mentioned above.

This resolve to find additional sources of enriched uranium became even more of a priority item when on January 22, 1973 the United States announced revised criteria for the ordering of U.S. enrichment services (implemented in May 1973) and because of the U.S. action in July 1974 not to conclude any new supply agreements for the period after 1982.[60] The principal points of the new criteria include the following: (1) a precontract for enrichment services eight years prior to delivery of the fuel (as opposed to one to two years notice in the past), which according to the Japanese requires users to plan 10 years in advance, as uranium must be bought and shipped to the United States as feeder or resupply material, a process that is usually started two years in advance;[61] (2) advance payment of $3.3 million per million kw; (3) a "high-rate" penalty if orders are canceled; and (4) the United States no longer guarantees a supply of uranium to Japan at the same price as those in the United States as under past agreements.[62] Coupled with the new criteria, the United States increased the price of services from $32 per kilogram SWU to $38.50.[63]

The United States moves will provide a long-term user process rate and may make it commercially profitable for the U.S. commercial atomic industry to provide these services; however, the new criteria and rate increase have forced other countries, particularly Japan, who only last year looked at the early 1980s with some degree of anticipation, to realize that project decision thresholds must be crossed soon to assure an adequate supply of enriched uranium in the mid-1980s.

Which partner Japan selects in the uranium enrichment field could affect possible policy options in the years to come. It would seem best from Japan's own interests to select commercial involvement in the U.S. enterprise while also becoming an active party in the British, West German, and Netherlands tripartite project. In that way, although denied access to the classified technology of the diffusion process, joint ownership of an enrichment plant (rated at from 5,500 to 9,000 tons SWU depending on the source; see Nuclear Engineering, January 1973; Denki Shimbun, November 29, 1972; and Nihon Keizai, May 27, 1973, for quotes of 5,500, 8,750, and 9,000 tons SWU) would assure the needed enriched uranium in the early to mid-1980s, when that commodity will be in short supply, and cover the enrichment requirements in the event technology for a commercially viable centrifugal system takes longer than expected to develop.

It would pay also to secure interests in the tripartite program to ensure access to advanced design concepts for centrifuges. The Tripartite Group plans to produce 300 tons SWU by 1976; 2,000 by 1978; and 10,000 by 1985.[64]

Participation with the French in an enrichment enterprise could indicate desires for greater independence from a single source supplier. This course has much to offer in light of experiences of the recent past, but the French do not have an established reputation in the large uranium enrichment field as does the United States. The plant proposed by the French would probably have an output from 6,000 to 7,000 tons SWU, close to the envisaged U.S. facility, but it might have advantages of greater access to the technology involved. As a French firm is cobuilding the reprocessing plant in Japan, this possibility cannot be entirely discounted. The selection of the French option could not go unnoticed as a strategic indicator for the future. It would probably offer a greater spectrum for Japanese autonomous action regarding nuclear matters and would be of keen interest to the nations of NEA.

Fuel Fabrication

The process of fabrication is necessary as the enriched uranium hexafluoride from the diffusion process cannot be directly adapted for power reactor use. The conversion process, usually into dioxide is accomplished, then the substance is formed into pellets, which in turn are heated, loaded into metal tubing, and assembled as fuel elements or bundles.[65]

The Japanese domestic fuel fabrication situation is quite bright. Domestic makers have reached the point where "Japan-fabricated fuel" has almost been realized completely. Tsuruga boiling water reactor (BWR) and Mihama-1 pressurized water reactor (PWR) are using fuel bundles fabricated in Japan and the industry is expanding with such rapidity that it is within reason to expect the entire needs of the Japanese nuclear power industry will be met by domestically fabricated fuel.[66]

Japanese manufacturers have adopted, for the most part, fuel fabrication technologies under licensing agreements, and must therefore pay royalties to foreign firms. This tends to make the domestic product slightly more expensive than foreign imports. Costs are also related to plant size and Japanese facilities have been initially smaller.[67]

The current major fuel fabricators are Japan Nuclear
Fuel Company, a combine consisting of Toshiba (30 percent),
Hitachi (30 percent), and General Electric of the United
States (40 percent); Sumitomo Electric Industries, which
has a license agreement with the U.S. firm Gulf United
Nuclear; and Mitsubishi Atomic Power Industries, another
combine with Mitsubishi Heavy Industries (20 percent),
Mitsubishi Metal Mining (40 percent), and United States
Westinghouse as members. There are two zircalloy tube
manufacturers, Sumitomo Metal Mining and Kobe Steel.[68]

In May 1972, it was announced that Furukawa Electric
Company of Tokyo and Sumitomo Electric Industries of Osaka
would form the first all Japanese-owned fuel fabrication
company. The new firm--tentatively named Nuclear Fuel Industry Company, Limited--represents the growing self-sufficiency and confidence of the Japanese in this phase of
the nuclear fuel cycle.[69]

Fuel facilities for processing 400 kg of plutonium
fuel per year are available within the Power Reactor and
Nuclear Fuel Development Corporation. There are some
plans to use Pu fuel in several reactors; however, most
will be fabricated overseas.[70]

While the foundation is broad for fuel fabrication,
the June 1, 1972 Revised Long-Range Program called for
greater efforts at technological development in this field
to ensure that the basis for domestic production is
"firm."[71]

Fuel Reprocessing and Waste Disposal

After the fuel (either uranium or plutonium) has been
"burned," it is removed and replaced. The average life-
time of nuclear fuel in a reactor is approximately three
years. After this three-year period, the fuel, even
though spent for reactor purposes, is still highly irra-
diated and contains residual fissionable material. Being
too valuable to be discarded, it is transferred to a reprocessing plant, where it is dissolved in order to recover and purify the residual uranium and plutonium (some
of which is produced in the reactor). Radioactive wastes
are also extracted at the reprocessing plant.[72]

The Power Reactor and Nuclear Fuel Development Corporation is building Japan's first reprocessing plant.
Japan Gasoline Company, Ltd. and the French firm Saint-
Gobain Techniques Nouvelles are cocontractors for the
plant, which was scheduled to begin operation in October

1974 but has slipped to a 1975 operational date. This facility, located at Tokai Mura, will have a capacity of
only 0.7 tons of spent fuel per day, or 210 tons per year.
On a yearly basis, 670 kg of U03 and 7.5 kg of Pu will be
recovered when the facility is operating at full capacity,
making it, for all practical purposes, a pilot plant.[73]
Subsequent plants will be constructed and operated by private corporations, as it is believed even the first facility will reprocess at a cost competitive with foreign
plants.[74]

It is anticipated the spent fuel from reactors by
1975 will reach 200 tons per year, pressing to the limit
the capacity of the pilot plant. By 1980, spent fuel will
reach 600 tons and by 1985 approximately 2,000 tons;[75]
the need for follow-on facilities is already quite evident.

All is not well with the reprocessing plant, as there
has been considerable local opposition to its construction.
Some of the opposition takes the form of the accusation
that "the plant might produce plutonium for military purposes." There is a legal struggle being waged, and it remains to be seen if an environmentalist, antiwar activist,
fisherman coalition will force further delays. The opposition has been successful enough that some recommendations
for the second plant to be located outside of Japan have
been made.[76]

Pressure within the atomic industry is mounting in
order to have the government establish basic policy concerning the second plant. The JAIF, for example, has already established committees to discuss preliminary steps
to prepare public opinion.[77]

Disposal of waste is being considered both at sea and
on land by the JAEC. The wastes will be solidifed and,
pending the results of tests, which should be available by
1975, a firm disposal policy will be determined.[78] One process developed by the JAERI places the waste in a round
steel container, which is compressed to 5 cm and then
packed in concrete.[79]

THE NUCLEAR FUEL CYCLE IN JAPAN

In general, Japan can be seen to have three major problem areas in regard to the nuclear fuel cycle. First and
foremost is the lack of natural deposits of uranium. This
is a fundamental problem but may be alleviated somewhat by
the FBRs of the 1980s. Second is the present inability to
enrich uranium to a degree necessary for the reactor pro-

gram (not to mention a weapons program). A solution to this problem is being sought by development of a centrifugal enrichment R and D program while attempting to keep options open regarding gaseous diffusion. The hoped-for "get-well" date is 1985. A determined attempt to achieve a centrifugal process by 1985 will be undertaken after initial tests conducted in 1973-74.[80] The third and last technical problem is the lack of a domestic reprocessing capability. This deficiency could be rectified by early 1975 but might be subject to some further slippage due to local opposition to the plant's construction.

The dreamlike desires for a complete nuclear fuel cycle, independent and self-sustaining, for Japan is not attainable in the current political context in this century. It is entirely feasible, after the massive introduction of FBRs, that some substantial progress toward self-sufficiency can be imagined, as, according to John W. Landis, president of the American Nuclear Society, ultimately fast breeders will "stretch our nuclear fuel reserves by a factor of about 40."[81] Even in this case, with Japan's limited uranium supply, the fast breeder is still a most finite solution. Real self-sufficiency cannot be realized until controlled thermonuclear fusion is possible. In this regard, Japan is proceeding with research that includes construction of experimental facilities to study the process of nuclear fusion.[82] The fusion method of creating energy is based on the way nuclei are combined by the sun, and as the fuels used are almost limitless and radioactivity is almost nil, it is a most attractive course for any energy-hungry nation.

In May 1972, a nuclear reaction was achieved at Osaka University that attained a temperature of 50 million degrees centigrade for several microseconds.[83] Another testing facility, the newly constructed JFT-2 of the Japan Atomic Energy Research Institute, succeeded in confining plasma at 3 million degrees centigrade on December 2, 1972 for 300ths of a second.[84] This unit reportedly ranks along with U.S. and USSR facilities in terms of scale and performance; cost was estimated at 530 million yen.[85]

Until controlled fusion can be realized, the more reasonable desire for Japan is to possess "the complete facilities for all processes involving nuclear fuel." Such a capability, circa 1985, even though obtained will be severely circumscribed by the stated basic lack of nuclear ore deposits and dependence on overseas sources of supply.

OTHER PROGRAMS AND THE JAPANESE
NUCLEAR INDUSTRY: THE FBR

Development of the fast breeder reactor is generally
sought by the nuclear industries and powers of the world
as it literally "breeds more plutonium from uranium than
it consumes in the generation of power."[86] The breeder is
plutonium-fueled and converts a blanket of uranium 238
(which makes up 99.3 percent of natural uranium), which
is placed around the fuel core, into plutonium. The U-238
absorbs neutrons from the plutonium core and becomes plutonium 239 itself. It is not exactly a rapid process but
is called "fast" because a fast neutron is absorbed by a
plutonium nucleus in the fission process. In a period of
approximately 10 years, the sodium-cooled fast breeder
can accumulate, or breed, enough extra fuel to start
another breeder of identical size.[87]

As optimistic as this seems, it still is a finite
answer to the energy demands of the world, since the
starting point must be U-238, the only fissionable material
occurring naturally.[88]

The Japanese Ten-Year Development Plan of the Central
Electric Power Council forecasting through fiscal 1980
(ends March 31, 1981) has no FBR indicated for completion
as a commercial facility; however, the report "Nuclear
Vision for the Year 2000" indicates that introduction of
FBRs will begin in 1986 and by the year 2000 all new installations and replacements will be FBRs.[89]

Currently the Power Reactor and Nuclear Fuel Development Corporation is engaged in two development programs for
fast breeders: the Joyo, a 50-mwe-plus sodium-cooled
loop-type experimental FBR, and the 300-mwe prototype
Monju also a sodium-cooled loop-type FBR. It was planned
that Joyo would reach criticality in 1973 and Monju in
1977;[90] however, this was slightly overoptimistic, and the
construction target for Joyo is now 1974, with criticality
(see Figure 3.7) coming somewhat later.[91]

Plans for a commercial FBR with a capacity of 1,500
mwe were announced in January 1971. Tokyo Electric Power
Company, Hitachi, Mitsubishi-Heavy Industries, and Tokyo
Shibaura Electric Company have prepared conceptual designs
for a FBR with a 1977 construction start. Completion is
scheduled for 1982.[92]

129

FIGURE 3.1

Operational Schedule for Advanced Reactors

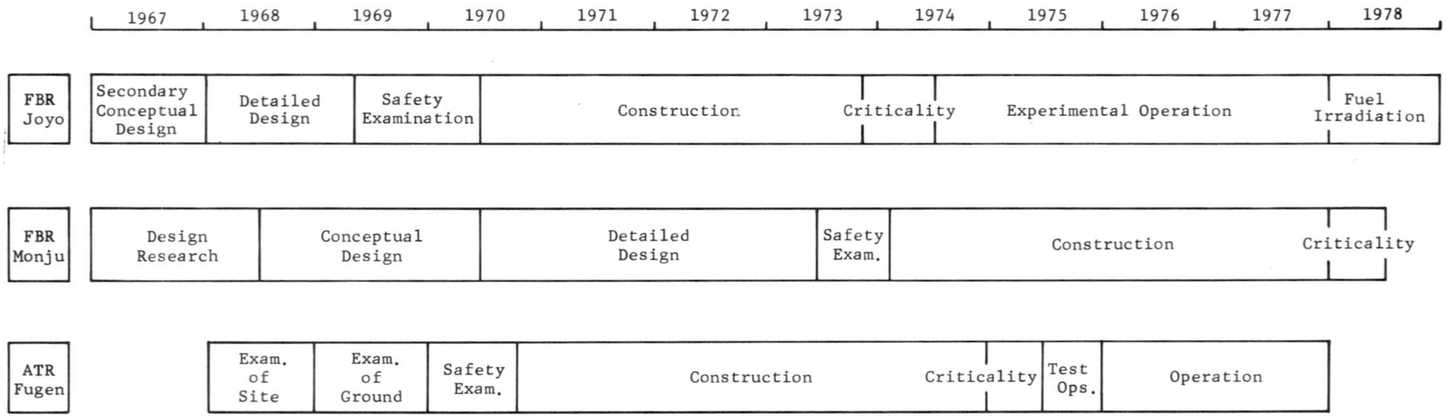

	1967	1968	1969	1970	1971	1972	1973	1974	1975	1976	1977	1978
FBR Joyo	Secondary Conceptual Design	Detailed Design	Safety Examination		Construction			Criticality	Experimental Operation			Fuel Irradiation
FBR Monju	Design Research		Conceptual Design		Detailed Design			Safety Exam.	Construction			Criticality
ATR Fugen			Exam. of Site	Exam. of Ground	Safety Exam.	Construction			Criticality	Test Ops.	Operation	

Source: Atomic Energy Bureau, Science and Technology Agency, Atomic Energy in Japan (Tokyo: Science and Technology Agency, 1971), p. 5.

Advanced Thermal Reactor (ATR)

The advanced thermal reactor being built by PNC is a heavy-water moderated boiling light-water-cooled pressurized type.[93] Use of the ATR will reduce the demand for uranium as these reactors will burn a fuel of natural uranium slightly enriched with plutonium produced in Japan and have a capacity to irradiate the natural uranium, thus producing plutonium as in a fast breeder. In the long-range plan, provisions are made for a 10, 20, or 30 percent use of the ATR, depending on the progress of the FBR. The ATR will be used for new installations and replacements, except where fast breeders are planned. The prototype ATR (Fugen) is expected to reach criticality by October 1975, one year later than originally planned, due to engineering modifications that were made in order to simplify the design.[94]

Maritime Reactor

The Japan Nuclear Ship Development Agency was established in 1963. The main purpose of the agency, as the name more than adequately implies, was to oversee the construction of a nuclear ship utilizing the shipbuilding technology of Japan. The hull was started in November 1968, and in June of 1969 it was launched and named "Mutsu." The fitting-out work is complete and the fuel assemblies, consisting of 32 rods of enriched uranium weighing 2.77 tons, were loaded in early September 1972.[95] Criticality tests were scheduled to begin in October 1972, after which training was to continue, and the maiden voyage was scheduled for April 1973.[96] However, the Mutsu did not go critical until September 1974, primarily due to opposition from fishermen, who felt the price for their catch would go down even if there was no proven contamination.[97]

When the ship finally put to sea on its first trial run, a minute radioactive leak was discovered in the reactor. The Japan Nuclear Ship Development Agency was quick to point out that a polyethylene cover was all that was needed to correct the problem, but damage to public confidence concerning the nuclear ship program was obvious.[98]

A second nuclear ship was to be started during the first half of the 1970s but was dropped due to economic considerations. However, plans to construct a high-speed container ship were announced in Tokyo in the spring of

1973. The ship, to be designed by the Ship Builders Research Association, will be powered by a 333-mwe reactor (almost 10 times the power of the <u>Mutsu</u>), will be 270 meters in length, will have a displacement of 43,000 tons and a maximum speed of 33 kilotons (kt), and will have a capacity to carry almost 2,000 7 x 7 x 7 containers.[99]

The long-term plan for nuclear ships of the JAIF published in May 1971 predicted the construction of a total of three nuclear-powered vessels by 1980 as well as an almost unlimited future for nuclear-powered container ships. Some 280 were forecast by the year 2000.[100]

THE STATE OF JAPANESE NUCLEAR
POWER SUPPLY INDUSTRY

By May 1971, the ratio of domestically produced equipment to that imported was 9 to 1 for plants under construction. This represented a marked reverse of the industrial support situation in just 10 years. In engineering, for example, all plants with Japanese prime contractors have "overall planning, nuclear thermal design, kinetic analyses, safety analyses, shielding design and anti-seismic design" accomplished domestically.[101] The availability of Japanese-manufactured instruments is increasing, as are fuel conversion and fabrication. Fuels for initial loadings and replacement are being produced by Japanese manufacturers.

The overall capability of Japanese suppliers is graphically indicated in Appendix C. At this point it can be noted that a Japanese domestic capability exists in overall planning, plant design, reactor components, turbine generators, and reactor containers as well as supporting equipment.

MILITARY APPLICATION

The Japanese civilian nuclear program has obvious strengths and weaknesses, but it is clear that Japan possesses the base from which to manufacture nuclear explosive devices. It has been estimated that Japan has already produced approximately 1,000 kg of plutonium from currently active reactors.[102] Such an amount of plutonium could yield as many as 166 20-kt weapons or as few as 116 depending on the purity of the plutonium. Besides the plutonium, which Japan has produced already (the 1,000 kg) it has, in terms of current reactors, the capacity to produce enough plutonium to fabricate "about ninety 20 KT warheads annually."[103]

Can it be assumed automatically that Japan, with such a plutonium reserve and reactor capacity, has the capability to produce nuclear weapons in the above numbers? No, for several reasons:

1. The plutonium used in explosive devices is plutonium 239. This can be obtained from a reactor only by "burning" the uranium 235 at a very specific rate for a relatively short period of time. Plutonium that is obtained from a normally functioning power reactor will have been in the reactor for much too long a time (approximately three years) and will have become "contaminated" with plutonium 240 and plutonium (Pu) 242;[104] from 15 to 30 percent of the Pu would be nonfissionable isotopes.[105] "The military usefulness of plutonium decreases as the proportion of nonfissionable isotopes increases." The problems involved are the increase of the critical mass by the nonfissionable isotopes and the fact that these two isotopes fission spontaneously, causing predetonation,[106] not a feature much desired in bombs.

2. To recover a greater percentage of weapons-grade plutonium from the reactor, the operator would have to expose it to irradiation for an unusually short period of time. This procedure, a very uneconomical one, does not lend itself to commercial reactor operation and would be discovered by the International Atomic Energy Agency (IAEA) safeguards system in effect in Japan.

3. A reprocessing facility to extract and purify the plutonium from the spent fuel does not exist to date. Until there is reprocessing, the capability for diversion is negligible. The year 1974 is the date for the plant, but, when built, it too will become subject to the safeguards of the IAEA; it will produce only 7.5 kg of Pu yearly.

4. Any surreptitious program to divert fissionable materials into a weapons program would run headlong into the fact that today's Japan is not a politically homogeneous entity. Any attempt to manufacture covertly a device, let alone an entire weapons program, would, in all probability, be exposed by members of the scientific/technical corps itself.

Taking the above points into consideration, there is still something to be gained by estimating Japan's capabilities in a nonpolitical context, and a study of this nature would be somewhat remiss if it did not attempt to calculate the weapon stockpile that conceivably could be Japan's if she so desired.

As most available data on plutonium holdings in Japan do not specify the degree of Pu purity, several estimates will have to be made. Pure Pu-239 will be considered as the highest quality for weapons production and will be calculated at 6 kg for one 20-kt weapon. That would roughly equate to 166 weapons from the 1,000 kg of Pu estimated to be on hand.

Typical plutonium taken from spent reactor fuel contains about 15 percent of Pu 240 or Pu 242, and the amount of nonfissionable matter might increase to as much as 30 percent, as reactor fuels are improved. Therefore, a high and low range of probable weapons output will be reflected for commercial reactor Pu that has not been purified or reprocessed. In the case of 1,000 kg, the number of weapons might be as low as 116 or as high as 141.[107]

A fourth possible rate, which will be called the military production rate, is that Pu that would be produced by rapid and frequent cycling of the fuel in commercial or research reactors. In this case a militarily usable Pu could be produced with perhaps 5 percent nonfissionable isotopes present. A possible output of 158 weapons could be achieved from the same 1,000 kg.

Figure 3.2 graphically depicts the potential for Japanese nuclear weapons production. It is based on the annual increase in electrical generation capacity from nuclear generators and the direct relationship between mwe capacity and plutonium production (Figure 3.3). For each mwe produced by a nuclear reactor, one-third kg of plutonium is produced;[108] therefore, the potential in 1974, based on reactor capacity, would range from 287 weapons (20 kt) if the plutonium is purely Pu-239 to a low of 201 if 30 percent impurities existed. (To achieve the higher weapons output, all reactors would have to be run to maximize Pu-239 production to the detriment of power generation. The lower weapons figure could only be achieved if sufficient reprocessing facilities existed.)

The role of reprocessing plants that remove the unwanted isotopes from the pultonium can be seen as critical. In the above example, showing possible weapons for 1974, it must be remembered that weapons could only be produced if some means to purify the Pu existed or if the reactors were run to produce military grade Pu. Realistically, no such weapons capability based on reprocessed fuel will exist in 1974.

FIGURE 3.2

Weapons Production Potential

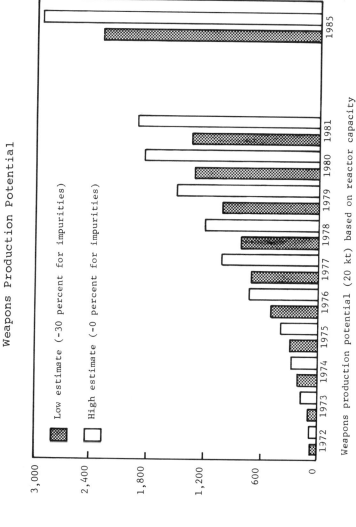

Weapons production potential (20 kt) based on reactor capacity

Source: Compiled by author.

FIGURE 3.3

Japan: Nuclear Power Plants
(nwe output)

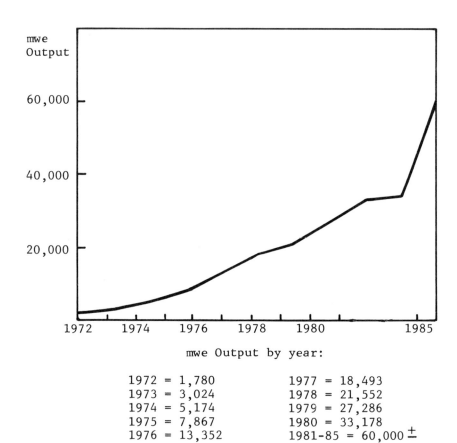

mwe Output by year:

1972 = 1,780	1977 = 18,493
1973 = 3,024	1978 = 21,552
1974 = 5,174	1979 = 27,286
1975 = 7,867	1980 = 33,178
1976 = 13,352	1981-85 = 60,000 $\pm$

Sources: Based on data presented in Atoms in Japan,
May 1972, and other sources.

To estimate more accurately the possible weapons production output capability of Japan, the annual separative
potential of the reprocessing facility soon to become
operational in Japan must be examined. As was pointed out
previously in the chapter, the pilot plant scheduled for
October 1974 operation can only extract 7.5 kg of Pu annually. If this 7.5 kg is contaminated with 15 percent
impurities, only 6.375 kg remain, or, just about enough
for one 20-kt bomb. If this Pu is reduced by a 30 percent
rate, the yearly Pu-239 output becomes a scant 5.25 kg.

The expected flow of spent fuel to reprocessing plants
for 1975, 1980, and 1985 has been estimated at 200 tons
for 1975, 600 tons by 1980, and 2,000 tons by 1985.[109]
By the year 2000, the reprocessing requirement will approximate a low of 3,500 tons or a high of 5,100 tons, depending on the success of the fast breeders.[110]

Assuming the output of the pilot plant is typical of
successive facilities--that is, the output from all reprocessing plants will not exceed 0.004 percent of the total
spent fuel input--the expected future annual output of Pu
can be put into meaningful terms. This, of course, assumes that additional reprocessing plants will be built
to handle the projected increase in spent fuel. If additional plants are made to handle the fuel, by 1985 output
would reach 2,000 tons or enough for 10 weapons per year
(based on a low impurities factor). By the year 2000 with
spent fuel being processed at a rate of 3,500-5,100 tons,
approximately 18 to 26 weapons would be possible.

By the year 2000, the cumulative reprocessing estimates run from a low figure of 43,000 tons to a possible
high of 65,000 tons.[111] This would allow for a potential
weapons stockpile (20 kt) by 2000 of from 221 to 335 weapons based on a 15 percent impurities factor or from 182
to 275 weapons based on a 30 percent rate.

These figures, however, are not independent in themselves, as it must be remembered that the plutonium produced in the power reactors will be used in the ATRs as
well as the fast breeders as fuel. If all the plutonium
were put into weapons, the estimated reprocessing requirements would be markedly reduced.

When discussing the reactor capacity of the commercial power plants, the potential plutonium capability does
look awesome indeed, but practical obstacles would make
the realization of the theoretical output difficult but
supposedly not impossible. Of all the Japanese reactors,
the one most suited to quick conversion to the production
of military grade Pu 239 is the Japan Atomic Power Company's

Reactor #1 at Tokai Mura. Reportedly it could produce 240 kg of weapons-grade Pu every year,[112] or enough for over 30 weapons.

It would appear that any program, other than a crash program, would have to consider seriously the potential of the Tokai Mura facility. Indeed, with a 30-plus weapons rate, it could serve as the center around which a nuclear arms program could be designed.

It seems from the above data that any crash program to provide a nuclear capability to Japan's military would have to be based on something other than the reprocessing capacity or Tokai Mura, which together could only produce approximately 65 20-kt weapons over the two-year span supposedly required.[113] In this regard, however, it should be remembered that when the fast breeders come into operation, about half of the Pu that comes from the blanket material will be very low in the isotope 240. Such plutonium "is adaptable to military use much more easily than plutonium normally produced by a commercial thermal reactor."[114] The rate with which the FBRs prove themselves will have a direct impact on the availability of military-grade plutonium. Three FBRs with a total output of 1,850 mwe have been announced. With completion scheduled for the mid-1980s, they will make readily available military-grade plutonium from normal operation of the reactors.

While the capability to produce plutonium weapons can be presented in a relatively clear-cut fashion, the situation as it relates to enriched uranium, also used in fusion as well as fission weapons, is not so clear. The uncertainty has to do with the fact that Japan has decided to perfect the centrifugal system to produce enriched uranium for its power reactors. It is hoped that this system will meet the 3.5 percent enrichment level needed for the reactors and allow Japan to avoid the gaseous diffusion method, which involves technology that is still held under classified procedures.

The production goals for slightly enriched uranium have been set at 40 tons per year by 1980 from a pilot plant and an internationally competitive facility by 1975.[115] What is meant by "internationally competitive" is not spelled out, but the European Tripartite group is planning to have a 10,000-ton capacity plant by 1985 using the centrifugal method.[116]

Theoretically, the centrifugal system can produce highly enriched uranium by lengthening the cascade and increasing the number of centrifugal separation machines; however, in practice this has yet to be done.

Therefore, projections on the development of highly enriched uranium permitting the manufacturing of nuclear weapons will have to be based on a great deal more speculation than in the case of plutonium warheads. If the pilot plant is successful by 1980, it might be assumed that the higher level of enrichment could be reached by the 1983-85 time frame. If two tons of 98 percent enriched uranium could be produced annually from such a facility, approximately 200 warheads could be manufactured.[117]

Japan has an anticipated reserve of 13,000 tons of natural uranium, the stock fuel to produce the enriched uranium. It takes approximately 18,000 tons of natural uranium to produce 20 to 30 tons of highly enriched uranium. If a linear relationship is assumed, total Japanese enriched uranium production for weapons based on domestic resources could reach from 14 to 22 tons. On the basis of 10 kg per weapon, this would permit the manufacturing of from 1,200 to 2,000 weapons.[118]

It might be too early to speculate further as to the output levels of a possible Japanese program to produce nuclear weapons from enriched uranium. Too little is known as to the centrifugal system and if it proves unsuccessful, Japan's entire force would be dependent on plutonium weapons until the gaseous diffusion technique becomes more commonly available.

Japan's current inability to enrich uranium to a 98 percent level will not affect materially its capability to produce "triggers" for thermonuclear weapons. These weapons combine fission and fusion effects to produce weapons yields several times greater in intensity than from fission alone.

As either Pu-239 or U 235 can be used to trigger a thermonuclear weapon, it might be asked what is the principal difference between these bombs and the fission kind, and where does Japan stand with respect to production capability. The main difference, of course, in the two weapons is the use of heavy hydrogen lithium to surround the fission-triggering device so that, when temperatures are high enough, a fusion reaction will begin.[119] Tritium (the heaviest isotope of hydrogen) is used, as well as deuterium, or a mixture of both, in combination with the fission device to initiate a thermonuclear fusion reaction.[120]

The main problem that is unique to the hydrogen bomb is that of separating the (double or triple) heavey hydrogen. This process can be accomplished in Japan by Showa Denko. There have been questions raised as to the efficiency of the method used by that firm, but as demand is so low for the commodity, no particular move has been made toward improvement.[121]

It would appear that Japan would be faced with a serious matter of testing a thermonuclear device, much more so than for a low-yield fission weapon. Of course, a program could be executed in which no tests are conducted, but one of the most important aspects in the theatrics of deterrence--demonstration--would be lost.

The problem of personnel engaged in the atomic industry who would work on a weapons project is also a very difficult question to assess in more than general terms. However, if a visible threat existed to Japan's security, it is possible to believe that enough personnel would be motivated either through financial rewards or a feeling of patriotism. There are now some 19,050 individuals "engaged in nuclear and related fields";[122] one might argue that a core of personnel could be found among the almost 2,000 engineers working in electric power-related tasks and the 6,400 engineers in mining and manufacturing[123] to ensure the success of a program. It might even be possible, as the number of personnel increases, to build one bomb surreptitiously. However, it must not be forgotten that Japan is not in the same strategic position as Israel; one nuclear bomb, no matter how powerful, would be about as useful to the Japanese as an umbrella with one rib in a typhoon.

For the present and until fast breeders make military-grade plutonium plentiful, the analysis of Ryukichi Imai is appropriate: "The only weapons activity Japan can engage in under [the] present system is a crash program against imminent danger--with tacit approval of major nuclear suppliers."[124]

How long would a crash program take before a nuclear device could be detonated? In conversations with U.S. and Japanese officials, this is a question never answered with a great deal of clarity, but Robert Oppenheimer in 1945 estimated that any country with a peaceful nuclear program could convert to a weapons program within one year.[125] We must estimate, in view of the high level of technology in Japan, that a nuclear device capable of detonation in a time frame of from 9 to 18 months after project initiation would be possible.

Much would depend on the urgency with which such a program might be approached. In a recent article Imai Ryukichi held that Japan is in a position of being able to build a "nuclear weapon minus two years."[126] This threshold concept also has been advanced by other political-strategic analysts in Japan who feel that Japan has more to gain politically from its current recognized capability to build the bomb in a certain period of time.

By the late 1970s to mid-1980s this finite threshold time would definitely tend to move toward the lesser side of the required time estimate, especially after a domestic capability for high-level enrichment is realized.

In summary, any autonomous nuclear program in Japan during the late 1970s or early 1980s would have to concentrate on a fission weapons program but would have ever increasing stockpiles to draw on. After successful large-scale testing of the centrifugal system of enrichment is completed for scantly enriched uranium, a program for highly enriched uranium might be possible. The number of trained personnel who would work on development of a bomb remains a gray area, and the reader would be advised to recall the outcry from concerned scientists when the National Defense Council membership was altered (as described in the previous chapter). Nevertheless, as the number of individuals involved in nuclear science continues to increase, it must be assumed that incentives, either patriotism or financial, could assure a sufficient number if a threat were present and perceived. Lastly, it seems reasonable, based on the data presented, to estimate that Japan would require 9 to 18 months from project initiation to denote a weapon. This time would tend to move toward the lower end of the spectrum as the post-1985 period is reached.

The existence of a nuclear base with a potential for weapons manufacture must be supported by a means of delivery or it falls into insignificance. In the next chapter, the Japanese capability for turning a weapons potential into a meaningful tool of military power will be discussed.

NOTES

1. The Atomic Energy Basic Law, Law No. 186, December 19, 1955, partially revised by Law No. 72, July 20, 1967. (Texts held by the author. Emphasis by the author.)

2. Atomic Energy Bureau, Science and Technology Agency, Atomic Energy in Japan (Tokyo: Science and Technology Agency, 1971), p. 2.

3. Atoms in Japan (Japan Atomic Industrial Forum), June 1972, p. 29.

4. Seinosuke Hashimoto, Atomic Energy of Japan--Her Course of Research and Development since Orientation 15 Years Ago (Tokyo: Japan Atomic Industrial Forum, 1970), pp. 21-35 (in Japanese).

5. Victor Gilensky and Paul Langer, The Japanese Civilian Nuclear Program (Santa Monica, Calif.: RAND Corporation, 1967), pp. 15-17.

6. Atomic Energy Bureau, op. cit., p. 14.

7. Gilensky and Langer, op. cit., p. 3.

8. Ibid., p. 5. This trend may continue into the 21st century, according to a study completed by Professor Yamamura of Tokyo University. By the year 2000, from a total electrical power demand of 2,527,000 million kilowatt hours (kwh), 78 percent will be produced by nuclear reactors, 15 percent by fossil fuels, and only 7 percent by hydropower (plus subterranean heat and nuclear fusion). See Atoms in Japan, December 1970, pp. 23-25.

9. Atoms in Japan, May 1972, p. 10.

10. Gilensky and Langer, op. cit., p. 2.

11. Atoms in Japan, May 1971, Supplement, p. 2.

12. U.S. Atomic Energy Commission, "Remarks by Clarence E. Larson, Commissioner, U.S. AEC at the Symposium on Energy, Resources and the Environment, Kyoto, Japan," USAEC News Releases, August 9, 1972, p. 3.

13. Ibid., pp. 3-4.

14. Ibid., p. 4. The Japanese forecast was 9,000 short tons (ST) by 1980 and 21,000 ST by 1990. If advanced thermal reactors (ATR) make up 50 percent of the power-generating capability, the requirement would be reduced to 8,000 ST and 16,000 ST respectively. Atoms in Japan, May 1971, Supplement I, p. 12.

15. Atoms in Japan, May 1972, p. 26.

16. Ibid.

17. Ibid.

18. Ibid., January 1971, p. 33.

19. Ibid., June 1971, p. 12.

20. Ibid., May 1972, p. 37; and Asahi Evening News, February 22, 1972.

21. Atoms in Japan, May 1972, p. 37; April 1972, p. 46; and June 1971, p. 34.

22. Larson, "Remarks," p. 4.

23. Atoms in Japan, July 1972, p. 33.

24. Ibid., May 1971, p. 31.

25. Ibid., May 1971, Supplement I, p. 31.

26. Ibid., August 1972, p. 47; and Genshiryoku Tsushin, July 17, 1972, pp. 4-6.

27. Genshiryoko Tsushin, July 17, 1972, pp. 4-6.

28. Larson, "Remarks," p. 4.
29. Ibid., pp. 4-6.
30. Atoms in Japan, March 1973, p. 5.
31. Ibid.
32. Ibid., August 1971, p. 2.
33. Ibid., October 1971, p. 28.
34. Ibid.
35. Denki Shimbun, November 13, 1972.
36. Nihon Keizai, May 27, 1973, U.S. Embassy translation; and Asahi Evening News, August 12, 1974.
37. Asahi Evening News, August 12, 1974.
38. Foreign Broadcast Information Service (FBIS), August 23, 1974.
39. Asahi, May 31, 1973, U.S. Embassy translation; and Sankei, July 24, 1974.
40. Sankei, July 24, 1974, U.S. Embassy translation.
41. Denki Shimbun, November 29, 1972.
42. Kyodo, July 11, 1971, 0915 GMT.
43. Yomiuri, May 17, 1973, U.S. Embassy translation.
44. Ibid.
45. Asahi, May 19, 1973, U.S. Embassy translation.
46. Asahi Evening News, February 17, 1973.
47. Denki Shimbun, November 29, 1972.
48. Atoms in Japan, August 1972, p. 10.
49. Ibid.
50. Ibid., February 24, 1973.
51. Ibid., pp. 19-20 and 24.
52. Ibid., August 1972, p. 10.
53. Nuclear Engineering, January 1973.
54. Atoms in Japan, February 1973, p. 23.
55. Ibid., p. 10.
56. Atomic Energy Bureau, op. cit., p. 8.
57. Asahi Evening News, January 19, 1972.
58. Atoms in Japan, August 1971, p. 30.
59. Nuclear Engineering, August 1972.
60. Sankei, July 24, 1974, U.S. Embassy translation.
61. Yomiuri, May 17, 1973, U.S. Embassy translation.
62. Mainichi, April 3, 1973; and Yomiuri, May 17, 1973, both U.S. Embassy translations.
63. Denryoku Jiji Tsushin, February 16, 1973.
64. Atoms in Japan, March 1973, p. 15.
65. Larson, "Remarks," p. 6.
66. Atoms in Japan, June 1971, p. 14.
67. Ibid.
68. Ibid., p. 16.
69. Ibid., June 1972, p. 28.
70. Ibid., p. 16.

71. Ibid., p. 17.
72. Larson, "Remarks," p. 7.
73. Conversations with AEC, November 1973; and FBIS, June 25, 1974.
74. Atoms in Japan, July 1972, p. 47, and p. 17.
75. Ibid., February 1971, pp. 27-32.
76. Ibid., May 1972, Supplement, p. 86.
77. Ibid., March 1973, p. 13.
78. Ibid., June 1972, p. 21.
79. Ibid., November 1972, p. 49.
80. Ibid., August 1972, pp. 10-13.
81. Ibid., April 1972, Supplement, p. 46.
82. Ibid., July 1972, pp. 31-32.
83. Ibid., p. 53.
84. Ibid., December 1972, p. 43.
85. Genshiryoku Sangyo Shimbun, March 16, 1972, p. 1.
86. V. Gilinsky, Fast Breeder Reactors and the Spread of Plutonium (Santa Monica, Calif.: RAND Corporation, 1967), p. 2.
87. Ibid., pp. 4-9.
88. Ibid., p. 8.
89. Atoms in Japan, May 1971, Supplement I, p. 30.
90. Atomic Energy Bureau, op. cit., p. 5.
91. Nihon Keizai, March 27, 1972, p. 11.
92. Atoms in Japan, January 1971, pp. 37-38.
93. Ibid., August 1971, p. 13.
94. Nikkan Kogyo Shimbun, February 8, 1972, p. 18.
95. Japan Times, September 7, 1972.
96. Atoms in Japan, August 1972, p. 47.
97. Nuclear News, December 1972, p. 54; and Daily Yomiuri, September 4, 1974.
98. Daily Yomiuri, September 4, 1974.
99. Nuclear News, April 1973, p. 60.
100. Atoms in Japan, May 1971, Supplement 2, pp. 1-10.
101. Ibid., Supplement 1, p. 23.
102. Victor Gilinsky, Where Is Nuclear Reactor Technology Taking Us? (Santa Monica, Calif.: RAND Corporation, 1967), p. 4.
103. Iwashima, op. cit., p. 7.
104. Gilinsky, Where Is Nuclear Reactor Technology Taking Us?, p. 1.
105. Gilinsky, Fast Breeders, p. 45.
106. Ibid.
107. Ibid., p. 45.
108. Ibid.
109. Atoms in Japan, February 1971, pp. 27-32.
110. Ibid., May 1971, Supplement 1, p. 20.

111. Ibid., May 1971, Supplement 1, p. 19.

112. Anzenhosho Chosa Kai, <u>Nihon no Anzenhosho 1970 nen e no Tembo</u> (Tokyo: Asagumo Shimbun Sha, 1968), p. 314.

113. Perhaps a warhead inventory of this nature could satisfy Japanese requirements. See Chapter 4 for further discussion.

114. Galinsky, <u>Where Is Nuclear Reactor Technology Taking Us?</u>, p. 9.

115. <u>Nuclear News</u>, December 1972, p. 53.

116. <u>Atoms in Japan</u>, March 1973, p. 15.

117. <u>Nihon no Anzenhosho</u>, pp. 316-17.

118. Ibid. The actual Japanese was <u>susen</u>, which translates as several thousand.

119. Ibid.

120. Samuel Glasstone, ed., <u>The Effects of Nuclear Weapons</u> (Washington, D.C.: Government Printing Office, 1962), p. 22.

121. <u>Nihon no Anzenhosho</u>, p. 316.

122. <u>Atoms in Japan</u>, December 1972, p. 3.

123. Ibid., p. 21.

124. Ryukichi Imai, "Japan and the World of SALT," <u>Bulletin of Atomic Scientists</u>, December 1971, p. 15.

125. E. R. Zilbert, <u>The Chinese Nuclear Explosion, N-Nation Nuclear Development and Civil Defense</u> (Santa Monica, Calif.: RAND Corporation, 1965), pp. 2-3.

126. Ryukichi Imai, "The Changing Role of Nuclear Technology in the Post-NPT World: A Japanese View," in Johan Jorgen Holst, ed., <u>Security, Order, and the Bomb</u> (Oslo: Universitetsforlaget, 1972), p. 121.

CHAPTER

4

DELIVERY SYSTEMS

The purpose of this chapter is to discuss the possible delivery systems that could be available to Japan during designated time frames to accomplish certain objectives if only technological and mission requirements are considered. Many of the assumptions upon which this chapter is written are projections of data collected but disassociated from this particular review due to their specific technical nature. Therefore, the interested reader is encouraged to refer to Appendix D, regarding the status of Japan's space program.

While Japan has the technology to produce nuclear weapons, given a certain lead time, a matter of equal importance is the existence of a delivery capability. In the UN Report Effects of the Possible Use of Nuclear Weapons and the Security and Economic Implications for States of the Acquisition and Further Development of These Weapons, a modest nuclear capacity was defined as one represented "by a force of from thirty to fifty jet bomber aircraft, together with fifty medium range missiles of 3000 kilometer range in soft emplacements and 100 plutonium warheads."[1] Is a force of this dimension possible for Japan? Can Japan "put together a serious strategic capability which could make a useful contribution to satisfying . . . security aspirations?" Can Japan realize more than a "suicidal threat against the cities of a potential foe" or is such a capability in itself considered enough to provide deterrence? Would a Japanese decision to attain a deterrent capability be aimed only at the PRC or would it also include a desire to deter the USSR? Would a capability to deter the USSR also imply a similar potential vis-à-vis the United States?

146

In order to assess adequately the ability of Japan to deliver nuclear weapons, a review of possible missions, or jobs to be done, must be accomplished. Prior to such a review, however, fundamental assumptions must be stated or at least implicitly understood or the following pages will border on the incredible, in light of what was said regarding Japan's domestic attitudes toward nuclear weapons in Chapter 2.

Any scenario that projects a Japanese nuclear defense posture must recognize, above all, that some dramatic political or economic change has occurred in the international system. While it is not necessary to spell out, at this time, the numerous possibilities of a reoriented international system, it must be assumed, at the least, that significant change has occurred in U.S.-Japanese relations. Perhaps a change in the perceived credibility of the U.S. nuclear guarantee would occur; possibly the change would be more clear-cut. Once a change in the U.S.-Japan relationship is admitted, a second basic assumption, that of a clearly perceived adversary, must also be accepted. With these two premises, it is possible, given the basic thesis of this study, to proceed with an examination of possible missions.

One role or mission that the government of Japan has consistently refused to rule out involves defensive nuclear weapons. Just what is a defensive nuclear weapon? Perhaps it would be possible to use the definition outlined previously in Chapter 2, which noted that a device not able to cross borders or threaten neighbors would technically not contravene the Japanese Constitution.

Given the extremely sensitive nature of nuclear armaments in Japan, this option would represent the one probably most acceptable to the Japanese body politic in early stages of a growing adversary relationship. Through a declaratory policy of nuclear armament for purely defensive reasons, in line with what has been declared constitutionally acceptable by the LDP, a future Japanese government could at least begin a test and warhead development program with minimal public opposition.

It would appear, however, that the first task of Japanese defense planners, after the perception of the loss of a U.S. commitment to come to her nuclear defense, would be to examine the possible non-nuclear alternatives that have been espoused by Japanese and foreign observers for many years. Namely, the leaders of Japan would most likely consider the appropriateness of such security guarantee systems as non-nuclear zones, nonaggression pacts, unarmed neutrality with the United Nations guaranteeing her security, armed neutrality (but short of nuclear armament), possible attempts to find a new nuclear patron--either the PRC or the USSR--or a policy of advanced "strategic accommodation" (so recently evidenced in the Japanese change of policy toward the Arab oil states).

After an adequate appraisal of the alternatives has been made, it might be found that only by developing the ability to inflict unacceptable losses on an aggressor could the sovereign independence of the Japanese state be maintained. In such a case, the objective of the military would clearly and simply be to stop the aggressive action of other powers once begun. Theoretically, such a mission by virtue of its inability to "cross borders" could only react to aggressive forces once clearly committed to an attack on the Japanese islands; they would have to stop short of "defensive" strikes against the source of the aggression, and, in essence, the attacker would enjoy a free and lasting sanctuary in his own territory.

The technical requirements for creating such a defensive military force would be minimal. Intelligence of an impending attack could be obtained through existing warning systems, and targets could be located by aerial reconnaissance or make themselves evident in the form of beachheads. Preemption, as such, could not exist as an option in the defensive environment. Command and control of defense forces would make use of available relay systems and land-line communications. Delivery systems, the F104Js, F4EJs, possibly the FT2, and VTOL fighter bombers could, if not destroyed on the ground, deliver 20-kt, or smaller, warheads to all possible targets on the islands or in close proximity.

It might be asked immediately what good is such a low-level nuclear force? Would it not be destroyed in the first moments of the war in the rush of oncoming missiles? Not necessarily. It could be justified as a force to prevent the USSR or PRC from seizing the industrial plant of Japan to replace that devastated in a war. (This would presuppose the absence of a great missile offensive, as the object of the attack would be to acquire the industries intact.)

While specific scenarios are endless, the possibility does exist for Japan to decide to create a tactical defensive nuclear force. Japan, especially with a vertical takeoff and landing (VTOL) force, could make aggression extremely costly; possibly so costly that deterrence--the decision not to embark on hostilities or a course of action implicitly harmful to the continued existence of the Japanese state--would occur. The antagonist would then possibly seek some nonhostile means to exploit the Japanese industrial capability. In light of the theory of strategic accommodation, the Japanese would collaborate to any extent stopping short of the reoccupation of the home islands.

While it is possible to conceive of a strictly defensive option for Japan in which damage is inflicted only on invading forces, it is a defense policy bordering on self-abnegation, which, in this writer's terms of reference would seem quite unrealistic. Therefore, while a self-abnegating, strictly defensive option is raised as one of the possibilities for Japan, this study should move to more specific possible adversary relationships and an appraisal of Japan's delivery capabilities in more pragmatic terms.

We must consider the very real future possibility that both the USSR and the PRC make contesting demands for "X" percent of the industrial output of Japan. At the same time these two adversaries could further demand that Japan completely abrogate commercial intercourse that would aid its enemy. In such an event, the policy of strategic accommodation could not succeed. The choices open to Japan would be alliance with the PRC against the USSR, alliance with the USSR against the PRC, or commercial intercourse with neither, which would mean war with both. (Another alliance, that with the United States against both, has been ruled out already as a factor in the changed international system.)

Other situations could arise in which bilateral relations deteriorated with either the USSR or the PRC at a time when the U.S. nuclear guarantee would be unreliable or nonexistent. In the context of this paper, it will be assumed that a policy of "aggressive expansion"[2] will be rejected by Japanese leaders and the object of a nuclear force will be to inhibit or deter the Chinese or Soviets from the unlimited exercise of power that would threaten the very existence of Japan.

A policy of deterrence must have hardware that is reasonably capable of threatening, in a second-strike situation, the destruction of major political, industrial, and cultural centers of the enemy. A brief examination of Japanese delivery systems currently in the inventory and those that could reasonably be expected to be introduced based on the technology level of the country follows. First the systems will be reviewed with respect to the PRC and then as related to capabilities against the USSR.

AIRCRAFT: CURRENT CAPABILITIES

Military Air

Japan has approximately 160 F-104Js and 230 F86Fs in the Air Self-Defense Force (ASDF).[3] Using a high-low-high flight profile (in this case, flight conducted at 35,000 feet when permitted by the defensive environment and 100 feet while penetrating active defense envelopes) for the F-104J with a 2,000-pound bomb load and launching from active airfields located from Hokkaido to Okinawa, the following areas in China are within range: the northeastern territory of Heilungkiang Province, the eastern tip of the Shantung Peninsula, Shanghai, Hangchow, and Chekiang Province, plus a major portion of Fukien Province. All of Korea save for the Yalu River area could be brought under attack.

Leonard Beaton and John Maddox state in their comprehensive review The Spread of Nuclear Weapons (published in 1967) that the "F-104G Starfighters . . . would make a good supersonic striking force over short to medium ranges."[4] Of course, as demonstrated, range is the main limitation with the F-104J. Of the major industrial regions in China, only portions of the lower Yangtze industrial base could be placed at risk. Seven cities with populations over 200,000 fall within the potential range of the F-104J strike aircraft. These are Chuanchow, Foochow, Hangchow, Ningpo, Shanghai, Soochow, and Wenchow with a total population of approximately 10 million, slightly more than 1 percent of the population of the PRC. While Shanghai does offer concentrations of textile, iron and steel, shipbuilding, electrical equipment, chemicals, and fertilizer production facilities, the other prime industrial centers of Peking-Tientsin, Mukden, Harbin, Nanking, Wu-Han, Pao-t'ou, Hsiang-t'an, Chungking, and Ch'ang-Ch'un would remain beyond effective combat radius of the F-104J.[5] If one-way missions were used, many of the mentioned areas would be vulnerable, but such a tactic would have to be the subject of Japanese declaratory policy in order to be effective and would seem only a stop-gap measure at best.

Civil Air

The current commercial jet aircraft inventory held by Japan Airlines consists of 8 Boeing 747s; 47 Douglas DC-8s;

150

2 Boeing 727s; and 2 NAC YS 11s.[6] Even if the 727s and YS 11s are excluded from the calculations, there are 55 long-range jet aircraft available to Japan. These aircraft with modifications could be made to carry nuclear weapons internally; however, the DC-8s (and 707s) have wing stressing strong enough to carry a weight of 5,000 pounds under each wing.[7] The Boeing Pod Pak, for example, which was designed for the 707 to carry extra engines externally, typifies the potential inherent in such aircraft.[8] The navigation systems, ground mapping radars, and available room for further "black box" modifications make these civil airliners potentially better weapons delivery aircraft than the military F-104J. Each DC-8 could carry, as a minimum, two atomic devices against targets as far away as 4,000 miles.

It should be noted that the UN Secretary General's report on the possible uses of nuclear weapons (mentioned above) considered "any system employing unorthodox means of delivery, such as a ship or commercial aircraft . . . as not a viable course for any nation to pursue."[9] It is clear that to accept such a view is to ignore the lessons of history. The attacks on Osaka Castle, Port Arthur, and Pearl Harbor, to mention only three, were instances of great unorthodoxy but impressive military results. However, in the sense of being capable of surviving a first strike and being used in retaliation, it is clearly possible to agree with the UN finding and discount commercial aircraft as contributing to deterrence.

CAPABILITIES OF THE PERIOD
1974-85

The Fourth Defense Build-Up Plan, which was announced on April 27, 1971, by the then director-general of the Defense Agency, Nakasone Yasuhiro, was to go into effect in April 1972.[10] However, keen domestic pressure has forced the delay of certain programs as well as the final determination of the full program itself. The original draft of the program called for the establishment of two new F4EJ squadrons (76 aircraft), the acquisition of 18 RF4E reconnaissance aircraft, 126 FST ground-support fighters plus 80 T2 trainers and 30 transports. The program was to cover a five-year period starting in fiscal year 1972 (April 1, 1972).

As it is now quite possible due to the oil crisis that some of the hardware that was to be included in the Fourth

Defense Plan will be slipped to the Fifth, it is appropriate to deal with these midterm capabilities as lasting through fiscal year 1985. During this period, which would be covered by the fourth and fifth programs, plus several years for insurance, the ASDF had hoped to produce 158 F4EJs by Mitsubishi Heavy Industries, Ltd. Originally, 54 of these were to be based in Okinawa. Eighty T-2 two-place trainers and 126 FS-T2 aircraft, the single-seat version, were also included in the plan. Prototypes of these FS-T2 fighters are scheduled for flight tests in 1974, and series production is planned for sometime during the fifth defense program.[11]

It was announced by the ASDF on July 1, 1972 that the FS-T2 would be equipped with a modern bombing computer "virtually the same" as the computer used in current U.S. aircraft (A7D). This would increase the air-to-ground capabilities of the aircraft as the bombing system automatically releases ordnance if the aircraft is over the target. (A bombing computer of a similar nature, but not as sophisticated, was rejected for the F4EJ in 1967 when the opposition parties contended it would seem provoking to Japan's neighbors.)[12]

The FS-T2 is reported to have a range of 345 miles with a bomb load of 4,000 pounds.[13] John H. Hoagland in World Combat Aircraft Inventories and Production: 1970-1975 makes an interesting observation about the XT-2: "This aircraft, like the Jaguar, is powered by two Rolls Royce-Turbomeca Adour engines, and its configuration is difficult to distinguish from the Jaguar. (The absence of protest from Britain or France suggests the possibility of informal technical collaboration in exchange for selection of the Adour engine.)"[14]

The FS-T2 with a range in excess of 400 miles with only 2,000 pounds would be available for defensive air-to-ground or air-to-sea missions in the proximity of the home islands while the F4EJ with a similar bomb load could be effective over a combat radius of 800 nautical miles (nm).

Using the ranges listed above from launching points mentioned previously, the F4EJ can reach Heilungkiang Province including Harbin, Ch'ang-ch'un in Kirin Province, Mukden, and Anshan. Tientsin and Peking are clearly within range as well as Tsinan, the Shantung Peninsula, Hsuchou, Nanking, and to as far south as Canton. The F4EJ, therefore, offers the prospect to Japanese defense planners of a delivery vehicle capable of a combat radius of 800 nm and beyond.

While it can bring within range the major cities of the PRC for targeting consideration, it does not provide a secure second-strike capability unless the Japanese would be willing to make the investment required to keep a major portion of the F4EJ fleet on air and ground alert.

All cities in Japan are exposed to the PRC's TU-16s including, of course, the political, industrial, and economic centers of the nation. Two forces of TU-16s penetrating the Japanese Air Defense Zone for strikes on Osaka and Tokyo, place, in these metropolitan areas, as many as 30 million at risk. (These figures include satellite cities such as Yokohama, Yokosuka, and Higashiosaka, in the municipal areas.) An expanded target list designed to include the use of the PRC medium-range ballistic missile (MRBM) force followed by TU-16 employment would effectively cripple a nation so dependent on ports and industrial capacity for its livelihood.

Diversified basing of the Chinese TU-16s at facilities normally out of range for F4EJs could effectively prevent a first-strike option unless one-way missions were contemplated, and with practically any functioning warning system at all, as well as a system of ground alert, the PRC could launch their TU-16s prior to anticipated time-over-target by the penetrating aircraft. The use of commercial aircraft could be possible in a first-strike scenario but admittedly would be most difficult in view of the open nature and lack of uniform political consensus in Japan.

More important, PRC medium-range/intermediate range (MR/IR) missile strikes against the known basing structures of the F4EJs could, in a matter of minutes, eliminate the threat of a Japanese second strike save for those aircraft on airborne alert. If the Japanese were to develop a VTOL attack force by 1985, capability to survive a missile first strike would be enhanced by the greater potential for dispersal; however, the questions of command and control and weapon availability over such dispersed forces would become extremely complicated. A medium-range bomber force-- on the scale of the FB-111--might also be possible; it would need to operate from more developed facilities than a VTOL but might have greater orbit time for air-alert roles.

Of much greater utility to the Japanese than more manned delivery systems, be they either with greater range or dispersal capabilities, would be an MR/IRBM capable of striking a greater spectrum of targets than that offered by the F4EJ or VTOL and offering greater survivability than medium bombers. It would appear from technical data presented in Appendix D that the Japanese, if they sought a second-strike capability against a growing Chinese nuclear threat, could develop a solid-fuel missile with acceptable accuracy for attacks against urban areas in the PRC.

Such a missile could be in the 1,000-1,500-nm range and could be deployed in launch sites dug into sparsely populated mountain regions of Japan; these launch sites would serve to draw PRC missiles away from urban areas, if a PRC damage-limiting first strike were contemplated. Missiles so deployed would seem to offer a credible second-strike capability against the PRC, as it has been stated that the destruction of only 12 of the major urban industrial complexes in China would set that nation back 50 years.[15] Such a capability would probably be within the range of possibilities of a hardened MR/IRBM force in Japan.

The missiles themselves would be the outgrowth of Mu and N rocket development programs (see Appendix D for the current status of the Japanese rocket program) and could be so targeted to threaten the destruction or severe dislocation of the very concentrated modern industrial base in the PRC.

It has often been mentioned by Japanese defense analysts that the earthquake nature of the Japanese islands precludes the use of missiles in hardened sites. While precautions would, of course, be required, it seems most logical to assume that hardened silos capable of resisting earthquake tremors could be technically feasible when silos capable of surviving nuclear near misses have already been fashioned in both the United States and the USSR (and possibly China).

It has been estimated that if a sophisticated industrial state spends 5 to 10 years on sounding rockets and has requisite test ranges, "then the development of strategic delivery vehicles would be an additional eight-to-twelve-year undertaking."[16] Japan spent 11 years, from 1955 to 1966 developing and firing sounding rockets from the Pencil to the Lambda-3H. The Lambda-4S represented a vehicle that eventually gave Japan a satellite-orbiting capability. It was first used in 1966, which was the same year the Todai Institute moved its launch site from Michikawa Beach in Akita (dangerously close to the Soviet Maritime Provinces) to the impressive Kagoshima Space Center located at Uchimoura, Kagoshima. The year 1966 plus 11 would be 1978, three years after the first operational N rocket is scheduled for launch (the N rocket is equivalent to a 1968 Thor-Delta).

While guidance represents the present most difficult hurdle for the Japanese to pass, problems of reentry would,

154

of necessity, also need to be addressed. Although no specific reentry objectives are highlighted in the midterm space plan, considerable data and experience are already being gained concerning reentry phenomena.[17]

Protective materials that could be used for rocket nose cones and rocket nozzles are currently being manufactured in Japan. Carbon fiber compound, particularly useful because of its light weight and strength, is being produced by four Japanese firms.* This kind of production capability combined with the advanced state of the rocket industry in Japan indicate that the 1978-80 period would be more than adequate for the possession of all the necessary technical skills for a strategic ballistic delivery vehicle in Japan. An assessment of its utilitarian nature, when programmed against the People's Republic of China, will be attempted in the next chapter.

If Japan's primary adversary is seen not as China, but as the USSR, delivery systems deemed acceptable to deter the PRC would seem less appropriate. The force level necessary to inhibit the USSR from aggressive actions against Japan must be examined in the light of the changing requirements forced by geographic considerations. Where a capability to inflict significant damage to approximately 12 urban areas in China might prove to be of deterrent value (if such a capability exists in a second-strike situation) and could be achieved with weapons systems within reach of the Japanese technological base, the problem of deterring the Soviet Union is quite a different matter.

If the principal instrument in deterrence is to possess the ability to threaten one's adversary with some assured measure of destruction including major political centers, urban/industrial complexes, and cultural points, it is clear that unless Japan were to develop long-range systems, the capability of successfully penetrating as far as Moscow would not exist.

Current systems including F4EJs offer little against Soviet targets deep in the European part of the USSR. For example, the F-104J could reach all of south Sakhalin, the

---

*The four firms are Toyo Rayon, Nippon Carban, Kurebane Chemical Industries, and Tokai Electrode Manufacturing Company. Toyo Rayon can produce from 10 to 20 tons per month, Nippon Carbon about one ton per month, and the remaining two firms at lesser rates. (Gentsu, November 20, 1972.)

Maritime Provinces including the cities of Komsomolsk,
Sovetskaya-Gavan, Khabarovsk, Lesoavodsk, Spassk-Dal'ny,
Voroshilov, Vladivostok, and Suchan, among other Soviet
territory. However, of the seven major industrial and
populated regions of the USSR, only one, Vladivostok,
could be brought under attack by the F-104J. Only three
cities with populations over 200,000--Vladivostok, Komsomolsk, and Khabarovsk--with a combined population of
slightly over 1 million would be placed at risk out of a
total Soviet population of over 240 million. With the
F4EJ, penetration is increased significantly, but Vladivostok is still the only major industrial region at risk,
and no additional cities over 200,000 are added to the
threat list.

Against the USSR Japan could not threaten even as
many cities as the Soviets were willing to lose in World
War II. Only one major industrial region could be
threatened and the political centers of the USSR would remain some 2,500 miles beyond the range of Japanese military
aircraft. Even with the Maritime Province as hostage, it
is not reasonable to believe that the Soviets would be
inhibited from any actions it had conceived against Japan.
Further, any significant threat to the Maritime Province
must be considered only as a first-strike threat; it
would face serious degradation as a second strike.

What measure of threat must survive to form a credible deterrence with regard to the Soviet Union? It was
common practice in U.S. strategic/academic circles to maintain that destruction of 20 percent of the Soviet population with concomitant damage to the industrial base would
act as a brake on Soviet policy-makers. The Japanese could
probably be satisfied with a much lower percentage, while
concentrating on major urban centers vital to the industrial, political, and military effectiveness of the USSR.
The destruction of Moscow and several other key centers,
with ancillary damage to overall Soviet command and control might be considered a realistic deterrent for a small
nuclear power, for such an attack, if successful, could
upset the major U.S.-USSR relationship to an extent perhaps felt unacceptable to Soviet leadership. While it is
logical to believe the above, in all candor it must be
admitted that no one really knows what level of deterrence
is sufficient in such cases.

In seeking a force capable of inflicting damage on
key Soviet targets so that deterrence might be possible
without U.S. assistance, the Japanese would have to consider seriously the construction not only of missiles cap-

able of intercontinental ranges but also of launch platforms with some greater degree of survivability than land-
based systems. Land-based missiles, while possibly acceptable against Chinese systems that could conceivably
have greater inaccuracies than Soviet systems, would seem
to offer less of a guaranteed second-strike capability
against the USSR. The great number of Soviet missiles
available for use against Japan plus their accuracies and
potential for multiple warheads during this period underline the need for Japanese development of a nuclear submarine capable of launching missiles.

Although there is an underlying desire on the part of
the Japanese Maritime Defense Force to possess nuclear
powered attack submarines, there are no plans (known to
the author) for a Japanese military nuclear powered submarine capability within the coming decade; however,
whether it would be technologically feasible by 1985, if
desired, is another question.

The subject of nuclear-powered submarines has been
discussed often enough. Yasuhiro Nakasone, while director
general of the Defense Agency, said that when nuclear propulsion is common for ordinary cargo liners and tankers,
it would be possible to use it to power submarines. He
was quoted as saying that it would not contravene the Basic
Atomic Energy Law as it had been "unanimously approved on
the understanding that defense ships could use atomic energy as power."[18]

The above was not in full accord with the 1965 unified
position of the government as in April of that year a
Science and Technology Agency spokesman had stated,

> At present when nuclear propulsion of ships is
> not a common practice, we do not think that using
> atomic energy for propulsion of defense vessels
> can be permitted. . . . At present, general uses
> of atomic energy for ship propulsion is nothing
> more than a [figment of the] imagination. We are
> unable to express the Government's policy on the
> basis of such [a dream] imagination.[19]

Much later, in May 1972, Admiral Kenichi Kitamura of
the Maritime Self Defense Force (MSDF) stated, "From an
operational point of view, conventional submarines have
many unsatisfactory aspects. I suppose that Japan may
come to have nuclear submarines in the future. Nuclear
ship propulsion and nuclear weapons are entirely different
matters."[20] This statement was followed on the first of

June by a reply by the incumbent director-general of the Defense Agency, who stated, "It is inconceivable that Japan will come to have nuclear submarines within ten years or so, such as under a fourth-term or fifth-term defense buildup program." He added that "if, in the future, nuclear propulsion of merchant ships becomes common knowledge, then there will naturally be room for consideration."[21]

By the early 1980s, a greater technological base will exist in Japan in the nuclear submarine field. This will happen as a result of the development of the nuclear ship Mutsu and a large containerized cargo ship. Other research also is currently under way in relation to commercial nuclear-powered ships.[22] Research that can be tied closely with a future nuclear-powered submarine capability is the R and D project to develop a new 2,200-ton submarine incorporating super high tensile steel (NS-90), which is scheduled to begin sometime after 1976.[23] Development of an inertial navigation system for submarines is also currently being sought. At this point, funds are only being requested to initiate certain limited feasibility studies.[24]

It would seem that attainment of an operational capability could be achieved within 8 to 10 years of project initiation, perhaps less. The missiles fired from such a nuclear submarine would need the minimum characteristics of the Polaris A-2 system; any greater range would enhance the choice of operating zones and perhaps allow for introduction of sophisticated penetration-aid packages for the Moscow antiballistic missile (ABM) defense.

To this point in this review of delivery systems, unmanned systems such as MR/IRBMs, intercontinental ballistic missiles (ICBMs), and submarine-launched ballistic missiles (SLBMs) have been stressed over manned delivery vehicles, primarily from the standpoint of prelaunch survivability. However, another area that must be of increasing concern to defense analysts is the penetration capability of manned aircraft in the face of the ever growing redundancy of defensive systems. The panoply of ground-to-air missiles such as the Soviet manufactured SAM-2, 3, 6, and 7 bring into serious question the capability of retaliatory aircraft charged with responsibility for carrying out a second strike of ever reaching their targets. (This question will be addressed in the next chapter, which will be devoted to an empirical analysis of possible Japanese defense options.) It is no longer unreasonable to foresee 60 to 70 percent attrition rates, or even higher, when a nation is responding to a first strike.

This naturally brings up the question of stand-off missiles and would seem to indicate that there may well be a role for an aircraft capable of fairly deep penetration with a good payload capability. While this may be a possibility with respect to the PRC threat, the major problem with any manned system that Japan might have vis-à-vis the USSR is the proximity of the ocean. A surprise Soviet first strike launched from submarines off the coast of Japan would never have to proceed further than 75 miles over land to reach its targets. Reaction time is almost nonexistent, and only manned systems already airborne would survive.

If the most favored systems seem to be hardened land-based missiles, and the SLBMs, what is the prospect of their interception prior to impact on target? Currently the Soviet Union possesses the Galosh ABM, which defends Moscow. The Galosh is an exoatmospheric interceptor, which might be confused by possible exoatmospheric nuclear detonations; however, if we deal in terms of the 1980s and 1990s, an atmospheric intercept capability must be allowed.

An even more serious contingency that Japanese defense planners must consider are provisions in SALT I for Soviet deployment of a 100-missile ABM system to defend a portion of its offensive missiles, and the secondary provision that permits ABMs to be located at missile test centers.[25] Depending on the placement of the new ABM field, Japanese missiles could be exposed to ABM intercept at two points along the Japan to Moscow trajectory. If Japan develops a SLBM force and launches from the Arabian Sea, Kapustin Yar, one of the Soviet rocket test centers, lies across the potential trajectory to Moscow. Therefore, if planners were to consider the ABM threat in a most realistic manner, some capability must be given to these additional sites. This, of course, theoretically degrades the second-strike capability.

The PRC does not possess an ABM system but could possibly be given a point defense capability in the late 1980s. While the ABM system does not seem of major concern in relation to China, there are reports of a comprehensive personnel bomb shelter program in Peking. If, indeed, Japan had to react to a Chinese first strike the advantage of being first could actually result in considerably fewer casualties (deaths and injuries) among the Chinese than in corresponding Japanese urban areas. Secondly, if the Japanese second strike were delivered by manned aircraft the hours available to the Chinese before the retaliatory aircraft are on target would allow for possible evacuation of the more exposed areas.

Possibly the one area that seems least subject to innovative defensive measures is that of antisubmarine warfare (ASN), but it is still a possibility that Japanese force planners will have to consider. If the objective of a Japanese nuclear force is to be able to guarantee the destruction of 10 to 20 major Soviet cities deep in the European zone of the USSR, even a small increase in ASW performance could affect Japanese plans.

As pointed out by Richard Garwin, ASW consists of four major functions: intelligence, detection, localization, and destruction.[26] Intelligence consists of knowing the capability and number of the various types of enemy submarines. Detection is the process of obtaining information on the general whereabouts of submarines. Localization is the function of refining of submarine position followed by destruction.

One-time Secretary of Defense Melvin Laird stated in 1970 that "the Soviet Navy today might be able to localize and destroy at sea one or two Polaris submarines."[27] A loss of two submarines to the U.S. submarine fleet is appreciable but, nonetheless bearable, especially in the era after multiple independently targeted reentry vehicles (MIRVs). However, if Japan had but three submarines at sea and had not yet developed a MIRV capability, the effect could be catastrophic.

A slight increase in ASW capability in five to seven years (by approximately 1977) was seen by Laird, but, generally, prospects for an ASW breakthrough are held to be extremely slim.[28] According to Garwin, the only "effective way to locate a submerged submarine from any distance is by the use of acoustic methods";[29] however, some hope, or threat, of an ASW breakthrough is possessed by the blue-green lasers that can penetrate water to some 300 to 400 feet.[30] Whether or not the threshold for an ASW breakthrough has been reached cannot be disputed, but defense planners must allow for some improvement and a corresponding degradation in SLBM effectiveness.

Against both possible adversaries, Japanese command and control and data acquisition programs must be updated in line with the modernization of their forces. The expected use of unmanned systems requires extremely accurate geodetic information. Such information might be obtained as a result of the space program; communication requirements would also be compounded further if the SLBM option were selected and forces operated thousands of miles from Tokyo. Delivery systems represent only the tip of the iceberg and demand adequate support systems to be made ef-

fective. This author would imagine that supportive in-
situtions would indeed be sufficient.

Before we conclude this particular investigation,
which deals with systems possible prior to 1985, it would
be useful to review the research and development programs
of Japan to understand better the current direction in
which major defense equipment procurement seems to be
heading.

JAPANESE R AND D GOALS PRIOR
TO THE 1980s

A review of the R and D objectives of the various government agencies reveals several general areas that are
receiving prime emphasis; these are as follows:

1. Atomic energy, especially uranium enrichment,
next-generation reactors, application of nuclear power to
shipping, and creation of a nuclear fuel cycle in Japan.
(See Chapter 3 for a more complete discussion.)

2. Military air, with special emphasis on avionics
development, advanced aircraft and power plants, and military missiles. Included in avionics development are an
airborne fire control system incorporating an advanced
phased array active radar unit for multipurpose roles
(prototype system by 1978-79); an advanced airborne electronic countermeasures system to be developed by the end
of 1976; general technology for an inertial navigation system to be developed post-1976 using as a base the license
manufacturing of the Litton ASN-63; and an integrated airborne "spy system" sometime in the early to mid-1980s for
incorporation into an upgraded F4EJ or the replacement
fighter of the future.[31] Projects included in the advanced
aircraft/powerplant field are STOL (short takeoff and landing) and VTOL-related projects; advanced rotary wing aircraft studies; an airborne early warning (AEW) aircraft
system; jet engine development including future turbofan
engines; and an advanced antisubmarine patrol plane.[32]

The Japanese Air Self-Defense Force (JASDF) has plans
to contract for the next main fighter post F4EJ during fiscal year 1977 so that delivery can take place before the
end of 1981.[33] Planes initially under consideration were
the F-15 (McDonnell), F-14 (Grumman), P-530 (Northrop),
Panagia 200 (a British, German, and Italian consortium),
and an improved F4EJ.[34] This list has been expanded to
include a plan for redevelopment of the Japanese developed
T-2, and it has been reported that the Defense Agency would

like to make its selection in 1974 so as to preclude the suspension of fighter production in Japan after 1979.[35]

3. Military missiles, aimed at obtaining a complete arsenal of advanced military missiles, R and D is scheduled for an air-to-ship missile, and a ship-to-ship system for use by hydrofoils, destroyers, and patrol boats. Both missiles are scheduled for force integration by the end of the 1970s.[36] Efforts may also be made to increase the range of the Model 30 surface-to-surface rocket used by the Ground Self-Defense Force (GSDF). This artillery rocket with a range of 30 kilometers may have its range extended to 40 or 50 kilometers.[37] A new air-to-air missile especially designed for close-range air-to-air combat is also on the planning boards but will be delayed somewhat pending development of other missiles.[38]

4. Space development. The National Aeronautical Laboratory is supporting studies in the following areas: general characteristics of rocket air frames, solid and liquid fuel rocket thrust vector controls, ion rocket engines, rocket guidance systems, flight attitudes and orbit controls, spin burning, solid fuel thrust cutoff, and so on.[39]

5. Maritime R and D. The fuel cell submarine (powered by an engine that produces electricity by the combination of oxygen and hydrogen as used in the U.S. Apollo spacecraft) is being developed,[40] as well as the previously mentioned high tensile steel submarine and feasibility studies for an inertial navigation system for submarines.

While only R and D projects related to systems that have obvious military application have been itemized, the desire is not to give the impression that the above represents an exhaustive recounting of all R and D being done in Japan. The above does connote, however, in this writer's opinion, an ever broadening scientific and technical base in Japan, which will, by the early to mid-1980s be fully capable of supporting practically a full spectrum of delivery vehicles. The one exception would seem to be a nuclear-powered missile submarine, which might be possible, from a technical standpoint in the mid-1980s to early 1990s time frame.

LONG-TERM CAPABILITIES:
1990 AND BEYOND

In our discussion of the long-term capabilities of the Japanese state regarding strategic weapons, the period beyond the 1990s and the year 2000, the temptation that must be resisted is to fall into the Jules Verne syndrome, leaving current reality far behind. However, as today has seen the practical application of many of his themes, it might not be a vain endeavor.

Railroad-based deterrent power: In the 1972 Rebuilding Japanese Archipelago written by former Prime Minister Kakuei Tanaka, a most interesting suggestion was made concerning the second generation of high-speed railways in Japan. The recommendation was that a total of 9,000 kilometers, or 6,120 miles, of high-speed railways be constructed to cover the Pacific Ocean side and Japan Sea coastal area with a main trunk running to the extremities of Hokkaido and Kyushu. Such a system of modern rails might permit the combination of solid-fueled nuclear-tipped missiles, with automated high-speed trains, normally on patrol but capable of being directed away from incoming reentry vehicles to safe mountain redoubts and tunnels by a national aerospace defense command center. Such a system could be supplemented by a system of land-based ICBMs positioned throughout the islands to take advantage of natural terrain features.

Of course, a Trident-type capability must not be overlooked, as such a system (albeit an improved version) would be well within the capability range of Japan within the scant 26 years to the next century.

It would be possible for the Japanese aerospace industry to turn out monster-air cushioned vehicles to patrol the seas, racing at fantastic speeds, armed with advanced antiair and submarine armaments, each carrying a battery of nuclear ICBMs patrolling a zone from Malacca to Kamchatka. Such a force, while highly visible for diplomatic purposes, would be capable of a most awesome power.

The weapons mentioned thus far represent, for the most part, extensions or refinements of weapon systems possible today, and each one would be possible only by embarking on an avowedly open nuclear policy. Such a policy depending on the international political situation might invite a hostile international reaction. Therefore, it is upon Weapon X that this author would assign a judgment of "most probable." Of course, Weapon X is the ultimate defensive weapon--the antimaterial laser beam.

The Japanese, interested primarily in defense, could rely on the U.S. nuclear umbrella and devote a major portion of its research and development to perfecting a laser ABM, and the period of offensive ascendancy would have ended. The Japanese would have avoided entirely the expenses inherent in a nuclear development program and would be in "on the ground floor" in the next generation of truly revolutionary weapons. According to Robert Barkan (a former electronics engineer) of the Pacific Studies Center, California, "the often-mooted laser 'death ray' and anti-aircraft guns are now actually being tested."[41] He noted that a

> laser "missile melter" would have significant ad-
> vantages over conventional anti-ballistic missile
> systems. The property of the laser beam to tra-
> vel at the speed of light gives the defence more
> time to detect and track warheads and to distin-
> guish them from decoys. Furthermore, the defence
> would not have to "lead" targets--that is, com-
> pute future intercept positions--because the de-
> lay from firing to impact is negligible.[42]

Where does Japan stand today in regard to current laser technology? In 1971 it was reported that "Japan may . . . have passed West Germany as the second-largest user of gas lasers" and that "the technology gap between the U.S. and Japan laser products is small."[43]

While no one can, with certainty, predict the course of events a full generation away, the above discussion has presented some possibilities. To continue, however, in this vein would be to contravene the well-regarded Japanese proverb: "When we speak of tomorrow, the devil laughs."

SUMMARY: JAPAN'S DELIVERY
CAPABILITIES

The delivery forces needed by Japan will depend upon the mission Japanese leaders assign to their nuclear forces. As stated above, the possible roles could range from a purely island defense mission to attempts to deter the PRC or the USSR by a sophisticated second-strike capability directed against major urban/industrial centers of those nations. Delivery forces could range from systems now in the arms inventory of Japan to SLBMs, which would be possible toward the end of the midterm period (1985). Of course, the arms actually selected would depend, in part, on the estimated comparative economic costs of the various systems and, as stated above, the ultimate missions to be accomplished.

In the following chapter the potential delivery systems of Japan through 1985 will be examined against various

164

possible levels of Chinese and Soviet defense posture to determine the viability of a Japanese second-strike force. It is hoped that by a close examination of key variables, a realistic appraisal of Japanese defense capabilities can be made.

NOTES

1.   United Nations, Effects of the Possible Use of Nuclear Weapons and the Security and Economic Implications for States of the Acquisition and Further Development of These Weapons, Report of the Secretary General (New York: United Nations Department of Political and Security Council Affairs, 1968), p. 23. (Hereafter, the UN Secretary General's Report.)

2.   See remarks of Takeo Fukuda in Newsweek, November 26, 1973, p. 43.

3.   International Institute for Strategic Studies, The Military Balance 1972-1973 (London: IISS, 1971), p. 50.

4.   Leonard Beaton and John Maddox, The Spread of Nuclear Weapons (New York: Praeger Publishers, 1967), p. 59.

5.   U.S. Congress, Joint Economic Committee, People's Republic of China: An Economic Assessment (Washington, D.C.: Government Printing Office, May 1972), pp. 61-73. Very useful for industrial capabilities data.

6.   Asahi Evening News, January 3, 1972.

7.   Beaton and Maddox, op. cit., p. 51.

8.   Malcolm W. Hoag, One American's Perspective on Nuclear Guarantees, Proliferation, and Related Alliance Diplomacy (Santa Monica, Calif.: RAND Corporation, 1971), p. 18.

9.   UN Secretary General's Report, op. cit., p. 22.

10.   Mainichi Daily News, April 27, 1971 and April 28, 1971.

11.   "New Hardware Planned for Japan Defense," Aviation Week and Space Technology, November 1, 1971, p. 48.

12.   Asahi Evening News, July 1, 1972.

13.   Ibid.

14.   John H. Hoagland, World Combat Aircraft Inventories and Production: 1970-1975 (Cambridge: Center for International Studies, Massachusetts Institute of Technology, 1970), p. 38.

15.   Comments of Professor Y. L. Wu addressing the 6th Arms Control Symposium, Valley Forge, Pa., November 1973.

16. Browne and Shaw Research Corporation, The Diffusion of Combat Aircraft, Missiles, and Their Supporting Technologies (Waltham, Mass.: Browne and Shaw, October 1966), p. B-21.

17. The optimizing of reentry trajectories of lifting vehicles has been studied by Kondo and Aihara. See J. Kondo and Y. Aihara, "The Optimum Reentry Trajectory of a Lifting Vehicle," in Proceedings of the Ninth International Symposium on Space Technology and Science (Tokyo: AGNE Publishing, 1972), pp. 265-72. Also refer to the work of Aihara, Nomura, and Watanabe, three scientists at the National Aerospace Laboratories who have used the arc-heated wind tunnel at the NAL to simulate spacecraft reentry environment including aerodynamic heating characteristics: Japan Society for Aeronautical and Space Sciences Journal, vol. 16, pp. 371-78.

18. Asahi, April 15, 1970.

19. Ibid.

20. Yomiuri, May 31, 1972.

21. Asahi, June 1, 1972.

22. Atoms in Japan, August 1972, p. 47.

23. Kokubo Keizai Tsushin, September 25, 1971, pp. 3-4; and Boei Tokushin, March 7, 1972, pp. 2-10.

24. Sekai no Kansen, October 1972, p. 115.

25. Richard G. Head and Ervin J. Rokke, eds., American Defense Policy (Baltimore: Johns Hopkins Press, 1973), pp. 149-52.

26. Richard L. Garwin, "Antisubmarine Warfare and National Security," Scientific American, July 1972, p. 15.

27. Melvin R. Laird, Defense Program and Budget for FY 1971 (Washington, D.C.: Government Printing Office, 1970), p. 40.

28. R. H. Smith, "The ASW Effort," Naval Institute Proceedings, May 1972, p. 129.

29. Garwin, op. cit., p. 16.

30. Chester H. Morgan II, "The Undersea Long Range Missile System, Cornerstone of Deterrence or Strategic Destablizer?" Unpublished paper, Fletcher School of Law and Diplomacy, Tufts University, November 26, 1972, p. 21.

31. Japan Press Exchange (JPE) Aviation Report Weekly, May 1972, pp. 8-9.

32. Ibid., April 1972, pp. 6-8.

33. Asahi, December 27, 1971.

34. Ibid.

35. Nikkan Kogyo Shimbun, June 16, 1972; and Asahi, December 27, 1971.

36. <u>JPE Aviation Report Weekly</u>, October 4, 1971, p. 4.
37. Ibid., November 15, 1971, pp. 7-8; also August 2, 1972.
38. Ibid., July 5, 1971, pp. 2-4.
39. Ibid., April 26, 1972, pp. 6-8.
40. <u>Nihon Keizai</u>, September 3, 1970.
41. Robert Barkan, "Laser for War," <u>Survival</u>, September/October 1972, p. 239.
42. Ibid., p. 241.
43. <u>Laser Focus</u>, July 1971, p. 30.

5

AN EXAMINATION OF POSSIBLE JAPANESE NUCLEAR OPTIONS, CIRCA 1985

In the Defense White Paper issued in October 1970 (and not, as yet superseded) entitled <u>Nihon no Boei</u> (The Defense of Japan) the then director-general of the Defense Agency of Japan (JDA), Yasuhiro Nakasone, stated quite emphatically that the vehicle to be used by Japan to counter any threat from a nuclear quarter would be the U.S.-Japanese security pact.[1] The integral part of dealing with nuclear blackmail and various degrees of atomic saber-rattling by either China or the USSR is reliance on the nuclear deterrent. This policy has not officially changed.

Masumi Esaki, director-general of the Defense Agency under former Prime Minister Sato, reaffirmed the utility of the U.S. nuclear deterrence on June 29, 1972, saying, "Few, I believe, can deny the fact that the U.S.-Japan security system has functioned as an effective deterrent for Japan's defense." However, in the next breath, he said, "Neither can anyone discover serious causes of conflict between Japan and other nations."[2] Esaki, noted "dove" and an influential member of the Dietmen's League for Restoration of Japan-China Relations, upon coming to office in December 1971, reportedly spurred considerable effort within the agency to define the nature of the "threats" over a 10-year period upon which Japan's Fourth Defense Build-Up Plan was formulated.[3] This plan, often called the Nakasone Plan, was introduced in draft form on April 27, 1971. Its main feature was the providing of defense against "restricted, direct aggression" and was programmed to encompass two Defense Build-Up phases each of five years' duration. Seventy to 80 percent of the plan was to be attained under the Fourth Build-Up, the remainder in the fifth or in yearly increments, as seems to be the current trend of JDA thinking. Particularly stressed in the plan were the objectives to realize the command of the seas and air space adjacent to Japan while having a sufficient capability to attack the invader with air power as he attempted to land. Also in the draft were resources to protect Japanese merchant ships from submarine attacks in the waters around Okinawa.[4]

To date, even though there has been no official change in the Japanese dependence on the U.S. deterrent, there is much private and semiofficial speculation touching on defense policy as introduced in Chapter 1; however, the military planning factors have not altered appreciably. The U.S.-Japanese Security Treaty remains the basis for Japanese strategic planning. This position was reaffirmed in the publication of July 1972 entitled <u>Kokkai Sanko Shiryo</u> in which the fundamental premises of the Fourth Defense Build-Up (five-year) Plan are identified as follows:

> Foundation of National Defense
> Our country's national defense, following the "Basic Plan of National Defense" (Cabinet decision of May 20, 1974), is to establish relations of friendship and cooperation with the many neighboring nations, follow a diplomatic policy, etc., that will lessen international tension and make necessary domestic policies for economic and social development, based on the system of the Japan-American security guarantee and consolidation of defense power that will check aggression. Moreover, the defense plan is a thing which will defend the freedom and independence of our country which is the basis for democracy.[5]

This general strategic doctrine, well reflected in the 1970 White Paper, remains unchanged as 1975 is entered.[6] However, what would be the policy if the United States did not play the role outlined above?

The purpose of this chapter is to examine some of the paths open to Japan if it were to become a nuclear weapons power. The time frame is 1985. The focus will be upon the strategic defensive role of nuclear weapons rather than the tactical defensive option, mentioned in Chapter 4, that depends on mines, antiair missiles, artillery warheads, bombs, and short-range ground-to-ground missiles.

This chapter outlines a simple model of certain Japanese nuclear options against two hypothetical target systems, one in the PRC and the other in the USSR. The model

is designed to show the comparative effectiveness of a
range of force levels when the number of deliverable warheads is fixed at a certain number. The targets against
which these delivery options will be ranged consist of a
limited number of Chinese and Soviet cities. The destruction of these urban areas would probably result in greater
losses to those states than could be offset by gains from
the destruction of Japan. Although the model does not consider a possible U.S.-Japanese nuclear confrontation, some
general comments regarding U.S. and Japanese strategic interaction will be made.

ASSUMPTIONS

For the purpose of this paper it will be assumed:
1. That the perception of U.S. nuclear guarantees
by Japanese leaders will force them to believe--whether
correctly or incorrectly--that nuclear defense would no
longer be provided by the United States. In essence,
the U.S. nuclear shield would be seen as not extending as
far as Japan in the eyes of Japanese leaders.
2. That political opposition to nuclear armaments
will be reduced by a general realization of some threat
to the security of Japan. A nuclear policy will be permitted after nonnuclear alternatives are considered but
found inappropriate.
3. That Japan will seek a capability to threaten a
certain minimum range of values held by China or the USSR
in the belief that destruction of these values would inhibit certain actions by either power, actions that Japan
would consider dangerous to its continued existence as a
state.
4. That the time frame for this study is the mid-
1980s. This period has been selected as it is that time,
from a technological sense, that a reasonable capability
exists for the delivery systems mentioned in Chapter 4,
excluding, of course, those systems feasible after the
1990s.
5. That the general strategic situation that sets
the framework of this study will allow for three potential
defensive and offensive levels for the Soviet Union and
the PRC in 1985.
(a) Force Level I will be considered a low or minimum-
level military posture and will reflect, as closely as
possible, a continuation of the strategic balance in effect
in the 1974 period of SALT I.

(b) Force Level II will reflect deployment of defensive and offensive systems to the level allowed by SALT I to include an antiballistic missile (ABM) site in the Siberian area of the USSR, an ABM capability in a test site area, and increased accuracy of Soviet offensive missiles.

(c) Force Level III will contain the highest level of military posture. It will reflect accurate Soviet multiple independently targeted reentry vehicles (MIRVs), a limited ASW breakthrough and greater intercept capability for ABMs.

6. That the basic strategic rivalry will continue between the United States and the USSR while the "spirit of détente" continues.

7. That Japan will be reluctant to become a major nuclear power but would consider a force equal to the combined strategic nuclear forces of France and Great Britain. In this case, it will be assumed that a program sufficient to deliver no more than 160 one-megaton (mt) warheads will be contemplated. (By choosing 160 as the maximum number of nuclear warheads, the study is assured of a reasonable range of damage probabilities regardless of the delivery vehicle considered. The total approaches the order of the combined French and British alert strengths and is felt to constitute the maximum outer limits of any Japanese nuclear armament program that seeks deterrence only. Of course, lesser numbers of warheads will be considered.)

8. That a preemptive attack by Japan will not be considered a possible policy option due to the size of the force (only 160) and the extremely exposed position of Japan.

9. That the damage levels believed sufficient to accomplish destruction of the urban targets will be considered as possible with 3 pounds per square inch (psi) overpressure. This overpressure can cause moderate to severe damage to wood-frame buildings, severe damage to unprotected parked transport aircraft, and moderate damage to wall-bearing masonry buildings.[7] While specific industrial facilities might not be destroyed by such overpressure, the capacity to operate such facilities would be considerably reduced by deaths and injuries to workers and losses in supporting services.

A POSSIBLE SCENARIO

The scenario selected for this examination will be similar to one referred to in Chapter 4. In essence, it pictures the Japanese as having followed a policy of strategic accommodation in international relations—disavowing aggressive expansion—during a period of increased international turbulence. While some nations voice criticism of such a policy, calling it opportunistic or cowardly, the Japanese, nevertheless, maintain their international trade position by meeting the demands of natural resource suppliers and concentrating on production of commodities in which they demonstrate a competitive advantage.

However, the Sino-Soviet ideological dispute will not disappear after the death of Mao and Chou but will instead intensify. As it does so, relations of all states in Northeast Asia will be swept into the vortex of the rivalry. The new leaders of the PRC, hoping to seek a solution to their population problems by expansion to the vast territories to the north, will abrogate all existing treaties with the Soviet Union and demand that the PRC be given access to land as far north as the Stanovoy Khrebet, claiming rights to the territory on which the Soviet cities of Vladivostok, Khabarovosk, Svobodnyy, Nikolayevsk, and Blagoveshchensk are located.

At the same time, China will see Japan's joint exploitation of Siberia and the Maritime Province as a grave threat to the national security of the PRC and eventually demand a halt to any joint enterprises with the Soviets.

While the Japanese will seriously consider the Chinese request, the Kremlin will issue a denunciation of the Chinese demands and inform Japan that termination of the enterprises would be seen as an unfriendly act that could not be tolerated. Any Japanese attempt to acquiesce in the Chinese demands would be considered a hostile act.

In such an environment, whether caused by these exact events or not, the Japanese—with good intentions—would stand "betwixt and between." Japan, not being able to turn to the United States, would see great value in a nuclear delivery capability to inhibit either side from using force. The purpose of the rest of the chapter will be to speculate on the type of force most likely to succeed as a deterrent against the two giant neighbors.

METHODOLOGY

A target system will be constructed for both the PRC and the Soviet Union. The impact of the offensive and defensive forces of the enemy will be examined as well as operational considerations of the Japanese delivery force. Some possible effects of each delivery system (as independent options) will then be estimated.

The possible effect of offensive, defensive, and operational measures will be estimated through the use of probability factors. Such figures for the 1985 time frame must be illustrative at best. These factors will be altered, as appropriate, to reflect the three basic military postures of the Chinese and Soviet forces as outlined in the Assumptions section of this chapter. Low, medium, and high levels will be considered possible by 1985. Low will represent an environment basically unchanged from 1974-75; medium will reflect a somewhat increased offensive potential plus significant ABM advancement by the USSR. High posture posits a Peking ABM system and a Soviet antisubmarine warfare (ASW) breakthrough. These levels will be reflected by a proportionate decrease in the probability factors for a retaliatory Japanese force.

The factors to represent the effects of offensive enemy forces--in this case a preemptive strike by the PRC or the USSR--will be called the survivability factors. These will reflect the likelihood of a delivery vehicle surviving an offensive first-strike so it can launch to carry out its retaliatory mission. Since the overall success of a particular delivery system is extremely sensitive to this factor, the assumed figures used in the study will actually represent a range of possibilities. They should help us understand what would happen if "X" or "Z" actually occurred rather than "Y." This will be accomplished through the vehicle of the three posture levels.

Each delivery system will be assigned survivability factors primarily based on their exposure, hardness, and mobility. Systems--that is, parked aircraft that are confined to easily defined geographical limits and are "soft" (can be rendered nonflyable by 3 psi overpressure) --will be given very low rates of survivability. This is in recognition of the threat and almost absence of warning time for Japan if missiles, especially submarine launched, are used in the attack. Parked aircraft will therefore receive 10 percent and lower in a retaliatory situation. The survivability factors for aircraft and missiles in the 1985 time frame are listed in Table 5.1. Special note should be made of the provision made for a possible medium bomber airborne alert. In that particular case it is hypothesized that the normal 10 percent survival rate can be increased to as high as 90 percent for the aircraft in the air. For those on the ground it is almost the same as for the advanced F4.

Operational factors will be reflected by in-commission rates for aircraft, launch rates and in-flight factors for

TABLE 5.1

Survivability Factors

Weapon	Defense Posture					
	China			USSR		
	Low	Medium	High	Low	Medium	High
Advanced F4	0.20	0.15	0.10	0.15	0.10	0.05
Medium bomber (on air alert)	0.90	0.90	0.90	0.90	0.90	0.90
Land-based mis- siles (in silos)	0.70	0.60	0.50	0.40	0.30	0.20
SSBN missiles	1.00	1.00	0.95	0.95	0.95	0.65

Source: Compiled by the author.

missiles, pilot target acquisition rates, and warhead reliability rates. These factors will remain basically unchanged in this retaliatory situation; in preemption or
planned first-strike, it might be argued that some of
these factors, especially in-commission rate, could approach a factor of 1.00, but this possibility has been
eliminated by the assumptions of this book.

The factors relating to the operational effectiveness
of the Japanese force are shown in Table 5.2. Since these
reflect the degree of training, maintenance, technological
competence, or what might be called the "professionalism"
on the part of the Japanese force and its general support
network, only one factor will be indicated for both China
and the Soviet Union. (Their actions could not appreciably
affect these factors.)

Enemy defensive factors, pertaining mainly to penetration rates, reflect the likelihood of the delivery vehicle's
reaching the target once it has successfully entered the
enemy air space. This factor is extremely sensitive to
actions taken by the opposition, as was shown in the October-November 1973 Middle East war, when newly introduced
surface-to-air missiles achieved technological surprise
in the early days of the campaign and cost the Israelis
dearly in aircraft losses. Therefore, these factors will
change markedly from low to high military postures. It
might be pointed out that, as the Japanese are retaliating,
the defense has been put on its highest alert--attrition
must be high. In the case of medium bombers, it is assumed

that they are equipped with four air-to-ground missiles each; therefore, their survivability is somewhat enhanced.

Missile penetration rates do not vary significantly against China until the high military posture allows for some degradation due to an ABM defensive threat. Particular emphasis has been placed on devising the factors for missile penetration against the Moscow ABM. If we assume that by 1985 the Moscow defense consists of 100 launchers, we must calculate the penetration rate based on the number of launchers the Soviets are willing to bring to bear against each incoming missile. If, for example, it is assumed that one launcher has a 50 percent chance of intercepting an in-coming reentry vehicle but that one successful warhead causes calamitous damage, it is imperative that the best probability obtainable be used to intercept the missile. Two interceptors would increase the likelihood of destruction to 75 percent, three to 88 percent, four to 94 percent, and five to over 97 percent.

If the first volley fired at Moscow consists of 20 missiles and if 5 ABMs are fired at each, the defenders could rest assured that they had a 97 percent probability of eliminating that particular in-coming missile threat. However, the 21st missile would have a free ride. Further, the Moscow defense must always be prepared to counter missiles launched from other possible adversaries who, upon seeing Japan deplete the Moscow ABM force, might launch their own attack to take advantage of the probable degra-

TABLE 5.2

Operational Factors

	Defense Posture
Aircraft in-commission rate missile launch rate	
Advanced F4	80
Medium bomber	75
Missiles (land-based)	75
SLBM	75
Target acquisition rate	
Advance F4	90
Medium bomber	95
Warhead reliability: all systems	99

Source: Compiled by the author.

dation in Soviet command, control, and ABM force. (One possibility that could result from a Japanese decision to develop a nuclear delivery force would be a Soviet decision to increase its ABM launchers appreciably.)

From the medium force posture onward, a capability is given to the Soviets to intercept Japanese missiles from a Siberian-based ABM field. Missiles fired from the Arabian Sea could also be degraded by a potential ABM site at the Soviet test facility at Kapustin Yar. The suggested penetration rates are found in Table 5.3.

Each delivery force will receive an overall factor to indicate the product of all factors thus far. For example, the product of all the aircraft factors for the Advanced F4 yields an answer of 0.06 for the low military posture against China. Thus, in this study, a ground-based aircraft in a retaliatory situation has a 6 percent probability of reaching a target in China and dropping its bomb.

The effectiveness of the bomb must also be demonstrated and incorporated into the overall success factor. The methodology to accomplish this step will be discussed below.

THE WEAPONS FACTOR

As stated in the assumptions, the one-mt warhead was selected as sufficient for Japanese deterrence goals. How-

TABLE 5.3

Penetration Factors

| | Defense Posture | | | | | |
| | China | | | USSR | | |
Weapon	Low	Medium	High	Low	Medium	High
Advanced F4	0.40	0.35	0.30	0.30	0.25	0.20
Medium bomber	0.50	0.45	0.30	0.40	0.30	0.20
Missiles (land-based)	1.00	1.00	1.00	1.00	0.50	0.40
Peking ABM	--	--	0.75	--	--	--
Moscow ABM	--	--	--	0.50	0.40	0.30
SLBM	*	*	*	*	*	*

*No change from land-based missiles.

Source: Compiled by the author.

ever, it was chosen after comparison with 20-kiloton (kt), 200-kt, and 500-kt weapons. Also, 3 psi was accepted after an examination of alternative overpressure levels of 16 psi and 8 psi. While either one of these overpressure levels would produce greater amounts of damage, the number of designated ground zeros (DGZs) required was significantly higher, requiring increased numbers of weapons. (Remember the constraint of 160 maximum warheads.)

The area over which 8 psi overpressure can be produced by a one-mt weapon was estimated using the RAND Bomb Damage Effect Computer. One weapon detonated at 900 feet scaled height of burst (SHOB) could produce 8 psi over approximately 33 square miles (3.14×3.22^2). The same weapon also detonated at 900 feet SHOB can produce 3 psi over 101 square miles (3.14×5.68^2). Total DGZs required to ensure complete overpressure coverage of the target areas could then be calculated by dividing 33 (for 8 psi) into the city area and using 101 to determine the number of DGZs at the 3-psi level.

The areas for Chinese cities were found by estimating population density to approximate 12,500 per square mile. This calculation is based on the fact that the density of other Asian areas was as high as 10,000 mi^2 in 1958. When we allow for the passage of 16 years, the figures may provide a rough approximation of the build-up area in China. To demonstrate the effect of city size on the number of DGZs, all city areas were calculated based on three density figures: 15,000, 12,500, and 9,000. As stated above, 12,500 was selected for the study but may be subject to further refinement.

No attempt was made selectively to place DGZs so that they would be colocated with certain primary installations within the target areas. It has been found, in previous studies, that randomly assigned DGZs are only slightly less effective in destroying industrial targets than if they were placed to maximize effectiveness.[8] Besides, such precise data are not available to the researcher who uses only open source materials.

By examining the results of the Hiroshima and Nagasaki strikes, as found in the U.S. Atomic Energy Commission's Effects of Nuclear Weapons,[9] it was estimated that areas receiving 16-psi overpressure from the detonations correlated with an 85.57 percent fatality figure and that 3-psi overpressure correlated with a 26.93 percent fatality rate, not counting the zone covered by 16 psi, or a combined rate of 37.67 percent fatalities for all people within the area from ground zero (GZ) to 1.6 miles from the GZ.[10]

Thus, it can be assumed that an overpressure of 3 psi in a target area can produce as high as 37.67 percent fatalities. While the specific characteristics of a target area can contribute to the overall magnitude of the detonation due to secondary fires or can reduce its effects in the presence of a shelter system, an overpressure range of 2 to 3 psi can shatter concrete or cinder-block wall panels 8 to 12 inches thick, blow in wood siding panels of the standard house construction, and cause major damage to transport and liaison aircraft and helicopters.[11]

Eight psi will destroy unreinforced brick wall panels 8 to 12 inches thick[12] and inflict moderate to severe damage to light steel-frame industrial buildings and multi-story wall-bearing buildings.[13]

While the 3 psi overpressure can be associated with 26.93 percent fatalities and the 16 psi with 85.57 percent, it must be assumed that 8 psi produces approximately 50 percent fatalities. The DGZ figures found in the following pages probably overstate, to a degree, the requirements to achieve the requisite damage of specific objectives. The reader is again cautioned about any fatality figures. Whereas building construction and atmospheric conditions did produce 37 percent fatalities from the Hiroshima-Nagasaki cases out to and including the area of 3 psi, it could reasonably be expected that in different circumstances (with considerable prior warning and a large-scale shelter system) fatalities would be much lower.

The affect of CEP (circular error probable) will not be seen to play a major role in this study primarily due to the size of the weapon chosen to be used throughout. The 1 mt is so strong that a weapon can be 6,000 feet from the DGZ at detonation and still produce 3 psi at the DGZ. Therefore, in all cases the weapons factor will be 0.99 (no CEPs are estimated to be greater than that in any of the delivery systems used in the study).

Once all factors are determined, each delivery system will be applied against the target system to determine the overall levels of damage to be expected from each system. The optimum system against the PRC and the USSR will then be selected and an estimate of costs made.

OPTIONS

The assumptions and methodology outlined will be used to examine the "effectiveness" of the possible options, of which there are five. The options to be considered will be (1) an advanced F4 aircraft option; (2) a medium bomber option; (3) a 1,500-nm MR/IRBM option; (4) an ICBM option; and (5) an SLBM option, 2,800 nm and 4,000 nm. The case of China will be examined first. In all cases the objective will be to examine the option in light of its capability to inflict damage upon the opponent in a retaliatory situation. To be considered credible, each option must have the capability of <u>threatening</u> the political capital of the adversary as well as a sufficient number of urban-industrial complexes. This will assure that industrial capacity has been materially reduced, either through the destruction of irreplaceable industrial plant, skilled workers, or the leadership cadre needed for a rapid recovery.

JAPAN VERSUS CHINA

China is generally considered to have three primary industrial zones, one concentrated in southern Manchuria around the industrial centers of An-shan and Shen-yang (Mukden), one located from the coast of the Po Hai Gulf to the capital, Peking, and a third located along the lower Yangtze River with Shanghai and Nanking as its two poles. Fifteen other major centers also exist. Of the three primary complexes, Shen-yang produces steel, agricultural equipment, electrical equipment, machine tools, heavy machinery, aircraft, and copper. The Peking/Tientsin area is noted for production of textiles, iron and steel, electronics, and agricultural machinery; the Shanghai/Nanking complex manufactures textiles, iron and steel, ships, electrical equipment, chemicals, fertilizer, and cement. The other, less significant, but important, centers are Ha-erh-pin (heavy machinery, electrical equipment), Ch'ang-ch'un (railroad equipment, trucks), Dairen (Luta) (steel, shipbuilding), Pao-t'ou (iron and steel), T'ai-yuan (fertilizer, chemicals, iron, and steel), Lan-chou (chemicals, rubber, and fertilizer), Yao-hsien (cement), Cheng-chou (textiles), Wu-Han (iron and steel), Chungking or Ch'ung-ch'ing (iron and steel), Ch'eng-tu (cement, iron, and steel), Chu-chou (iron and steel), K'un-ming (copper, iron and steel, cement), and Canton (sugar, newsprint, cement, shipbuilding).[14]

China, prior to the formation of the PRC, had as much as 90 percent of its industrial output capacity concentrated in centers along the coastal areas.[15] Destruction or capture of these coastal areas made the Chinese state highly vulnerable to naval bombardment, air attack, or invasion. Once these coastal facilities were destroyed or occupied, domestic production was crippled. The PRC shortly after formation of a new government embarked on a program of industrial diversification. By 1970, it was estimated[16] that coastal concentration had been reduced, so that it represented only 55 percent of the total industrial production of the PRC.

While progress has been recorded, the fact remains that some industries would be strategic bottlenecks if placed under successful attack. For example, 80 percent of China's crude steel production is produced by the 10 largest steel mills;[17] at least half of China's total crude oil production is from the Ta-ch'ing oil field in Heilungkiang Province,[18] with other major oil fields located in Kensu, Sinkiang, and Tsinghai.[19] The cities of Peking, Shanghai, Nanking, Tientsin, and Chengtu contain more than 50 percent of the electronic component manufacturers in China, and these same five cities account for 75 percent of the semiconductor, electron tubes, and passive components output.[20] Approximately two-thirds of the total production of electronic instruments are concentrated in Peking, Shanghai, Nanking, and Tientsin.[21] Digital and analog computer components are manufactured in five plants in Peking, Tientsin, and Shanghai.[22] More than 75 percent of communications equipment is produced in the four major concentrations of Peking, Shanghai, Nanking, and Tientsin,[23] and the production of trucks, a total of about 85,000 units, is concentrated at Ch'ang-ch'un Motor Vehicle Plant in Kirin Province.[24]

A critical examination of selected industrial commodity output reveals that in 1970 the seven coastal provinces of Liaoning, Hopeh, Shantung, Chekiang, Kiangsu, Fukien, and Kwangtung plus the three centrally administered municipalities of Peking, Tientsin, and Shanghai produced 56.6 percent of electric power, 40.3 percent of the mined coal, 13.3 percent of the crude oil, 55.5 percent of the crude steel, 50 percent of chemical fertilizer, 79.6 percent of the machine tools, 38.8 percent of machine-made paper, 61.3 percent of cotton cloth, and 47 percent of the nation's sugar.[25]

The population containing the skilled manpower to operate China's industrial base is concentrated to a degree. Of the 59,830,000 people who inhabit the 43 cities in the PRC with populations over 500,000, the total found in the 20 coastal metropolises is 35,750,000. Thus, almost 60 percent (0.5975) of inhabitants of the large cities of the PRC reside in coastal provinces or municipalities none of which are more than 240 nautical miles from the coast.

There are 29 province, autonomous region, and municipal government (governed by the central government) administrative centers throughout the country ranging in population from 100,000 to 7 million. In addition to these administratively important centers, there are 63 cities with populations in excess of 200,000 each (one over 2 million and four over 1 million). The total population in these 92 total cities amounts to approximately 74,195,000. (See Table 5.4 for a 1973 estimate as to the number of cities down to the 50,000-level class.)[26]

These 92 cities, each having over 200,000 population (except Lhasa), are shown in Figure 5.1, below, to indicate their proximity to Japan. Twenty-one of these 92 have been selected as being of particular significance, either from an industrial, administrative, or population resource standpoint. It is conceivable that China, as mentioned in Chapter 4, could be thrown back 50 years in its drive for industrialization with the destruction of these 21 urban areas. In a period of Sino-Soviet rivalry she could not risk their loss without the prospect of grave secondary consequences. (The possibility always exists of a Soviet desire to create another buffer state between the USSR and northern China.)

The Limited City Deterrent List (see Table 5.5) has a combined population of approximately 43,630,000 (1970), or almost 5.5 percent of the population of China in 1970. While 5 percent does not seem particularly damaging to a nation of about 800 million, the significance of the inhabitants of these 21 cities far outweighs the number involved. The technical, political, military, administrative elite would be placed at risk if an attack could be carried out in a retaliatory situation.

Admittedly, there are important military centers that will be omitted from this list, but all municipalities under central government administration and some major provincial capitals are incorporated. While the percentage of the total population placed at risk is only 5.5 percent, as stated above, if all 92 cities above 200,000 were attacked, the population percentage would increase only to 9.25 percent. At the same time an attack on all 92 cities would spread resources too thin and reduce probability figures appreciably.

Table 5.5 gives the Limited City Deterrent List, which shows population figures, possible density, and area rela-

FIGURE 5.1

Map of Potential Targets in China

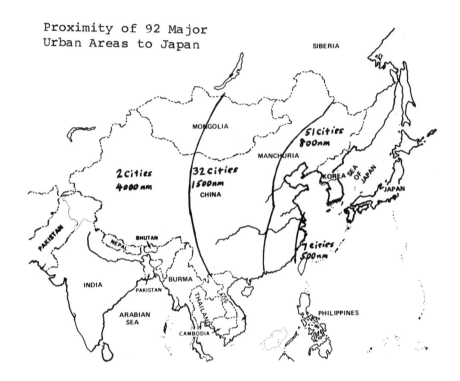

Proximity of 92 Major
Urban Areas to Japan

TABLE 5.4

Chinese Cities with Populations over Half Million, 1970

City	1936	1953	1957	1970
Shanghai	3,727,000	6,204,417	6,900,000	7,000,000
Peking	1,551,000	2,768,119	4,010,000	5,000,000
Tientsin	1,292,000	2,693,831	3,220,000	3,600,000
Mukden (Shenyang)	527,000	2,299,900	2,411,000	2,800,000
Wuhan	1,379,000	1,427,300	2,146,000	2,560,000
Canton	1,222,000	1,598,900	1,840,000	2,500,000
Chungking	446,000	1,772,500	2,121,000	2,400,000
Nanking	1,019,600	1,091,600	1,419,000	1,750,000
Harbin (Haerphin)	465,000	1,163,000	1,552,000	1,670,000
Luta (Dairen, Port Arthur)	445,000	766,400	1,508,000	1,650,000
Sian	155,000	787,300	1,310,000	1,600,000
Lanchow	106,000	397,400	699,000	1,450,000
Taiyuan	139,000[a]	720,700	1,020,000	1,350,000
Tsingtao	515,000	916,800	1,121,000	1,300,000
Chengtu	516,113	856,700	1,107,000	1,250,000
Changchun	228,744	855,200	975,000	1,200,000
Kunming	145,000	698,900	880,000	1,100,000
Tsinan	442,000	680,100	862,000	1,100,000
Fushun	118,000	678,600	985,000	1,080,000
Anshan	166,000	548,900	805,000	1,050,000
Chengchow	80,000[b]	594,700	766,000	1,050,000
Hangchow	589,000	696,600	784,000	960,000
Tangshan	85,000	693,300	800,000	950,000
Paotow	67,206[c]	149,400	650,000[d]	920,000
Tzepo	--	184,200	806,000	850,000
Changsha	507,000	650,600	703,000	825,000
Shihkiachwang	60,000	373,400	598,000	800,000
Tsitsihar	76,101	344,700	668,000	760,000
Soochow	389,797	474,000	633,000	730,000
Kirin	143,250	435,400	568,000	720,000
Suchow	160,013[c]	373,000	676,000	700,000
Foochow	359,205[c]	553,000	616,000	680,000
Nanchang	301,000	398,200	504,000	675,000
Kweiyang	117,000	270,900	594,000	660,000
Wusih	272,209	581,500	613,000	650,000
Hofei	70,000	183,600	304,000	630,000
Hwainan	--	286,900	370,000	600,000
Penki	98,203[e]	449,000	--	600,000
Loyang	77,159[c]	171,200	--	580,000
Nanning	88,900	194,600	264,000	550,000
Huhohot	83,732[c]	148,400	314,000	530,000
Sining	55,564[f]	93,700	300,000	500,000
Urumchi	80,000[g]	140,000	275,000	500,000

[a]1934 [c]1935 [f]1946
[b]1931 [d]1958 [g]1943
         [e]1941

Source: Cheng-Siang Chen, "Population Growth and Urbanization in China," Geographical Review, January 1973, p. 67.

TABLE 5.5

Limited City Deterrent List: China

City	In Range	Population (in thousands)	Area M² 15,000 M²	Area M² 12,500 M²	Area M² 9,000 M²	DGZ Requirements[b] 15,000 M² 8 Psi	15,000 M² 3 Psi	12,500 M² 8 Psi	12,500 M² 3 Psi	9,000 M² 8 Psi	9,000 M² 3 Psi
An-Shan	--	1,050	70	84	116	2	1	3	1	4	1
Canton	--	2,500	167	200	278	5	2	6	2	8	3
Ch'angchun	--	1,200	80	96	133	2	1	3	1	4	1
Chengtu	--	1,250	83	100	139	3	1	3	1	4	1
Chungking	--	2,400	160	192	267	5	2	6	2	8	3
Dairen	--	1,650	110	132	183	3	1	4	1	6	2
Fushun	--	1,080	72	86	120	2	1	3	1	4	1
Harbin	--	1,670	111	134	186	3	1	4	1	6	2
Hsiang-T'an (Changsha)	--	900	60	72	100	2	1	2	1	3	1
Kunming	--	1,100	73	88	122	2	1	3	1	4	1
Lanchou	--	1,450	97	116	161	3	1	4	1	5	2
Nanking	--	1,750	117	140	194	4	1	4	1	6	2
Paotow	--	920	61	74	102	2	1	2	1	3	1
Peking	--	5,000	333	400	555	10	3	12	4	17	5
Shanghai	--	7,000	467	560	778	14	5	17	6	24	8
Shenyang	--	2,800	187	224	311	6	2	7	2	9	3
Taiyuan	--	1,350	90	108	150	3	1	3	1	5	1
Tientsin	--	3,600	240	288	400	7	2	9	3	12	4
Tsinan	--	1,100	73	88	122	2	1	7	1	4	1
Tsingtao	--	1,300	87	104	144	3	1	3	1	4	1
Wuhan	--	2,560	170	204	284	5	2	6	2	9	3
Total	21	43,630,000[a]				88	32	111	35	149	47

[a]5.45 percent of total PRC Population.

[b]All DGZ requirements based on effectiveness of 1-mt weapon, air burst, 900 SHOB (RAND Bomb Damage Effect Computer).

Source: Compiled by the author.

184

tionships, and number of DGZs required based on the 1-mt weapon and 8 and 3 psi.

The Advanced F4 Option

When we consider the various delivery system options against the Limited City Deterrent List with the Advanced F4, the first problem faced is the combat radius, which might reasonably be expected to be 800 nm. With such a range, only 15 of the 21 cities are placed at risk. However, this particular problem is eliminated if one-way missions are considered possible. In such a case, all cities come within range.

By applying the Low Military Posture Factors (see Table 5.6 for the Advanced F4 factors) to weapons data it is seen that any one Advanced F4 has a 6 percent probability of arriving at the target and dropping a successful bomb. If more sorties are added to each target, the 6

TABLE 5.6

Advanced F4 Option, Circa 1985

	Military Posture		
	Low	Medium	High
Survivability	0.20	0.15	0.10
In-commission rate	0.80	0.80	0.80
Target acquisition rate	0.90	0.90	0.90
Bomb reliability	0.99	0.99	0.99
Penetration rate	0.40	0.35	0.30

Overall factors including weapon factor: low = 0.06; medium = 0.04; high = 0.02.

Weapon probabilities: 1 mt

500 CEP		2,000 CEP		4,000 CEP		6,000 CEP	
8 psi	3 psi	8 psi	3 psi	8 psi	3 psi	8 psi	3 psi
0.99	0.99	0.99	0.99	0.99	0.99	0.99	0.99

Note: CEP does not begin to degrade weapon effects until 7,000 off the DGZ.

Source: Compiled by the author.

185

percent might be increased to 12 percent (two sorties), 18 percent (three sorties), 22 percent (four sorties), or 27 percent (five sorties). Under the conditions outlined here, 20 of the 35 DGZs in the 21 cities could have five individual sorties programmed against them, and a 27 percent probability would exist that one aircraft would get to the target and destroy it. Fifteen DGZs could have four sorties each, with an expected probability of 22 percent. It seems most questionable whether a probability of from 22 to 27 percent would be considered appropriate for a deterrent force. The national leader who went to the "brink" with such forces would indeed be gambling with his nation's future in a most foolhardy manner.

As Chinese offensive power grows and is reflected in the medium military posture factors, the credibility of a successful Advanced F4 retaliatory strike lessens further. The product of aricraft and weapon factors decreases to only 4 percent the likelihood of any one strike being successful. The application of five sorties only results in a compound probability of 18 percent.

During Chinese high military posture, the probability of success for one sortie drops to 2 percent, which reduces the targets with five sorties each to an astonishingly low 9 percent. This option, in the face of what might be considered the "most probable" future Chinese military posture, would not exist.

The Medium Bomber Option

The Medium Bomber Option would have certain advantages (see Table 5.7 for factors). The plane would have sufficient combat radius to reach all 21 targets—and return—could carry as much as four air-to-ground missiles for a limited stand-off capability, and might be capable of performing an airborne alert role. In the event of long-term crisis airborne alert, possibly one-tenth of the 40 bomber force could be kept in the air constantly. (Of course, this figure is one that could be changed, and its selection is critical to the statistics of the option. As confrontation became progressively worse, the number of bombers on alert could be increased. This, however, has its limits as far as crew fatigue is considered.)

While the medium bombers on the ground have almost the same probability of reaching their targets as the Advanced F4 Option (save for the low posture, which reflects a 7 percent probability vice, 6 percent for the Advanced F4),

the four airborne aircraft show the real gains inherent in
such a defensive posture at the time of crisis. In the low
posture the four bombers have a 32 percent probability of
penetrating to fire their missiles. This could conceivably
permit 16 of the more essential targets to be targeted with
a 32 percent probability of success. (Actually, it would
be somewhat lower, as the variables of the air-to-ground
missile system would also have to be incorporated into the
overall calculation. If we could say such a system would
be 70 percent reliable, each target would have a 22 percent
probability of being destroyed. If it were 80 percent reliable, the chance of success would be 26 percent, and if
the missile had a 90 percent rate, the opportunity for
success would climb to 29 percent.)
    The ground bombers launched during a period of low
Chinese military posture could register a 7 percent probability of getting close enough to launch their missiles.
But, if those missiles were only 70 percent reliable, the
overall chance of success would drop to 5 percent, less
than that of the Advanced F4.
    It seems clear that the medium bomber system offers
the greatest chance for success if the portion of the fleet

TABLE 5.7

Medium Bomber Option, Circa 1985

| | Military Posture | | |
	Low	Medium	High
Survivability			
Nonair alert	0.20	0.15	0.10
Air alert	0.90	0.90	0.90
In-commission rate	0.75	0.75	0.75
Target acquisition rate	0.95	0.95	0.95
Bomb reliability	0.99	0.99	0.99
Penetration rate	0.50	0.40	0.30

Overall factors:

Nonair alert			Air alert		
Low	=	0.07	Low	=	0.32
Medium	=	0.04	Medium	=	0.25
High	=	0.02	High	=	0.19

Source: Compiled by the author.

actually airborne is maintained at the highest level possible. Otherwise, the air-to-ground missile can, at times, act to make the medium bomber option not as attractive as the Advanced F4. (There are so many variables with a multiweapon system that, at this point, all that will be done is to indicate the complexity of determining an adequate table of probabilities. The medium bomber could actually be degraded by further penetration factors, as it proceeds to other locations to release all on-board missiles.)

Basically, for the Japanese, with so little warning time when attacked by missiles, the only advantage of a medium bomber would be its capability to orbit for long hours during periods of tension; would not a fleet of modified civilian airliners do the job better?

1,500-nm MR/IRBM Option

This option, of course, is dependent on the development of a storable missile, either liquid or solid, the attainment of a good guidance system, and the development of hardened silos for a Japanese missile force. It is believed that all these requirements will be possible by the 1985 period.

With hardening of silos and deployment in mountainous terrain, the missiles fired in retaliation might enjoy a survival rate as high as 70 percent or as low as 50 percent (see Table 5.8) depending on the development of Chinese offensive systems. Adjusting for operational, enemy offense, and weapon factors, the IRBM in a retaliatory situation could have a probability as high as 49 percent in conditions of low Chinese military posture. Under high posture levels, this could drop to around 35 percent. (If Peking were to obtain an ABM capability, the success rate could go to 26 percent or lower depending on the number of ABM launchers and how realistic the factors are to begin with.)

Assuming that Japan had 160 launchers and was concerned only with guaranteeing that 3-psi overpressure damage be inflicted on the 35 DGZs in the 21 cities, four weapons per DGZ could be programmed for all DGZs and yield a 94 percent probability of success. Another 20 DGZs could have one additional weapon each to bring the probability on those 20 DGZs to 97 percent. With such a high level of probability, all 21 cities would receive the desired overpressure, Japanese decision-makers could at least be

TABLE 5.8

1,500-nm MR/IRBM Option, Circa 1985

| | Military Posture | | |
	Low	Medium	High
Survivability	0.70	0.60	0.50
Launch rate	0.75	0.75	0.75
In-flight reliability	0.95	0.95	0.95
Warhead reliability	0.99	0.99	0.99
Penetration rate	1.00	1.00	
Peking			0.75
All other			1.00

Overall factors: low = 0.49; medium = 0.42; high = 0.26 (Peking), 0.35 (all other).

Source: Compiled by the author.

confident that most of the major urban industrial centers of China would be significantly damaged if deterrence failed.

Even under conditions of high military posture in China, the probability of success with four missiles on each DGZ would be approximately 83 percent, and on those with five weapons, 89 percent. With such a high degree of confidence, it might be wondered if the target list might not be too restricted. What would be the case if 160 missiles were programmed against all major urban areas over 500,000 in population that were within range of the 1,500-nm vehicles?

An extended target list--the MR/IRBM Extended City Option (Table 5.9)--could possibly add an additional 23 cities for targeting consideration. All cities in China over 500,000 in population, except Urumchi, would be included. The number of additional city-dwellers could possibly be as high as 17 million (1970 figures). Overall fatalities from an attack on all 44 cities could reach approximately 23 million as opposed to roughly 16 million fatalities if only the 21 key cities were attacked. (These figures may be high given the retaliatory nature of the attack.) It can be observed that the point of diminishing returns is being reached. Strikes against the first list of 21 cities could possibly result in 16 million fatalities; however, by more than doubling the target list (to include 23 additional cities) only 7 million additional fatalities could be expected.

A total of 58 DGZs would be required to cover the 44 cities with 3-psi overpressure. All 58 DGZs could have two missiles programmed against them, the 35 DGZs of the most important centers could have three, and nine missiles would be available--possibly to be directed against Peking in the event of ABM developments. Thus, under conditions of low military posture, a 75 percent probability could be expected against all 44 cities in China over 500,000, except Urumchi. The 21 key cities would receive three missiles each and the probability could possibly reach 87 percent.

Under conditions of high military posture the expected success rate would drop to a low of 57 percent against the 44 cities, with 73 percent possible against the key 21. The Peking complex would have 13 warheads programmed against the 4 DGZs in that city. On the surface, it would appear that the IRBM Extended City Option could at least be seriously considered in periods of low Chinese military posture but might border on "adventurism" during high postures.

The nonextended IRBM Option seems to be the first option that gives Japan the capability to inflict serious levels of damage in retaliatory conditions with any high degree of assurance. It is possible that, facing a PRC with rational leaders, deterrence would be achieved.

ICBM Option

The development of an ICBM capability does not, on the surface, appear necessary if Japan becomes a nuclear weapons power with a desire only to deter the PRC; however, in the terms of the present scenario Japan would need a capability to deter either the PRC or the USSR. Only two additional administratively important cities fall within range of a costly ICBM. The cities of Urumchi and Lhasa would be added for a possible 600,000 additional population placed at risk. Certain prime military targets could be struck by a Japanese ICBM, and the kind and number of military targets placed in the zone inaccessible to the MRBM provides additional justification for a longer-range system, but as we are discussing terms of a limited deterrence capability, not damage limitation or preemption, it would not seem extremely profitable to attack such targets.

TABLE 5.9

IRBM Extended City Option

| City | Population (in thousands) | Area (M^2) | DGZs | |
			8 Psi	3 Psi
Chengchow	1,050	84	3	1
Chinchou	500	40	1	1
Foochow	680	54	2	1
Hangchow	960	77	2	1
Hofei	630	50	2	1
Hu-Ho Haote	530	42	1	1
Huianan	600	48	1	1
Kiamusze	500	40	1	1
Kirin	720	58	2	1
Kuei 'Yang	660	53	2	1
Lo Yang	580	46	1	1
Nin Chang	675	54	2	1
Nanning	550	44	1	1
Penki	600	48	1	1
Shih Chia Chuang	800	64	2	1
Sian	1,600	128	4	1
Sining	500	40	1	1
Soochow	730	58	2	1
Suchow	700	56	2	1
Tangshan	950	76	2	1
Tsitsihar	760	61	2	1
Tzupo	850	68	2	1
Wu Hsi	650	52	2	1
Total	16,775,000*	52	41	23

*Approximately 2 percent of total population.

Source: Compiled by the author.

An ICBM with a 1-mt warhead could produce results similar to those listed in the IRBM Option. Range, as such, the major benefit of an ICBM, is not a problem for Japan with regard to the PRC; more will be said in reference to ICBM options when discussing the Russian contingency.

SLBM Option (2,500 nm)

Ultimately, if Japan desires a secure second strike with an extremely high survival factor, a submarine-launched missile would be necessary (see factors in Table 5.10). One advantage of an adversary relationship with China would be that boats in port could possibly be maintained in a "fire" condition. If Japan maintained one port in Kyushu and one in northern Honshu, or southern Hokkaido, target coverage from port would be the same as the IRBM coverage.

Assuming enough submarines were built to use all 160 missiles, a fleet of at least 10 could be envisaged. When all 10 boats are operational, such a fleet could maintain seven boats on station, for a total of 112 missiles (see Figure 5.2). Each missile would have a 74 percent proba-

TABLE 5.10

PRC SLBM Option, Circa 1985

	PRC Military Posture		
	Low	Medium	High
Survivability	1.00	1.00	0.95
Launch rate	0.75	0.75	0.75
In-flight reliability	0.99	0.99	0.99
Warhead reliability	0.99	0.99	0.99
Penetration	1.00	1.00	--
Peking	--	--	0.75*
All other	--	--	1.00

*Peking ABM launcher factors: 1 launcher = 0.75; 2 launchers = 0.56; 3 launchers = 0.41; 4 launchers = 0.32; 5 launchers = 0.22. Overall factors: low = 0.74; medium = 0.74; high = 0.70 (non-Peking), 0.52 (Peking 1 ABM), 0.39 (Peking 2 ABMs).

Source: Compiled by the author.

bility of reaching the target; two missiles on one DGZ would bring the probability to 94 percent during periods of low military posture. During the high-posture periods, the expected figure would drop slightly to 92 percent (for non-Peking DGZs). If these levels could be accepted by Japanese planners as sufficient, all DGZs of the 44 Extended List (except two) of Table 5.4 could be attacked. (These could be dropped from the list to assure a uniform 94 percent [low posture] to 92 percent [high posture].)

During high-posture levels Peking could present a problem if an ABM capability is gained. The eight reentry vehicles aimed at DGZs in that capital would have a 75 percent probability of success if one ABM each was fired at them. Additional targets might be cut from the extended list to assure sufficient attack weight against Peking. This is all contingent on the ABM. (More will be said on this subject when the USSR is discussed.)

In all, the SLBM Option offers higher success rates than land-based missiles, but across a reduced spectrum of targets due to the reduction of submarines available at any one time. Against the 21 key cities, the SLBM could possibly achieve a 98 percent probability with three missiles on each DGZ, allowing seven missiles for Peking or—in medium posture—other targets.

Under the same conditions—medium posture—the land-based systems could achieve an 82 percent probability of success against the 21 cities and have 55 missiles left over for the 23 additional cities. If four missiles were fired against each of the 35 DGZs in the 21 key cities, the success rate would reach 90 percent. Twenty missiles would be left over for redundant coverage. Where the land-based systems fail is when the high posture is considered. Four missiles on each DGZ could only achieve 82 percent; the submarine force in the same period can obtain 92 percent with two missiles and could possibly achieve 98 percent with three.

What would happen, however, if the 70 percent on-station rate, which is considered very high, could not, in fact, be maintained? If the actual rate approached 40 percent rather than 70 percent, only 64 missiles would be available. This, of course, would not provide enough resource to cover each of the 35 DGZs with two missiles each. This being the case, it might be possible to reduce coverage of the six DGZs scheduled for Shanghai by three warheads, leaving 9 vice 12. The three saved could then be reapplied to three cities with one DGZ each. In the case of one weapon only on each DGZ (in this case involving six), the prob-

FIGURE 5.2

Possible Target Flow Chart

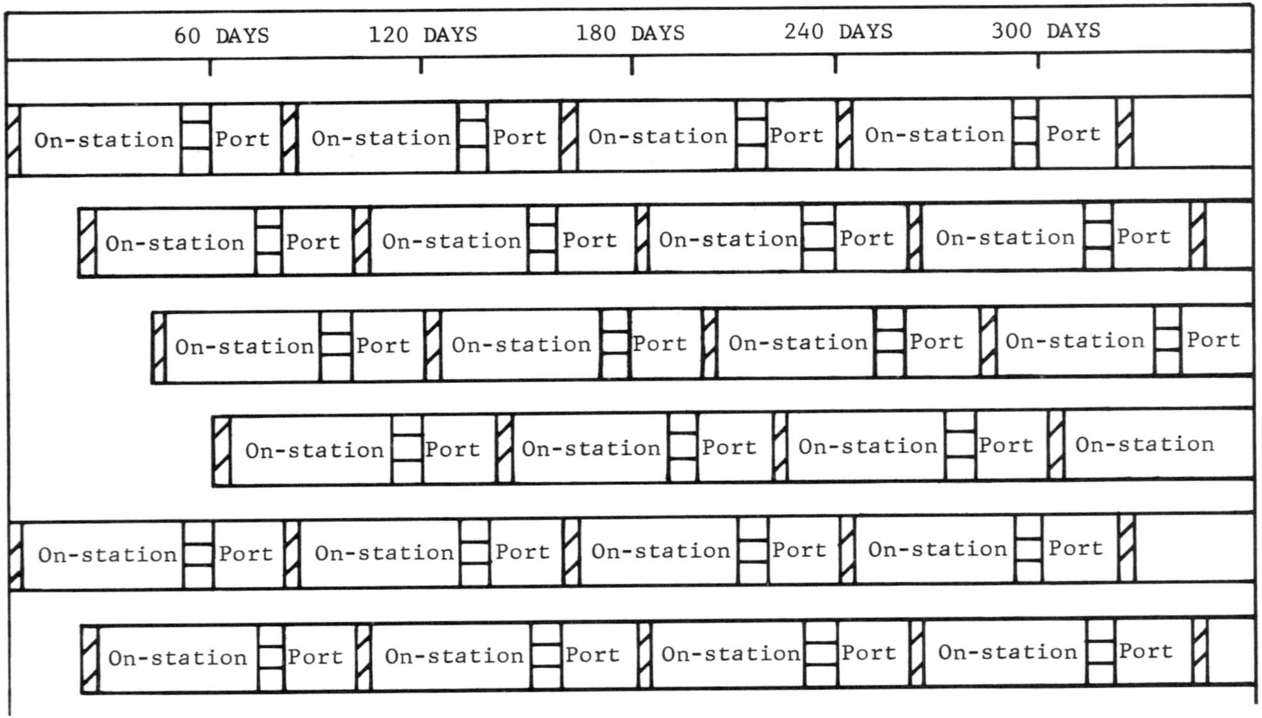

194

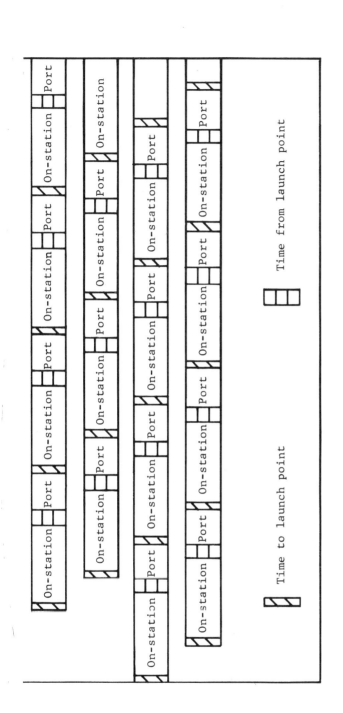

Note: Possible target coverage flow chart for a 10-boat force off China. Based on a 60-day cruise length followed by 20 days in port. Transit time shown can be included as "on-target" time, due to proximity of Japan to China.

Source: Compiled by the author.

ability would be 74 percent. The remaining 29 DGZs in 18 cities would maintain a 94 percent rate.

In this manner the readjustments would not reduce the areas or population placed at risk, only the probabilities. Of course, other retargeting could be affected, such as deleting the three targets adjudged least important to the overall success of the mission--deterrence.

It would seem, from a survivability standpoint, that a Japanese force of 10 nuclear submarines would be superior to land-based systems (given the environment assumed in this paper, see Figure 5.3) if its main purpose is to achieve a second-strike capability across a limited number of Chinese cities. It would seem that deterrence could be achieved even with 60 percent of the submarine force degraded.

If deterrence fails and any one of the options mentioned were executed, all cities in Japan would be exposed to PRC missiles and TU-16s, including the political, industrial, and economic centers of the nation. Just two forces of TU-16s penetrating the Japanese Air Defense zone for strikes on Osaka and Tokyo, place, in these metropolitan areas, over 30 million at risk. (These figures include satellite cities such as Yokohama, Yokosuka, and Higashiosaka in the municipal areas.)

The 3-mt weapon, on five occasions, has been tested in air drops by the Chinese Air Force.[27] A weapon of this size could effect a 3-psi overpressure over the entire 1,070 square miles of the populated area, with five successful weapons, and over Osaka-Kobe only three successful weapons would be required to cause as many as 11 million fatalities. Additionally, the targets so destroyed represent the two most vital targets in Japan. An expanded list designed to include the use of the PRC/MR/IRBM force followed by TU-16 employment would effectively cripple a nation so dependent on ports and industrial capacity for its livelihood, possibly below that point from which it is possible, without outside assistance, to regain economic viability.

JAPAN VERSUS THE USSR

In considering a possible attempt by Japan to embark on a program to reach a deterrent capability against the Soviet Union, the same general methodology will be used, but it soon becomes apparent that weapons and systems credible to some degree against the PRC have little significance against similar target criteria for the Soviet Union. The

FIGURE 5.3

China: Probabilities of Success for One Sortie
(percent)

Defense Posture

	Low	Medium	High
Advanced F4	6	4	2
Medium bomber ground	7	4	2
Medium bomber air alert	32	25	19
MR/IRBM	49	42	35 / 26
ICBM	49	42	35 / 26
SLBM	74	74	70 / 52

Non-Peking

Peking (ABM)

Source: Compiled by author.

target system used as a base for this part of the study
consists of 100 cities in the USSR. Each city has at
least 200,000 population, and the list includes cities
from all of the major industrial regions of the Soviet Union
namely:

- Leningrad--primarily the metropolitan Leningrad
area, covered by an arc from the Gulf of Finland,
south to the border of the Central region, and
north to the Finnish border.
- Central--essentially the entire industrial region surrounding Moscow, plus sections of the
"Central Black Earth" (Voronezh; Kursk) and of
"Volga-Vyatka" (Gor'kiy; Kirov).
- Donetsk-Dnepr Complex--the extensive industrial
areas located in the Donetsk-Dnepr Basin, running
from Kiev in the north to Rostov and the mouth of
the Don River in the south.
- TransVolga--the highly industrialized but narrow
Volga River region from Volgograd in the south to
Kuybyshev and Kazan in the north.
- Urals--essentially the entire Urals industrial
complex, running north to south from Perm to Oren-
burg.
- Baku--the area surrounding Baku on the Caspian
Sea to the central industrial cities in the north-
ern Transcaucasus Region (Tbilisi; Yerevan).
- Omsk--the Omsk oblast and adjacent areas.
- Novosibirsk-Kuzbass--the industrial complex con-
centrated along the Trans-Siberian Railway from
Novosibirsk to the Novokuznetsk-Kemerovo district,
and the Kuzbass coal-fields (some of which lies
in East Siberia).
- East Siberia--an angular region following the
railway from Krasnoyarsk to Irkutsk.
- Tashkent--the industrial area bordering the
Central Asia region and Kazakhstan, from the Tash-
kent oblast to Alma-Ata.[28]

A population totaling 63 million is accounted for in
the 100 cities or approximately 26 percent of the Soviet
population.[29] From these 100 cities (see Figure 5.4), a
list of 25 was compiled that represent key industrial,
political, administrative, and military centers in the
Soviet Union. The population included in these 25 cities
(1970 base) number approximately 37 million or 15 percent
of the population in 1970.

FIGURE 5.4

Map of Potential Targets in USSR

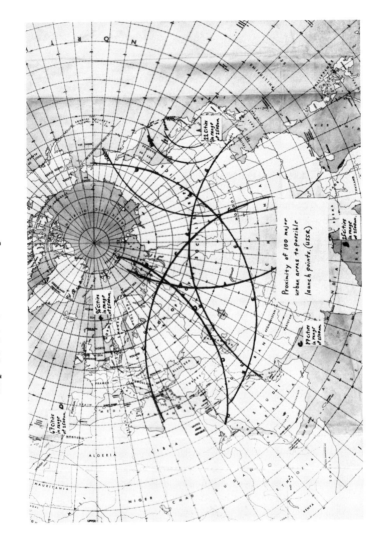

Damage levels, for attacks against these targets, will be calculated at 3-psi overpressure; data are furnished to indicate the effectiveness of several nuclear warhead yields (200 kt, 500 kt, and 1 mt). In the DGZ chart (see Table 5.11) it will be noticed that 31 DGZs are required for the 25 cities based on the 1-mt yield.

As Japan is seeking only to deter the Soviet Union from actions extremely harmful to Japan's security, the retaliatory environment will be the only one addressed; because of the scope of this book, only a limited question will be asked: Does it seem possible for Japan to be able to threaten the destruction of enough of the Soviet urban and industrial base to deter possible Soviet aggressive actions toward Japan?

Advanced F4 and 1,500-nm IRBM Options

The Japanese, if armed with Advanced F4s, medium bombers, or 1,500-nm MR/IRBMs, can bring under the threat of attack only Khabarovosk, Komsomolsk, Vladivostok, Chita, Irkutsk, and Ulan-Ude from the list of 100 possible targets with a population of 200,000 or more in the USSR. Not one of these six cities is considered critical enough to appear on the list of 25 key cities (see Table 5.12). It must be concluded that any attempt to threaten retaliation with such a force would be bound to fail. Systems so effective for the Chinese contingency are impotent before the particular problem of range that the Japanese must face in dealing with the USSR.

Three possible answers to this problem are the 5,000-nm ICBM, a 2,500-nm SLBM, or a system similar to the Trident with a 4,000-nm range.

The 5,000-nm ICBM Option

The first thing that is apparent in the ICBM option is the relatively high attrition rates of Japanese missiles in their silos (see the factors in Table 5.13). In a low military posture, the survival rate for Japanese ICBMs has been postulated as 40 percent, which, in essence, means that 6 out of 10 missiles would be destroyed by the initial Soviet strike. (It is probable that the Soviet attack could be delivered with greater accuracy than the Chinese. Of course, it is realized that this figure is extremely sensitive. It was devised by using the RAND com-

TABLE 5.11

DGZ Requirements for List of 25 Cities

Target Number	200 KT 16 Psi	200 KT 8 Psi	200 KT 3 Psi	500 KT 16 Psi	500 KT 8 Psi	500 KT 3 Psi	1 MT 16 Psi	1 MT 8 Psi	1 MT 3 Psi
1	69	31	8	34	16	5	21	10	3
2	50	22	6	25	11	3	15	8	2
3	58	26	7	29	13	4	18	9	3
4	25	11	3	13	6	2	8	4	1
5	17	8	2	9	4	1	5	3	1
6	15	7	2	8	3	1	5	2	1
7	20	9	3	10	5	1	6	3	1
8	36	16	4	18	8	2	11	6	2
9	27	12	3	13	6	2	8	4	1
10	30	13	4	15	7	2	9	5	1
11	11	5	1	5	2	1	3	2	1
12	20	9	3	10	5	1	6	3	1
13	19	9	2	9	4	1	6	3	1
14	19	9	2	9	4	1	6	3	1
15	19	9	2	9	4	1	6	3	1
16	19	8	2	9	4	1	6	3	1
17	19	8	2	9	4	1	6	3	1
18	18	8	2	9	4	1	6	3	1
19	18	8	2	9	4	1	5	3	1
20	17	8	2	9	4	1	5	3	1
21	17	8	2	8	4	1	5	3	1
22	18	8	2	9	4	1	6	3	1
23	16	7	2	8	4	1	5	3	1
24	16	7	2	8	4	1	5	2	1
25	14	6	2	7	3	1	4	2	1
Total	606	273	72	301	137	38	192	96	31

Source: Compiled by the author.

TABLE 5.12

USSR: List of 25 Cities

City	Target Number	Launch Point					Population (in thousands)	Area*
		A	B	C	D	E		
Moscow	1			x	x	x	9,150	346
Leningrad	2			x	x	x	4,350	250
Kiev	3			x	x	x	1,693	297
Gorky	4			x	x	x	1,535	128
Tashkent	5		x	x		x	1,424	87
Baku	6			x		x	1,292	77
Kharkov	7			x	x	x	1,248	105
Novosibirsk	8	x	x	x		x	1,180	182
Kuybyshev	9			x	x	x	1,200	134
Sverdlovsk	10	x	x	x		x	1,160	150
Minsk	11			x	x	x	955	55
Tblisi	12			x	x	x	907	103
Donetsk	13			x	x	x	901	96
Chelyabinsk	14			x		x	897	96
Kazan	15			x	x	x	881	95
Dneprope-trovsk	16			x	x	x	875	94
Perm	17			x	x	x	854	92
Odessa	18			x	x	x	832	90
Omsk	19	x	x	x		x	830	89
Rostov	20			x	x	x	885	87
Volgograd	21			x	x	x	797	86
Yerevan	22			x	x	x	791	90
Saratov	23			x	x	x	772	83
Ufa	24			x	x	x	755	81
Voronezh	25			x	x	x	655	70
Total	25	3	4	24	19	25	36,819,000	

*Based on Geoffrey Kemp, "The Strategic Requirements for European Nuclear Forces," unpublished manuscript, Fletcher School of Law and Diplomacy, August 1973.

Source: Compiled by the author.

TABLE 5.13

ICBM Options, USSR, Circa 1985

Option	Military Posture		
	Low	Medium	High
Survivability	0.40	0.30	0.20
Launch rate	0.75	0.75	0.75
In-flight reliability	0.99	0.99	0.99
Warhead reliability	0.99	0.99	0.99
Penetration			
Moscow	0.50[a]	0.40[b]	0.30[c]
All other	1.00	0.50	0.40

Multiple ABM launcher rate:

	[a]0.50	[b]0.40	[c]0.30
Launcher 0.50 (1st ABM)		0.40	0.30
Launchers 0.25 (2d ABM)		0.16	0.08
Launchers 0.13 (3d ABM)		0.06	0.02
Launchers 0.06 (4th ABM)		0.02	0.001
Launchers 0.03 (5th ABM)		0.01	0.001

Source: Compiled by the author.

puter and working backward from a 200-psi target and using
a 1=mt warhead for the Soviet delivery force. A 1-mt weapon, which is detonated on the surface of the ground, will
produce a 60 percent probability of 200 psi at the DGZ if
the CEP is roughly 2,300 feet. An 1,800-foot CEP will produce a 70 percent chance of 200 psi and a 1,600-foot CEP
an 80 percent probability. A 5 mt was also looked at, and
CEP needs only be 4,000 feet to obtain the 60 percent probability of destruction for a 200-psi target. It is felt
that such a range of CEPs is possible by 1985.)

Besides the impact of increased offensive capability
on the part of the USSR, the impact of ABM deployment could
also be quite dramatic. The interaction of these factors
indicate that missiles launched under low posture conditions
against the 25 cities could, in terms of this study, have
a 29 percent probability of reaching assigned targets and
achieving the desired 3-psi overpressure level in all areas
but Moscow. Two missiles on each DGZ would compound to
50 percent, three to 65 percent, and four to 75 percent.

With four missiles assigned against the 28 DGZs in the
24 cities (excepting Moscow) a total of 112 missiles would
be committed, with 48 remaining for Moscow's three DGZs.

A 50 percent penetration rate was postulated for the
Moscow ABM (refer to success factors, Table 5.14). However, as stated previously, actual penetration depends
on the number of launchers the Soviets are willing to com-
mit to their defense. If 48 missiles are committed to
Moscow DGZs by a Japanese force, the probability of penetration for any one missile would be about 7 percent (if
two ABMs are fired at each RV). However, by using 16 missiles on each DGZ, the probability becomes almost 70 percent that one missile will slip through to hit each DGZ.
(It can be seen that the success of this force option is
dependent on the number of weapons that this model assumes
as a given. It also suggests that states with a total
force of only three ballistic missile submarines must
think seriously about the advantages of avoiding Moscow
completely.)

While the possibility for a credible deterrent force
can be demonstrated by a Japanese force against a low Soviet military posture, if that posture becomes high and re-

TABLE 5.14

ICBM: Overall Success Factors

| | Military Posture | | |
	Low	Medium	High
Non-Moscow DGZs			
1st ABM	--	0.11	0.06
2d ABM	0.29	0.06	0.01
3d ABM	--	0.03	0.001*
4th ABM	--	0.01	0.001
5th ABM	--	0.01	0.001
Moscow DGZs			
1st ABM	0.15	0.09	0.04
2d ABM	0.07	0.04	0.02
3d ABM	0.04	0.01	0.01
4th ABM	0.02	0.004	0.001*
5th ABM	0.01	0.002	0.001

*0.001 is used rather than going any further.

Source: Compiled by the author.

flects the refinement of ABM techniques, the situation
changes radically. Under the high posture level factors,
the trajectories of missiles launched from Japan toward
non-Moscow targets could possibly come within range of an
ABM built to protect Soviet ICBMs. If this does, in fact,
occur, it could materially reduce penetration probabilities.
As the ABM created to defend an ICBM field would only possess 100 launchers, it is likely that no more than one shot
would be attempted at any one Japanese missile as it passed
on its way to a target. (Because the USSR must guard
against other possible adversaries.)

Another consideration arises from the proximity of
Japan to the USSR. It might be possible for Soviet in-
frared sensors to pick up Japanese ICBMs as they are
launched. Moving at 0 to 5.5 nm per second during the
boost phase, the missiles would generate temperatures in
the 1,000-2,000 kilo (k) range making them fairly easy to
locate.[30] Also, during this phase of engine burn, the ul-
tra-high frequency (uhf) radar cross-section increases to
almost 1,000 square meters, by far the largest of the entire flight.[31]

Whether or not a Soviet ABM will fire at passing Japanese missiles cannot be disputed at this time, but it is
a factor that Japanese military planners cannot ignore.
If the Soviet defensive force fired half of its ABMs at
missiles within range, it might be possible that intercept action would be attempted on 50 Japanese missiles.
Using the degradation factors for high military posture,
each one of the missiles would have only a 6 percent probability of satisfying its mission. If all these missiles
were aimed at non-Moscow targets (28 DGZs), the probability
of destroying a DGZ would stand at 12 percent for those
with two missiles. Other missiles going to non-Moscow
targets could possibly be intercepted by ABMs from test
sites (but the likelihood is low). If not, they would
have a 15 percent chance of reaching their targets. Missiles targeted on Moscow would face an improved ABM system
that might, with two ABMs fired at each incoming missile,
reduce one missile's chance to 1 percent. Even if 16 separate missiles were launched at each of the three Moscow
DGZs there would only be a 15 percent probability of destroying the DGZs.

It would seem that a "confidence zone" for Japanese
defense planners would not exist with the ICBM Option
against the much-improved Soviet offensive and defensive
power as reflected in the high posture factors of this
study. (One should be reminded at this point that these

factors are only illustrative and may not resemble reality either in 1974 or 1985.)

The SLBM Option (2,500 nm)

It becomes clear from an examination of the survivability factors in the ICBM option that an increase in Soviet missile accuracy would force the Japanese to seek some way to reduce the prospects of having their deterrent force disarmed by a Soviet preemptive strike. One way to increase the possibility of weapon systems survival markedly in the low and medium postures and appreciably in the high posture would be to turn to the SLBM option (see survivability factors in Table 5.15).

In the examination of the submarine-launched ballistic missile, five locations were selected as possible patrol zones for Japanese nuclear submarines: Point A was located in the Sea of Japan at 4300N 13630E; Point B in the Bay of Bengal at 1900N 8900E; Point C in the Arabian Sea at 2400N 6300E; Point D in the North Atlantic rather close to Portu-

TABLE 5.15

SLBM Option, USSR, Circa 1985

	Military Posture		
	Low	Medium	High
Survivability	0.95	0.95	0.65
Launch rate	0.99	0.99	0.99
In-flight reliability	0.75	0.75	0.75
Warhead reliability	0.99	0.99	0.99
Penetration			
Moscow	0.50[a]	0.40[b]	0.30[c]
All other	1.00	0.50	0.40

Multiple ABM launcher rate:

1st ABM	[a]0.50	[b]0.40	[c]0.30
2d ABM	0.25	0.16	0.08
3d ABM	0.13	0.06	0.02
4th ABM	0.06	0.02	0.001
5th ABM	0.03	0.01	0.001

Source: Compiled by the author.

gal at 3900N 2800E; and Point E in the Norwegian Sea at 6500N 0500E.

From Point A, desirable for its close location to Japan, only three of the key (25) Soviet targets could be placed at risk. These cities contain an aggregate population of about 3 million, of which a figure possibly approximating 1 million could be considered fatalities if a 3-psi damage level is obtained over the target areas.

Point B in the Bay of Bengal is approximately 14 days from Yokohama (submerged sailing) at an assumed rate of 15 kt. This launch point is within range of four key targets, only one of which was not placed at risk from Point A. The total population placed within the threat zone is 4.5 million, approximately 1.5 million greater than from A. Moscow, Leningrad, Gorky, Kuybyshev, and so on are not, as yet, within the threat zone, and deterrence potential seems not very promising.

In order to reach patrolling zone C, approximately 20 days are required. On the 19th day, as the patrol area is approached off the coast of India near the Gulf of Kutch, Moscow, for the first time, comes within range. This area has been identified as the First Possible Arabian Sea Firing Zone (FPASFZ). From the time FPASFZ is reached until the patrol point is gained, Moscow is within range. From Point C, all 25 key Soviet targets out of the 25 identified are within range. The population placed at risk amounts to 36,819,000 (1970) and includes practically all the principal targets of the western RSFSR.

While Point C is well-suited for action against the 25 key targets, the testing of the various points continues for the sake of comparison. The cruise through the Indian Ocean around Africa to Point D would entail a period of silent vigil of almost 30 days as the submarine leaves the point from which Moscow can be hit to the First Possible North Atlantic Firing Zone (FPNAFZ) off the coast of Morocco. It would require approximately 47 days submerged to arrive on station at Point D, and target coverage drops to 19. Overall there is a net loss of about 6 million persons from Point C coverage in terms of population at risk. The net loss in coverage plus the 47 days required to arrive on station make Point D less attractive than Point C. (Total transit time was also computed from Yokohama, across the Pacific, and around South America to the patrol zone. Total time was approximately 50 days; however, this route does offer possibly greater security while in transit. There also might be a polar route that would make points D and E more accessible.)

Point E, a patrolling zone off the coast of Norway, would require some 54 days of submerged cruising to reach. Once there, all of the 25 targets come into range. However, the 54 days and the demanding communications system that must be required in order to alert a Japanese force of Tokyo's intentions make Point E, like D, rather unattractive.

Assuming that a cruise length for the nuclear submarine force of approximately 90 days is feasible, the nuclear force required, in terms of Polaris-type boats, can be computed (see Figure 5.5). It is immediately apparent that from an on-station perspective, launch point A offers an unsurpassed 86 days' on station, while launch point E is so far removed from Japan that on a 90-day cruise basis, it is 18 days' short of the requisite round trip transit time. Such an inordinate transit time does not automatically eliminate launch points D and E from consideration as it would not be wise to concentrate the entire force in the Arabian Sea. However, active employment would require six-month cruises, a series of refurbishment vessels and possibly entire crew transfers at sea. Any attempt to maintain cover and not be detected would have to be realistically discounted during these periods, and this would have a tendency to degrade the system's reliability during times of emergency.

It would seem that unless international events precluded patrolling in the Indian Ocean, Point C would provide the most advantageous launching zone from which to threaten Moscow and the 24 other key cities. By assuming 90-day cruises,[32] 30 days in port, and a major refit every two years for nuclear submarines, it can be observed that four boats of a 10-boat force can be on station (see Figure 5.6). Frequently five boats are on station, and infrequently, there could be six boats available. Therefore, 64 missiles is the minimum and 96 the maximum number available to the Japanese in a retaliatory situation.

Due to the greater survivability factors for submarines, missiles not attacking Moscow have a 70 percent probability of success (see success factors in Table 5.16). With only four boats on station and 64 missiles to fire, it might be possible to fire seven missiles on non-Moscow DGZs from each ship and nine on Moscow for a total of 36 missiles programmed against Moscow DGZs. If the Moscow defenders tried to launch three ABMs at each reentry vehicle, they would deplete their supply. With two interceptors on each missile, a 17 percent probability of success exists for each missile. By firing 36 at three DGZs, the

FIGURE 5.5

Transit Times Required from Japan to Five Launch Points

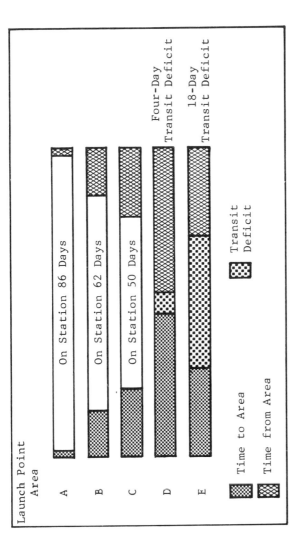

Note: 90-day cruise comparison of A, B, C, D, E launch points. Cruise originates at Yokohama and is based on 90 days' maximum.

Source: Compiled by the author.

FIGURE 5.6

Possible Target Flow Chart

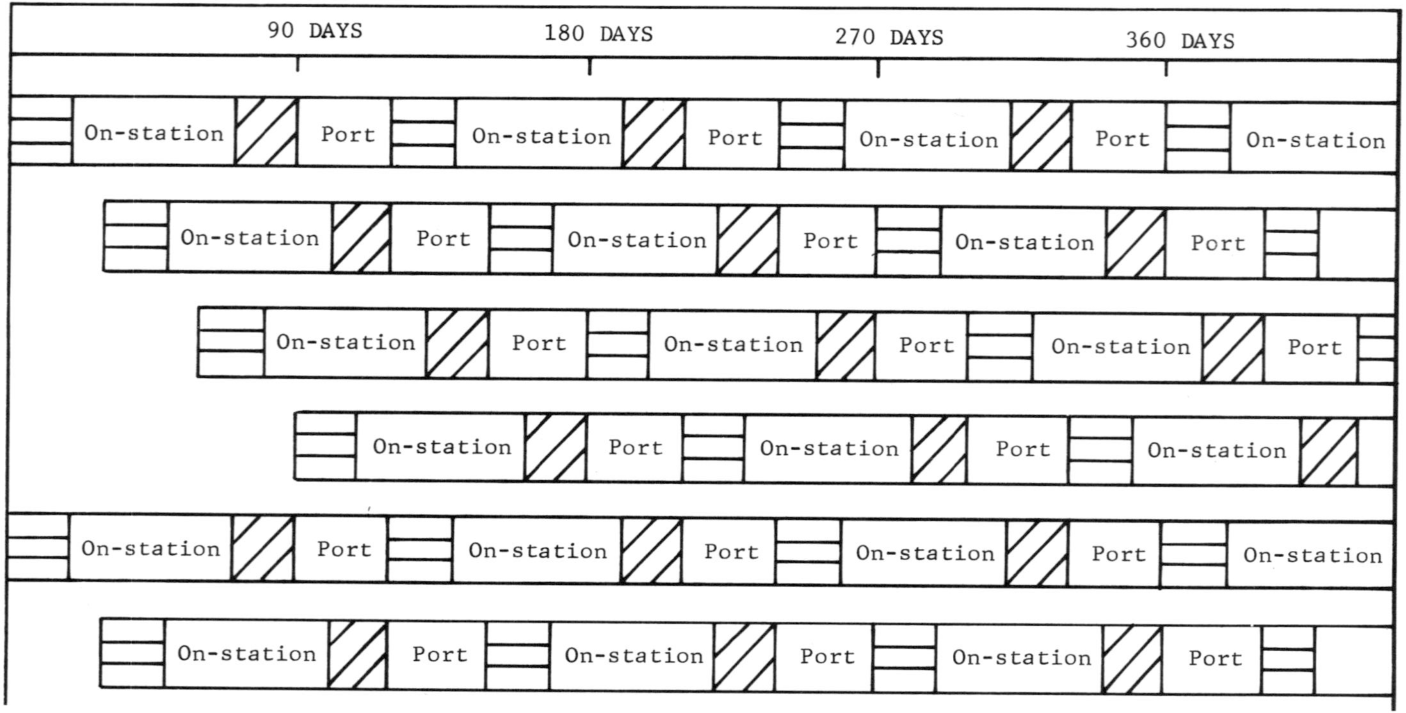

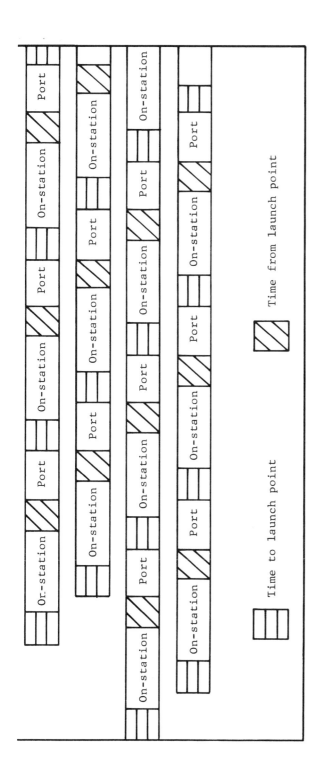

Note: Possible target coverage flow chart for a 10-boat force at Launch Point C (Arabian Sea). Based on 90-day cruises followed by 30 days in port. Transit time is approximately 20 days in each direction.

Source: Compiled by the author.

Japanese would have almost a 90 percent probability of
success. The situation would improve if more boats were
on station. The arrival of a fifth boat could send the
probabilities on non-Moscow DGZs to over 90 percent, and a
sixth boat, admittedly an infrequent occurrence, would permit over 90 percent probability on all targets, including
Moscow. (Given the nature of the many assumptions and
variables of this study.) This compares quite favorably
with the land-based ICBM, which could only achieve 75 percent on non-Moscow DGZs after placing four missiles on each
target and which by applying 16 missiles on each DGZ in
Moscow could only reach a 70 percent likelihood of success.

The same trend can be observed even in the high posture levels, which include some degradation in the survivability of submarines due to a limited ASW breakthrough.
In that case submarine-launched missiles register a 20 percent probability of success as compared with 6 percent for
land-based missile systems.

If the number of boats available for a retaliatory
mission were to drop to two, what effect would it have on
the likelihood of deterrence? In periods of low Soviet
military posture, 32 missiles would permit all DGZs to be
covered by one missile with one left over for redundancy.
In terms of probability, 70 percent could possibly be ex-

TABLE 5.16

SLBM: Overall Success Factors

	Military Posture		
	Low	Medium	High
Non-Moscow DGZs			
1st ABM	--	0.40	0.19
2d ABM	--	0.17	0.08
3d ABM	0.70	0.09	0.03
4th ABM	--	0.04	0.01
5th ABM	--	0.02	0.005
Moscow DGZs			
1st ABM	0.40	0.28	0.14
2d ABM	0.17	0.11	0.04
3d ABM	0.09	0.04	0.01
4th ABM	0.04	0.01	0.0004
5th ABM	0.02	0.006	0.0004

Source: Compiled by the author.

pected on non-Moscow DGZs. Moscow's three DGZs would have only a total of four missiles targeted against them. If the defense realized the degraded state of the Japanese force, sufficient ABMs could be fired to reduce penetration possibilities to almost zero. If they only fired one ABM the reentry vehicle might have a 35 percent chance; if two were fired 17 percent.

If the two boats faced a high-posture defense, the situation would be aggravated indeed. Against Moscow one reentry vehicle would have a 4 percent chance of penetrating against only one ABM; two ABMs would reduce it to 2 percent; and so on. If all 32 missiles were fired at Moscow's three DGZs, roughly 10 per DGZ, under these conditions the probability of success would only be 18 percent. It might be wise when resources are scant to avoid Moscow and concentrate on the other key cities of the USSR, where probabilities of success would run 47 percent for a missile that had not come within range of an ABM.

It would appear that, even with two boats on station, the Japanese would stand an almost even chance of destroying or severely damaging 24 key cities with fatalities out of the 28 million at risk as high as 10 million. This does not represent 20 percent* of the total population but does represent an appreciable blow to the Soviet state, which could not be borne vis-à-vis competition with the United States or China. It is quite likely that even with two boats, on-station deterrence, if Moscow is avoided, would be possible; however, it is a grey threshold area indeed (see Figure 5.7).

The 4,000-nm SLBM Option

What would be the situation, from a targeting standpoint, if Japan were to attempt to construct a 4,000-nm missile system for launch from a nuclear submarine? It is

---

*Secretary of Defense Robert McNamara attempted to quantify the damage levels the United States should seek to assure that the Soviets would be deterred from initiating nuclear war. He chose a level between 25 and 50 percent of Soviet population and industry. If Japanese forces could approach the lower limits of this range, it would appear more than adequate for a minimum deterrent force. See Colin S. Gray, "What RAND Hath Wrought," Foreign Policy, no. 4 (Fall 1971), p. 120.

FIGURE 5.7

Percent Probability of Success,
One Missile, USSR Military Posture

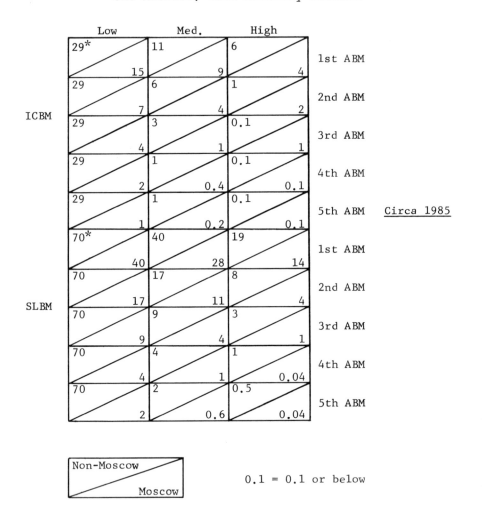

*No ABM threat.
Source: Compiled by the author.

not inconceivable to suppose that Japanese defense planners, fully realizing the defensive weaknesses of a 2,500-nm system could decide early in a development program to skip the 2,500-nm stage and concentrate on achieving an operational 4,000-nm system. If this were done, the Japanese deterrence could be substantial, since patrolling zones could be increased and security from antisubmarine warfare developments could be enhanced.

Using the 4,000-nm missile and firing from the referenced launch points in the Sea of Japan, Bay of Bengal, and Arabian Sea, 100 percent coverage of all key urban areas becomes possible. If patrolling zones were established in the North Pacific, in the Bering Sea, and so on, 100 percent coverage could be obtained. The desirability of points B and C is also enhanced due to greater patrolling zone potential.

The greatest advantages to the 4,000-nm missile would be the obviating of any need to seek a zone in the North Atlantic as well as the possible increase in patrol area. However, to add the remoteness of the mid-Pacific to the security of the Japanese deterrent force, another 1,000-to-2,000-nm range would be needed.

JAPAN VERSUS THE UNITED STATES

As has been pointed out, comments with reference to the Japanese and the United States will be general and brief. It is evident, at this point in the study, that the magnitude of any effort to engage a great land-mass industrial power must be significant. Any Japanese capability to strike at the heartland of the Soviet Union must also have the ability to strike the industrial center of the United States. The 2,500-nm SLBM that could cover 100 percent of the key Soviet targets from the Arabian Sea could easily place at risk all the 68 urban areas of 200,000 or greater in the United States from a launch zone some 300 nm off the coast of Canada and the northern United States.

The 4,000-nm missile would open the vastness of the Pacific to a patrol area as much as 2,000 nm off the U.S. west coast. Such a vast patrol area would offer much greater security to the submarine force than a similar range missile against the USSR. For U.S. military planners, a Japanese 4,000-nm capable program could cause more concern than a 5,000-nm system that would appear to more closely meet the needs of a force oriented toward deterrence of a Soviet threat.

THE OPTIMUM NUCLEAR FORCE FOR JAPAN

Within the very limited confines of this book, it is
not possible to determine what the optimum nuclear force
would be for Japan. In fact, it is almost presumptuous to
attempt an answer. What this paper has done, given a
stated number of warheads, is to test various delivery
systems thought to be within Japan's technological competence by 1985 against a limited spectrum of targets. It
was felt that a secure second-strike capability sufficient
to destroy certain cities in the PRC and the USSR could
act as a deterrent upon those states.

From the limited data that have been presented in this
work, the 2,500-nm SLBM seemed to meet the requirements
stated above when operated in a force of approximately 10
boats. It seemed to offer the best chance for Japan to
threaten an adversary with a second strike. Of course, a
second strike in Japan's case, or in any nation's case,
marks the failure of "nuclear diplomacy" as Japan, once
attacked, and depending on the severity of the attack,
could possibly not regain the requisites of a viable economy. Its possible opponents, on the other hand, if willing
to suffer the damage that could possibly be inflicted on
their advanced industrial bases could, in a one-on-one engagement, regain economic viability after a requisite period of time.

The likelihood, however, of a one-on-one situation is
very remote, and this, of course, is what Japan, or any
medium-size nuclear power, must rely on to increase the
diplomatic effectiveness of its deterrent. If Japan were
to engage the Soviet Union and execute the nuclear option,
great damage to the command and control structure and
internal communications would probably be inflicted on the
USSR in addition to the destruction of vital industrial
capacity. The leaders of the Soviet Union, realizing that
their nation had been placed in a weakened condition vis-
à-vis the United States and China, must at that time decide
whether or not to risk a period of strategic inequality
with the United States. In the worst case, the decision
would be to execute the nuclear force against the United
States, which would, in its train, stimulate the reality
of Armageddon. It is this kind of doubt that a medium-
size force could exploit as a diplomatic tool; however, if
the diplomatic ploy fails, the spirit of Yamato would continue to exist only in the rocks and barren mountain sides
of the Japanese archipelago.

There have been several estimates that have been developed, some relating specifically to Japan, others to
all states aspiring to be a medium-level nuclear power.
The Anzenhosho Chosa Kai estimated in 1968 that Japan,
over a five-year span, could develop an ICBM that included
50 vehicles for experiments on the ground, 100 for flying
experiments, 100 for parts experiments, guidance system
development, facilities and personnel for $1.464 billion
(1968 costs). Warhead and reentry vehicle costs were excluded.[33] A gaseous diffusion plant capable of 98 percent
enrichment was seen as costing $139 million plus annual
fixed and electric power costs of $59 million (annual out-
put--two tons).[34]

While the above estimate has considerable merit, conditions in Japan change yearly vis-à-vis nuclear program
costs and development, and an updated figure based on data
reflecting the U.S., French, British, and Japanese experience to date needs to be introduced.

Japan has or will soon have sophisticated air delivery
forces. No attempt will be made to include F4EJ costs in
this estimate as all such costs will have been absorbed by
the build-up of conventional forces. This estimate will
examine each of the primary components of the nuclear de-
terrent--missiles, subs, and warheads. It will be assumed
that the Japanese will not be interested in any system that
would act as a target attracting missiles to Japan itself
in a counterforce situation. Thus, an SLBM system that
best promises the ability to survive a first strike will
be examined. That number (10 carrying 1-mt x 16 warheads)
of nuclear submarines that seemed to offer at least the
threshold of deterrence in the empirical study will be
used as the base. It will further be assumed that no outside power will assist Japan, placing the constraint on
Japan of technology rather than money in its race to develop
a domestic uranium enrichment process, inertial guidance,
and a nuclear-powered submarine.

Enrichment

As Japan does not have access to the technology of
gaseous diffusion, concentration on the ultracentrifuge
to produce the highly enriched material for the 1-mt warhead would be necessary. This would be a most difficult
hurdle to leap and will take time. As was said by one

humorist, "You cannot produce a baby in one month by getting nine women pregnant," so Japan will not be able to speed the realization of the ultracentrifuge. Much of the basic research for the centrifuge method of enrichment, as has been pointed out earlier in the study, is already being or will be done on a national priority basis. It would seem that the R and D costs, therefore, need not be assigned to a decision to build the bomb. Possibly only those expenses incurred in increasing the enrichment level from 3.5 percent to 98 percent would be registered. These costs, since the concept requires only the lengthening of the cascade, would seem to be relatively small.

Missiles

The cost of Japanese-made rockets through the Mu series has been relatively inexpensive. The Kappa 6 cost only $11,000;[35] reports on the Kappa 8 ranged from $17,000 to $21,000. The Kappa 9L was reported as $35,000 (in 1963) and the Lambda 4S was estimated to cost close to $333,330 in 1968 ($461,538 in revalued yen rates).[36] With the development of the Mu, the price per rocket finally rose over the $1 million mark. The estimated price was $1.1 million in 1966 while in 1968 it was listed as being $1,388,888. (Due to the yen revaluation, that figure, based on 260 yen for the dollar, would be $1,923,076.)[37]

While these prices were reasonable, the rockets themselves lacked sophisticated guidance and secondary control systems, their only objective being to provide correct attitude for satellite insertion.[38] These simple requirements have been seen to produce simple results, which led to the demand for better guidance and accuracy. The N rocket, which may have development costs totaling 99 billion yen, represents Japan's attempt to achieve a fully guided rocket. While the 99 billion figure represents $275 million at 360 to 1 or 346 million at 260 to 1 and includes costs for experimental rockets and other miscellaneous equipment, it is known that the initial Japanese produced models will cost in excess of $7,564,000 (1972) for the first stage alone. These figures must include certain fixed capital costs for the Japanese manufacturers and the producing of certain tools and dies no longer held by the U.S. firms. Nevertheless, this figure represents a breathtaking $6,264,052 above the U.S. shelf price for similar first-stage equipment.

The N rocket promises to meet the range requirements
of a Japanese 2,500-nm missile, but its first two stages
are liquid and thus not appropriate for a missile launched
from a sub. Much technology learned from the N might be
adaptable to a SLBM, especially guidance, but, most likely,
a newly designed missile would be required. Considerable
propulsion and air-frame experience has been gained by
Japanese rocket manufacturers, but guidance, thrust vectoring, and reentry techniques would have to be developed
further or developed from scratch. To date, the low cost
of Japanese rocketry has been due, in large part, to the
limited number of test vehicles used prior to operational
use. This probably cannot be duplicated in a program to
develop a reliable nuclear delivery vehicle, although advanced telemetry instrumentation will keep the number of
test vehicles to an acceptable level (possibly as low as
30).

The cost of A-3 missiles, if bought from the United
States, would be approximately $1.6 million a piece by
1975.[39] The cost of a Japanese missile might be estimated
by using the Mu as a model. As this rocket would have
over a 1,600-nm range with a nuclear warhead,[40] it would
seem that it could serve as the technology base for a 2,500-
nm vehicle; the price, $1,380,000 (1968), could serve as
a base also. It would seem reasonable that the design
and testing of a solid follow-on to the Mu would benefit
from existing propulsion, frame, and project coordination,
ground support, and test range facilities extant or under
construction or development for the N rocket program. Even
guidance and reentry would have as a base recent studies
by the National Aeronautics Laboratory.

By using the model established in Browne and Shaw's
Diffusion of Combat Aircraft, Missiles, and Their Supporting Technologies,[41] the apportionment of costs for a standard 1,500-nm solid propellant missile can be approximated
as follows:

Item	Cost (percent)
Motor (case, nozzle, loading, project coordination	80
Guidance	16
Reentry body	4

If it is possible to work from the single known factor
that is currently available--the $1,920,000 (1973 costs) of

the Mu rocket--it would be possible to estimate that a
total missile system, including guidance and reentry body
on this same vehicle would be roughly $2.4 million, with
the guidance costing about $384,000 and the reentry vehi-
cle about $96,000. While this seems to be rather expen-
sive for a 1,500-nm missile in comparison to off-the-shelf
A-3 missiles produced in the United States, it is not un-
like other sophisticated weaponry where Japan does not
possess a competitive advantage but has embarked on production for reasons of "technological modernization."

Having developed a "reasonable" cost estimate for the
unit production costs of a 1,500-nm guided missile based
on Mu technology, it is important to determine the scope
of a development program to support a 2,500-nm vehicle.
Latest information available on development is in reference to the N rocket. Although it is partially a liquid
fuel enterprise, investigation might lead to some valid
conclusions as indicators. It has been reported that 99
billion yen or $380,769,230 (1973 at 260 to 1) is being
contemplated as the development cost of the N rocket;
however, an additional 77 billion yen, or $296 million
will be spent on facilities.[42] If a total of these figures
can serve as a base ($680 million) and the N rocket program
follows a typical liquid propellant development course, expenditures of $95 million for design and test of the pro-
pulsion, $95 million for design and test of the frame and
project coordination, $95 million for the guidance system,
$48 million for development of the reentry vehicle, $95
million for ground support, and $244 million for testing
and range facilities would follow. (Notice that the announced figure for facilities is not too far from that
projected by a hypothetical breakdown of costs.)

If it is possible to accept about $700 million (1973
costs) as a representative development cost for a country
that has already a rather substantial rocketry base, it
is possible to make some further assumptions about a
2,500-nm delivery system. Assuming research and development programs for thrust vector controls, guidance, and
improved solid fuels materialize in line with the progress
of the N rocket and applicable upper stage test rockets
by the 1977-78 time frame, Japan would be in a very bal-
anced position to design and test a rocket system that
would meet the specific requirements of SLBMs. Such a development program would cost in the neighborhood of the N
rocket program adjusted for inflation, or approximately
from $800 million to $1 billion. The unit cost of the
rocket could be expected to be at least what the Mu would

cost with guidance and reentry features ($2.4 million) plus inflation, or roughly $2.9 million. Thus, using the model provided in the _Diffusion_ study, an estimate of costs involved can be made (see Table 5.17).

Nuclear Submarines

Development of the Polaris system cost the United States an estimated $10 billion over the fiscal years 1956 to 1967,[43] and latest figures for a British-built single Polaris boat runs $93 million. It has been estimated that by 1975, a new SSBN might run $123 million.[44]

While there are no similar data based on Japanese experience for nuclear submarines, there is considerable in-

TABLE 5.17

Estimate of Costs in 2,500-nm Solid-Propellant Missile Program

	Cost (dollars)
Design and test	
Propulsion	130,000,000
Frame and project coordination	130,000,000
Guidance	170,000,000
Reentry vehicle	90,000,000
Ground support equipment	60,000,000
Testing and range facilities	420,000,000
Total	1,000,000,000*
Production	
Motor (case, nozzle, loading project coordination)	2,320,000
Guidance	464,000
Reentry body	116,000
Total	2,900,000
160 operational units plus 20 percent	556,800,000
Total system cost	
Development	1,000,000,000
192 missiles (warhead costs excluded)	556,800,000
Total	1,556,800,000*

*1978.
Source: Compiled by the author.

221

formation available concerning Japan's experience in the construction of a nuclear-powered surface ship, the <u>Mutsu</u>.[45] Initial work on the ship's hull was begun in 1968, with launching in 1969. The nuclear reactor was delivered in August 1972, and the fuel was installed the following month. Construction cost was approximately 2.9 billion yen for the hull and 2.67 billion yen for the reactor, for a total of 5.57 billion yen. At 1973 exchange rates, that would amount to $21,423,000.

Besides some maritime nuclear reactor experience, and admittedly 11 years after the launching of the USS <u>Savannah</u>,[46] the Japanese have produced a modern "teardrop" submarine, <u>Uzushio</u>, which bears a striking resemblance to the U.S. Polaris submarines. Procurement costs of this diesel-powered vessel in revalued yen would be $23,750,000; yearly maintenance costs run at an estimated $1.2 million per ship.

While Japan has thus had some experience with maritime reactors and modern design using the newest high-strength steels, they have not attempted to put all these elements together--nor does Japan currently possess an inertial guidance system for submarines. It is this researcher's opinion that since much experience has been gained about maritime reactors and submarine design by the Japanese already, the program costs would not approach those of the U.S. Polaris system--perhaps the program will be about one-third as expensive as that estimated for the United States. Such program costs for Japan would bring the cost of systems development to almost $300 million per boat. A possible cost breakdown follows.

Submarine development program	3,000,000,000
Approximate unit cost of boats	175,000,000
Total submarine buy	1,750,000,000
Total costs	4,750,000,000

Atomic Warheads

As the main premise of this cost estimate is based on a program starting in the 1977-78 time frame, it is very likely that by that time Japan will have succeeded in its pilot enrichment projects and would be able to assign to civilian programs all R and D costs except those necessary for the specific requirement of going from 3.5 percent enrichment to 98 percent. While this researcher must admit of no knowledge concerning the cost factors involved in going from the lower- to the higher-grade uranium, it is possible to gain an idea of cost by reviewing the British and U.S. price for warheads. U.S. Atomic Energy Commission (AEC) warheads for the Poseidon missile have been estimated at $5 million per missile;[47] however, each missile has as many as ten 50-kt warheads.[48] Warhead costs for the Polaris A-3 type (three 200-kt warheads) have been estimated as being between $400,000 and $500,000 for each warhead.[49]

The pilot plant to contain 10,000 centrifuges by 1980 and have a capacity of 40 tons per year will cost about $384 million (1972 costs).[50] This sum will not be included in the development costs but will be considered as assigned to the atomic power program. Since we do not know the actual cost of the higher enrichment process, the warhead will be considered to cost $1.7 million, slightly higher than that cited above for the Polaris A-3. The total cost for 160 warheads would run close to $304 million.

The total cost for a 10-boat deterrent force carrying a one-megaton nuclear warhead might approximate the following:

Missiles (192)	$1,556,000,000
Submarines (10)	4,750,000,000
Warheads (160)	304,000,000
Total costs	6,610,000,000

Annual operating costs based on the British experience could approximate $35 million per year per boat by the early 1980s.

The total costs are fairly close to the $2-4 billion figure mentioned by the Japanese analyst Ryukichi Imai, who wrote, concerning medium-size nuclear capabilities, that certain countries, like Japan, could achieve such a level with the expenditure of from $2-4 billion based on an industrial base that had already accomplished most of the necessary R and D.[51]

It is obvious that the date chosen to make the cost estimate is crucial (the end of the 1970s--to make it applicable to 1985, an inflation factor would have to be added, but to be available by 1985, some sectors would need to be on their way by the late 1970s). Without such a date, many of the items funded against civilian space or atomic power programs would have to be applied to the calculations, for Japan to go nuclear. After 1985 the costs might be expected to reduce (exclusive of inflation) as

Japan's aerospace industry gains in avionics experience and Japan's atomic power industry gains competence in enrichment technology.

Until the 1980s it is folly to speak of a Japanese autonomous nuclear capability, as her potential weapon yields and delivery capability would both be limited.

Time Frame

Tables 5.18-5.20 and Figure 5.8 show graphically the rate at which Japan could develop a nuclear capability. All benchmarks are based on the continuation of present development schedules for atomic power and space programs. As pointed out before, these technical development programs seem to be proceeding at a pace possibly 80 to 90 percent of that which Japan is capable; hence a great infusion of additional money would only have marginal effects on the overall progress. Only unexpected aid from foreign nations, included as possibilities on the flow chart, could alter the forward momentum measurably. On the flow chart allowance was made for a possible U.S.-supplied license for missile guidance systems and French gaseous diffusion technology. Neither time schedule is appreciably affected by the actions, as they would probably come close to a Japanese technological breakthrough point.

It would appear, because of the lack of a major reprocessing facility, that Japan could not go nuclear in a fission sense until 1975. From that point, events would permit the realization of a 20-kt weapon by 1976 or early 1977. This low-yield weapon stage must be transited as the smaller-fission weapons serve as triggers or detonators for the larger fusion devices, which would be possible a year to 18 months later.

An MR/IRBM capability of 2,500-nm range would occur sometime shortly after 1978, with a complete nuclear submarine-launched force possible by perhaps 1982 at the earliest and 1985 at the latest, assuming a project start in 1974.

Many of these events are predicated on the basis of the recent Chinese experience,[52] and much depends on the perceived adversary. If the USSR is considered prime, or the United States, the minimum acceptable system becomes the submarine-launched 2,500-nm missile system. If China alone were considered the major adversary, it might be possible to accept an IRBM land-based deterrence force.

Tactical weapons for air delivery in defense of the Japanese islands might be seen as providing needed flexi-

TABLE 5.18

Feasible Japanese Military Nuclear Program

	1974	1975	1976	1977	1978	1979	1980	1981	1982	1983	1984	1985	1986	1987	1988
Nuclear warheads	*Prototype re-processing facility operational. *Development program for nuclear devices begins.			*Detonation of first device.		*Improve warhead design--achieve 200-kt yield for MR/IRBM delivery.			*More compact thermonuclear device possible.						
Plutonium	*Certain power/research reactors converted to production of weapons-grade Pu.		*Fabrication of device components.		*Develop, fabricate, test nuclear warheads for manned delivery vehicles.	*Achieve higher yield warheads and thermonuclear detonations.			*Thermonuclear warheads possible for missiles.						
Enriched uranium	*Dual development of enrichment technology		*R and D facility produces 3.5 percent enriched uranium. *National priority project for development of centrifugal enrichment enters 2d year. *Advanced rotary drums developed for centrifugal method.	*France offers gaseous diffusion collaboration; Japan accepts. *Prototype facility completed. *Testing continues.	*Production begins of slightly enriched U by centrifugal method.		*Prototype gaseous diffusion facility completed.		*Highly enriched U produced by centrifugal method. *20-kt device detonated.		*Design of thermonuclear device. *Production of weapons-grade U possible by gaseous diffusion method.		*Higher weapon yields achieved.	*Megaton device tested.	

Note: This table represents possible capabilities only and is predicated on a 1974 weapons program. Such a likelihood is not a finding of this book.

Source: Compiled by the author.

TABLE 5.19

Feasible Japanese Development Program for Missiles

| 1974 | 1975 | 1976 | 1977 | 1978 | 1979 | 1980 | 1981 | 1982 | 1983 | 1984 | 1985 | 1986 | 1987 | 1988 |

*"N" Rocket development continues from 1973. Thrust is 170,000 pounds and is 1968 model Thor.
  *Japanese space industry places emphasis on guidance and achieves adequated technology to produce Thor.
*Reentry vehicle research pressed for 200-kt warhead payload.

  *Guidance technology given boost by license agreement with United States or France.

*Development of solid-fuel MRBM pressed using the "M" rocket with improved Japanese guidance.

*Thrust-augmented Thor of 330,000 pounds thrust fired successfully (N Rocket).
  *Crew training begins.
    *Deployment of a force of 50 MRBMs possible.
      *RV for 200-kt warhead possible.

*Original "N" rocket of 700,000 pounds thrust reactivated. Possible backup in event nuclear submarine program slips.
  *Development of 2d-generation solid fuel rocket beings--for use in submarines.

*Development program for submarine-launched IRBM succeeds. Series production begins.

  *Development of 1-mt payload RV begins.

    *Development program for 4,000-mile SLBM begins.

Note: This table represents possible capabilities only and is based on a program start date of 1974. Such a likelihood is not a finding or this book.

Source: Compiled by the author.

TABLE 5.20

Feasible Japanese Development Program for Missile-Firing Submarines

Submarines	1974	1975	1976	1977	1978	1979	1980	1981	1982	1983	1984	1985	1986	1987	1988
Conventional	*Program begins to adapt modern conventional submarines (that is, Uzushio class) to missile-carrying role. *Commencement of hull design and construction of new submarines for China patrol.		*First new submarines (stretched Uzushio class) launched.	*Fitting-out begins.	*Sea trials for new conventional submarines begins.		*New class of submarines ready for recently developed MRBMs.	*System testing complete.		*Submarines on-station.					
Nuclear	*Japan's first nuclear ship Mutsu goes critical and test navigation begins. *Nuclear submarine reactor detail design and development begins. *R and D conducted; shielding tests begin. *Hull designed.		*Hull construction begins. *Inertial guidance system R and D begins. *Command and control studies and requirements data accomplished.	*Trial operations of prototype submarine begins. *Inspection of reactor and verification of test data.		*Final design of operational reactor. *Production of operational versions of prototype submarines begins.		*Production submarines undergo extensive shakedown and inspection trials. *Missiles and submarines undergo system tests.			*Boat 1 of nuclear submarine force on-station.				

Note: This table represents possible capabilities only and is based on a program start date of 1974. Such a likelihood is not a finding of this book.

Source: Compiled by the author.

FIGURE 5.8

Japan: Opportunity-Capability Spectrum

	Year								
Nuclear Base	72	73	74	75	76	77	78	79	80
Mining and milling of uranium	5,000-ton capacity by								
Enriched uranium R and D	Decision on national priority			Concerted centrifugal development					
Fuel fabrication	Expansion of capability in								
Fuel reprocessing	Pilot plant operational by October 1974			Follow-					
Fast breeder reactors	Joyo critical				Manju critical				
Advanced thermal reactors	Fugen critical			Incorporation					
Maritime reactors	Critical target date October 1972--not realized								
Delivery systems									
F86F	287 aircraft			Probable phase-out period					
F104J	192 aircraft			Probable					
F4EJ	46 aircraft								
FST-2	Prototype flights								
T-2									
M rocket	Operational--180,000 lbs. thrust								
N rocket	166,000 lbs. thrust			330,000 lbs. thrust					

81	82	83	84	85	86	87	88	89	90	91	92	93	94	95

─────────────────────────X────►

40-ton SwU 5,000-
──────────── ────── X─────────────────────►
capacity   ton SwU

line with demand──────────────────────────►

on plants needed by 1975───────────►

        Probable com-   Massive incorporation of FBR into
        mercial FBR   power-generation capabilities

of ATR 10-20-30 percent depending on FBR success

Possibly 3 ships   Possibly 200 by
by 1980   the year 2000

phaseout period

158 aircraft   Replacement fighter
                 begins by end of 1981

126 aircraft

80 aircraft

Source: Compiled by the author.

FIGURE 5.9

Estimated Yearly Expenditures for Nuclear Weapons System

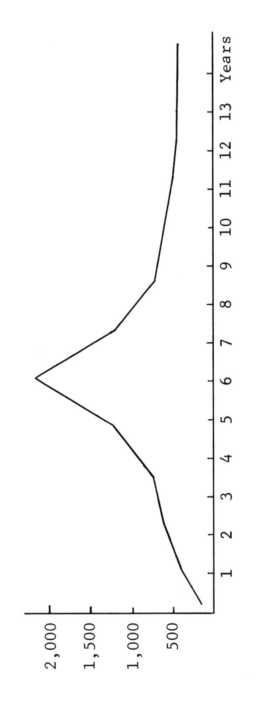

Note: Estimated yearly expenditures for nuclear weapons program over a 10-year period. Note an estimated $350 million per year for operational expenses after the 10th year.

Source: Compiled by the author.

bility. Further, it would be in Japan's interest to develop nuclear warheads for the extant air defense missile systems, as well as nuclear depth charges for ASW purposes. The cost of such programs would be additive but could reasonably seem to develop from the technical advancements made during the initial strategic deterrence phase.

The fiscal 1972 budget for national defense was 803,004 million yen[53] (approximately $2.62 billion--306 to 1), compared to a GNP of $293 billion, or roughly 0.89 percent of the GNP. Under the Fourth Defense Build-Up Plan, 1976 could possibly see expenditures in excess of $4 billion for the conventional force build-up.[54] If the time frame of this program were 10 years and the total cost were in the neighborhood of $6.6 billion, it could be reasonable to expect that costs would peak at a figure close to 2 billion halfway through the program, with the 10-year annual average, of course, near $660 million. Such an amount is feasible if an expanding economy is assumed that would increase the one percent of GNP in absolute terms. (However, there has been much trouble in convincing the Diet of the continuing need for current spending levels for defense purposes. Also, the government of Japan is not pleased with the 1 percent limitation and would rather advocate a concept of budget sufficiency rather than a simple 1 percent.) See Figure 5.9 for a chart of possible 10-year annual expenditures.

These figures represent only the tip of the iceberg, as Japan would need to bolster its command and control, intelligence, and warning systems to make the nuclear tool a meaningful instrument in international politics. In an era when the very existence of the Self-Defense Force has been called a contravention of the constitution, it is difficult to foresee such a drastic change as envisaged above.

NOTES

1. Boei Cho (Defense Agency), <u>Nihon no Boei</u> (Tokyo: Boei Cho, October 1970), p. 30.
2. Masumi Esaki, June 29, 1972 speech at the Foreign Correspondents' Club--transcript held by author.
3. <u>Asahi Evening News</u>, December 15, 1971.
4. Ibid., February 29, 1972.
5. <u>Kokkai Sanko Shiryo</u> (Diet Reference Materials) (Tokyo: Boei Cho, July 1972), p. 6.
6. Correspondence with official of the JDA.

7. Samuel Glasstone, ed., The Effects of Nuclear Weapons (Washington, D.C.: Government Printing Office, 1962).

8. See G. Sidney Winter, Economic Viability after Thermonuclear War: The Limits of Feasible Production (Santa Monica, Calif.: RAND Corporation, September 1963).

9. Glasstone, op. cit., p. 550.

10. Ibid.

11. Ibid., pp. 163 and 167.

12. Ibid., p. 163.

13. Ibid., p. 639.

14. U.S. Department of State, Issues in United States Foreign Policy (Washington, D.C.: Government Printing Office, 1969), no. 4, p. 12; and U.S. Congress, Joint Economic Committee, People's Republic of China: An Economic Assessment (Washington, D.C.: Government Printing Office, May 1972), p. 72.

15. Donald Hsia, "Changes in the Location of China's Steel Industry," in Industrial Development in Communist China, ed. Choh-Ming Li (New York: Praeger Publishers, 1964).

16. Robert Michael Field, "Chinese Industrial Development: 1949-1970" in Joint Economic Committee, op. cit., p. 71.

17. Ibid., p. 61.

18. Ibid., p. 66.

19. Harold Fullard, ed., China in Maps (London: George Philip and Son Limited, 1968), p. 16.

20. Philip D. Reichers, "The Electronics Industry of China," in Joint Economic Committee, op. cit., pp. 91-92.

21. Ibid., pp. 94-95.

22. Ibid., pp. 98-101.

23. Ibid., p. 103.

24. Philip W. Vetterling and James J. Wegy, "China: The Transportation Sector, 1950-71," in Joint Economic Committee, op. cit., p. 163.

25. Compiled from data presented on page 84, Joint Economic Committee, op. cit.

26. I have relied heavily on new population data compiled by Cheng-siang Chen for this study. See "Population Growth and Urbanization in China, 1953-1970," Geographical Review, January 1973.

27. Chosa Geppo, September 1973, p. 33.

28. Geoffrey Kemp, "The Strategic Requirements for European Nuclear Forces," unpublished manuscript, Fletcher School of Law and Diplomacy, August 1973, pp. 33-34.

29. Many of the updated population figures have been taken from ibid.

30. Space/Aeronautics, September 1968, p. 48.

31. Ibid.

32. Herbert Scoville, Jr. states that "nuclear sub-duty involves 60-day underwater cruises." I have chosen 90-day increments to optimize time on station due to the rather long transit time to the desired launching area. See Herbert Scoville, Jr., "Missile Submarines and National Security," Scientific American, June 1972, p. 17.

33. Anzenhosho Chosa Kai, Nihon no Anzenhosho--1970 nen e no Tembo (Tokyo: Asagumo Sha, 1968), pp. 327-28.

34. Ibid., pp. 301-02.

35. Browne and Shaw Research Corp., The Diffusion of Combat Aircraft, Missiles, and Their Supporting Technologies (Waltham, Mass.: Browne and Shaw, 1966), p. D-28.

36. Chosa Kai, op. cit., p. 327.

37. Ibid.

38. Ibid., p. 323.

39. Kemp, op. cit., p. A-17.

40. Chosa Kai, op. cit., p. 323.

41. Browne and Shaw, op. cit., pp. B-32, B-33.

42. Nihon Roketto Kaihatsu Kyogikai Kaiho, November 1970, p. 23.

43. Harvey M. Sapolsky, The Polaris System Development: Bureaucratic and Programmatic Success in Government (Cambridge, Mass.: Harvard University Press, 1972), pp. 162-63.

44. Kemp, op. cit., p. A-17.

45. See Takenobu Yokomura, Nihon Zosen Gakkaishi, March 1973, pp. 26-33.

46. Ibid.

47. Kemp, op. cit., p. A-24.

48. International Institute for Strategic Studies, The Military Balance: 1972-73 (London: IISS, 1971), p. 65.

49. Kemp, op. cit., p. A-17.

50. Nuclear News, December 1972, p. 53.

51. Imai in Johan Jorgen Holst, Security Order and the Bomb (Oslo: Universitetsforlaget, 1972), p. 125.

52. Murphy, op. cit., pp. 28-35.

53. Budget Bureau, The Budget in Brief, Japan (Tokyo: Ministry of Finance, 1972), p. 38.

54. New York Times, November 2, 1970, p. 3.

CHAPTER

6

WILL JAPAN EXERCISE
A NUCLEAR OPTION?

During the course of Japan's history, there has been
a pronounced cyclic characteristic regarding the country's
interaction with and response to the international environment. Periods of great acceptance and importation of foreign ideas and techniques alternated with periods of introspection, assimilation, and awareness of the uniqueness
of native Japanese society. The concept expressed as
Nihonshugi, or Japanness, was cultivated during periods of
self-reflective and insular existence. Often such introspection took on security-related connotations and was fos-
tered by a military/bureaucratic elite attempting to maintain its own oligarchic position in society. After the
longest period of self-imposed isolation, which ended
during the twilight of the Tokugawa, 1853-58, the Japanese
entered upon a period of active importation of new ideas
and new machines. After the Meiji and Taisho eras, the
movement that placed major emphasis on the uniqueness of
Japan and its society gained in strength. International
economic depression coupled with a decline in trade eventually led to a situation of internal strife that permitted
the ascendancy of the militarists and the events of the
late 1930s and early 1940s.

After the conclusion of the Great Pacific War, the
Japanese embarked on another phase of foreign importation.
This period of infatuation with things modern and Western
began to wane in the early 1970s. In fact, the death in
late November 1970 of the Japanese novelist and political
extremist Yukio Mishima signaled the beginning of a growing desire once again to explore the essential nature of
the Japanese and their country. This period has been
marked by a rapid decline in interest in European books

and a corresponding concentration on books that examine the Japanese psychology. A great interest has also been realized in the history of Japan often taking the form of archeological pursuit.

What has the new introspection of the 1970s to do with nuclear weapons? The subject can be viewed in two ways, each of which produces diametrically opposed results. On the one hand, it can be conjectured that as the Japanese did not "go nuclear" during the period of the great infusion of foreign ideas and techniques, the period most likely to bring about military nuclearization has passed. (The failure, of course, is closely related to the story of the U.S. occupation.) The Japanese, having rejected or failed to introduce nuclear weapons during the era prior to the 1970s, will not, at this time, attempt to reproduce the machines of war created during World War II but will press forward in a self-reliant manner, developing their national future in a cooperative, but not submissive, spirit in association with the United States.

On the other hand, this period of renewed Japanese self-assurance could be viewed as one that fosters the creation of a nuclear deterrence so that the Japanese state can be independent in its diplomacy and reflect, in political terms, the power it has in the economic sphere.

In either case, it is this researcher's opinion that a Japanese decision to embark on a nuclear weapons program will be postponed until a serious international threat is perceived that cannot be countered by existing bilateral or multilateral mechanisms. Such a threat, in all likelihood, would involve a grave danger to the physical security of Japan, and the very existence of what is considered the Japanese way of life. However, one would be naive not to include in these conditions of grave peril the possibility of irresponsible economic warfare that could threaten calamitous ruin to the Japanese economy. Japan as an independent sovereign state will ultimately act in a manner to preserve its inherent sovereignty but will attempt to delay a decision to possess nuclear weapons until it is the last policy alternative. Of especial importance will be the continued perception of viability on the part of the Japanese leadership of the U.S. nuclear guarantee.

What is the status today of Japan's nuclear option? On the basis of the data presented in this study, certain broad conclusions can be drawn:

1. The Japanese government and the intellectual elite are engaged in a comprehensive security policy debate. The outcome of this debate will depend most significantly

on changes in the external environment that tend to degrade the efficacy, as perceived by the Japanese, of the current U.S.-Japanese security system.

2. Based on currently announced planning schedules, the Japanese are developing and will possess by 1985 a broadly based nuclear industry experienced in performing all the major technical processes inherent in the nuclear fuel cycle--mining and milling, refining, enrichment, fabrication, power reactor use and construction, reprocessing, and disposal. This industry, as of today, is highly developed and sophisticated in its own right, permitting innovation of technological refinements and the introduction of new processes, but it is almost totally dependent on external sources of uranium.

3. Under current international safeguards, and, very possibly, also due to the domestic political environment, a surreptitious program for diversion of plutonium to a weapons program is not feasible, at least, until 1975, and probably not before fast breeder reactors become commonplace (late 1990s), and in the strategic environment in which Japan is situated, a few surreptitiously produced fission weapons would be of no concrete military value.

4. Japan faces significant <u>potential</u> threats from the Soviet Union and People's Republic of China (PRC), but in this period of détente her leaders have had problems articulating the nature of these threats. Against these nations, the air arm of the Japanese Self-Defense Force (JASDF) with the acquisition of F4 aircraft and equipped with nuclear weapons, could threaten a spectrum of Chinese targets but would not be more than marginally credible through 1982, due to the absence of a secure second-strike capability. The same is true, and to a far greater degree, against the Soviet Union. Japan, on her part, would face national disaster if she initiated hostilities against either state based only on a manned-aircraft-delivered weapons capability.

5. The Japanese aerospace program, considerably advanced in solid fuel missile propulsion technology, dropped plans for boosters capable of long-range flight and instead embarked on the production, under license, of liquid-fueled Thor boosters. This was interpreted (by the author) as an effective means of closing the technology gap that exists between Japan and the rest of the world in guidance and secondary-thrust technology. A technical capability to produce a militarily viable missile should exist not later than the 1978-79 period, but any move to deploy such missiles prior to the development of an underwater launch platform would be unwise.

236

6. All costs, such as R and D, normally associated with the development of a nuclear weapons capability (including delivery systems) are being absorbed by the civilian nuclear, space, and conventional force buildup programs so that costs incurred in "going nuclear" would be, comparatively speaking, moderate, imposing little strain on the nation in terms of percentage of the gross national product (GNP).

7. Numerous domestic legal and international treaty constraints stand in the way of a Japanese nuclear weapons program; however, insofar as domestic constraints are concerned, interpretation by incumbent administrations of these restrictions has played a significant role in the past, and may in the future, vis-à-vis defense requirements. In the case of international restraints, the Nuclear Nonproliferation Treaty (NPT) lacks any enforcement mechanism without unanimity in the UN Security Council, but the various bilateral agreements have stipulations that could strip Japan of most existing nuclear physical plants and deny access to vitally needed uranium supplies, enriched or natural.

8. Domestic political opposition to nuclear weapons remains a hallmark of all the so-called progressive political parties as well as a significant portion of LDP members. However, the NPT has enough of the nature of an "unequal treaty" to cause general opposition to its ratification by the "Progressive" parties and the members of the influential right-wing Soshinkai Seirankai of the LDP. The Japanese will delay ratification as long as possible, seeking to obtain the maximum quid pro quo. This objective could indeed be access to data on gaseous diffusion, but, in any event, the treaty is likely to be ratified by 1976.

9. In the normal political climate, the body politic is highly critical of nuclear weapons, but from polls taken during the period of intense Chinese irrational behavior that followed the testing of the first Chinese nuclear devices, there was an indication that the Japanese public might support a nuclear program in the face of an extremely hostile and visible foreign threat.

10. It seems most unlikely that Japan could unilaterally become armed with nuclear weapons without a patron, due to her extreme dependence on foreign suppliers for uranium. Also to do so without the benefit of a nuclear shield would expose the nation to possible preemptive strikes during the most vulnerable early stages. Such is the nature of the Japanese defense dilemma. Domestic oppo-

sition prevents Japan from "going nuclear" in a peacetime environment, and even the status of "nuclear power minus two years" would not permit realization of a crash program if the international environment deteriorated to that point necessary to assure public support for a nuclear force. A possible result of an autonomous Japanese national priority program to develop such a capability would be a preemptive attack by the adversary who was seen as the impetus for the program.

11. One of the most critical decisions to be made in the Northeast Asian political environment could be one of the ruling elite of the PRC. If it is decided to deploy an operational ICBM and do so in numbers sufficient to threaten the U.S. command and control system, the international situation could well be altered to that degree that precipitates a Japanese desire for a nuclear weapons capability independent of the U.S. decision-making process.

It is admittedly difficult to be certain in answering this question, which can be affected by so many external variables. First, however, a time frame must be established for the estimate, and secondly, the most important trends must be singled out to establish those points upon which the estimate will be made. The period established is to 1990, and the events chosen to help determine the most significant trends include (1) the slow but steady movement toward ratification of the NPT, (2) the continued opposition of the Japanese people to nuclear weapons, an opposition that stays above 66 percent of nationally polled respondents, (3) the proven stability of the U.S.-Japanese security community, which has weathered the worst of the 1971 crisis period and has entered a season of more productive relationships, (4) the recent U.S. congressional moves to ensure a lasting U.S. nuclear deterrent capability, most firmly expressed by the endorsement of the Trident program, (5) the continuing decline of the LDP, and the rise of opposition parties who are focusing attention on Japan's environmental problems, (6) the growing awareness on the part of opposition parties that the U.S.-Japanese Security Treaty has become accepted, even by the PRC, as a means to ensure stability in Asia even though its present form may be altered, and (7) finally, the probability that, if U.S. forces completely withdraw from Japan as a result of a modification of the Security Treaty, the JASDF will be equipped with the F4EJ, thus ensuring that similar U.S. aircraft could redeploy with minimum support equipment in event of a security crisis in Northeast Asia.

These points help in the conclusion that Japan will continue to avoid the necessity of becoming just another medium-level nuclear power at a time when certain defensive systems (the laser ABM) offer the prospect of putting all advanced-technology states within reach of systems that will end the one-sided preponderance of offensive weapons. Indeed, it might be hoped that Japan would concentrate on the development of this promising defensive system and avoid, altogether, the costs, political and economic, of a nuclear arms program.

APPENDIX A

Nuclear Power Development Plans for 1971–80
(as of November 30, 1972)

Region or Agency	Plant	Output (mwe)	Type	Construction Starts	Operation Starts	Remarks
Hokkaido	N	350	--	1973.04	1977.11	
Tohoku	Onagawa	524	BWR	1971.02	1975.12	Under const.
	N 1	784	--	1975.12	1979.12	
	N 2	784	--	1978.12		
Tokyo	Fukushima 1	460	BWR	1966.12	1970.12	In opera.
	Fukushima 2	784	BWR	1968.03	1973.05	Under const.
	Fukushima 3	784	BWR	1970.03	1974.12	Under const.
	Fukushima 4	784	BWR	1971.12	1975.12	Under const.
	Fukushima 5	784	BWR	1972.03	1976.08	Under const.
	Fukushima 6	1,100	BWR	1971.12	1976.10	Under const.
	Fukushima No. II.1	1,100	--	1972.10	1978.01	Under const.
	N 1	1,100	--	1973.02	1977.12	
	N 2	1,100	--	1975.04	1979.08	
	N 3	1,100	--	1975.09	1980.01	
	N 4	1,100	--	1975.10	1980.08	
	N 5	1,100	--	1975.12	1980.10	
	N 6	1,100	--	1976.09		
	N 7	1,100	--	1977.03		
	N 8	1,500	--	1977.07		
	N 9	1,500	--	1977.07		
	N 10	1,500	--	1978.06		
	N 11	1,500	--	1978.06		
	N 12	1,500	--	1979.07		
	N 13	1,500	--	1979.07		
	N 14	1,500	--	1979.07		
	N 15	1,500	--	1980.07		
	N 16	1,500	--	1980.07		
	N 17	1,500	--	1980.07		
Chubu	Hamaoka 1	540	BWR	1971.03	1974.11	Under const.
	Hamaoka 2	840	BWR	1972.03	1976/77	
	Q	1,100	--	1973.12	1977.12	
	R	1,100	--	1975.01	1979.01	
	S	1,100	--	1976	1980.09	
	T	1,500	--	1977		
	U	1,500	--	1978		
	V	1,500	--	1980		
Hokuriku	R	500	--	1972.12	1976.12	
	S	800	--	1975.08	1979.08	
	T	800	--	1978		

Region or Agency	Plant	Output (mwe)	Construction Type	Construction Starts	Operation Starts	Remarks
Kansai	Mihama 1	340	PWR	1966.12	1970.10	In opera.
	Mihama 2	500	PWR	1968.05	1972.06	In opera.
	Takahama	826	PWR	1969.12	1974.08	Under const.
	Takahama 2	826	PWR	1970.11	1975.07	Under const.
	Mihama 3	826	PWR	1972.03	1976.07	Under const.
	Oh-ii 1	1,175	PWR	1976.04	1976.07	Under const.
	Oh-ii 2	1,175	PWR	1972.04	1977.01	Under const.
	X 1	1,200	--	1973.02	1978.07	
	X 2	1,200	--	1973.02	1979.01	
	X 3	1,200	--	1974.01	1980.07	
	X 4	1,200	--	1975.07	1981.01	
	X 5	1,200	--	1976		
	X 6	1,200	--	1976		
	X 7	1,200	--	1977		
	X 8	1,200	--	1978		
	X 9	1,500	--	1978		
	X10	1,500	--	1979		
	X11	1,500	--	1979		
	X12	1,500	--	1980		
	X13	1,500	--	1980		
Chugoku	Shimane	460	BWR	1970.02	1973.11	Under const.
	F	750		1975.07	1979.07	
	J	750	--	1978.07		
	L	1,000	--	1979.07		
Shikoku	Ikata	566	PWR	1973.03	1977.04	Under const.
	A	566	--	1976.07	1980.07	
	B	800	--	1978.11		
Kyushu	Genkai	559	PWR	1970.12	1975.07	Under const.
	P	559	--	1974.03	1978.07	
	Q	826	--	1975.07	1980.07	
	R	826	--	1977.07		
	S	826	--	1979.07		
JAPC	Tokai 1	166	GCR	1950.02	1966.07	In opera.
	Tsuruga	357	BWR	1966.03	1970.03	In opera.
	Tokai 2	1,100	BWR	1972 early	1976 end	
PNC	Tsuruga (Fugen)	165	ATR	1970	1975	Under const.

Total: 75 plants, 75,272 mwe

Note: Listed are the nuclear power plants in operation, under construction, or scheduled for construction throughout Japan. Since this is a plan that spans a decade, the reader will note that there are substantially more plants scheduled for construction than are currently in operation.

Source: Atoms in Japan, December 1972, pp. 44-46. By permission.

Power Reactors in Operation or under Construction

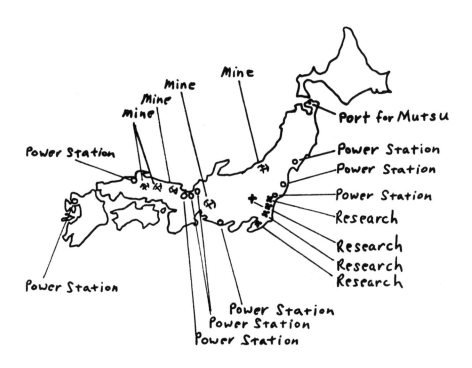

Source: Science and Technology Agency, <u>Atomic Energy in Japan</u> (Tokyo: Atomic Energy Bureau, Science and Technology Agency, 1971), p. 1.

Domestic and Overseas Contribution to Nuclear Power Plant Construction

	Reactor Type				
	GCR	PWR	PWR	PWR	BWR
Plants	Tokai	Mihama	Mihama	Taka-hama	JPDR
Output (mw)	166	340	500	826	12.5
Construction starts (ed)	1960.1	1966.12	1968.5	1969.12	1960.10
Operation starts (ed)	1967.7	1970.10	1972.6	1974.8	1965.3
I. Engineering					
Overall planning	x	x	0	x	x
Plant design					
Core design	x	x	x	x	x
Kinetic analysis	x	x	x	x	x
Safety analysis	x	x	x	x	x
Shielding design	x	x	0	x	x
Antiseismic design	0/x	0/x	0	0/x	x
II. Instruments, Equipment					
Reactor components					
Pressure vessels	0	x	0	0	0
In-core structure	0/x	x	x	x	0/x
Control rod and driving mechanisms	x	x	x	x	x
Recirculation pumps	x	x	x	x	--
Steam generators	0	x	0	x	--
Pressurizers	--	0	0	0	--
Isolation values and safety valves	x	x	x	x	x
Emergency cooling system and turbines	--	--	--	--	--
Fuel handling equipment	x	x	0/x	0/x	x
Rad-wastes disposal facilities					
Gas	x	0/x	0/x	0/x	0/x
Liquid	0	0/x	0/x	0/x	0/x
Solid	--	0/x	0	0/x	--
Instrumentation and control					
Nuclear instrumentation	x	x	x	x	x
Process instrumentation	0/x	x	0/x	0/x	x
Process computers	--	x	x	x	--
Turbine generators					
Turbines	x	0	0	0	0
Condensers	0	0	0	0	0
Feed water heaters	0	0	0	0	0
Generators	x	0	0	0	0
Reactor containers	--	0	0	0	0

(continued)

| | Reactor Type | | | | | |
	BWR	BWR	BWR	BWR	BWR	PWR
Plants	Tsu-ruga	Fuku-Shima	Fuku-shima	Fuku-shima	Shi-mane	U.S. Mutsu
Output (mw)	357	460	784	784	460	36
Construction starts (ed)	1966.4	1966.12	1968.3	1970.1	1970.2	1967.11
Operation starts (ed)	1970.3	1971.3	1973.3	1974.12	1974.6	1973-74
I. Engineering						
Overall planning	x	0/x	0/x	0	0	0
Plant design						
Core design	x	x	x	0	0	0
Kinetic analysis	x	x	x	0	0	0
Safety analysis	x	x	x	0	0	0
Shielding design	x	x	x	0	0	0
Antiseismic design	x	x	x	0	0	0
II. Instruments, Equipment						
Reactor components						
Pressure vessels	0	0	0	0	0	0
In-core structure	0/x	0/x	0/x	0	0	0
Control Rod and driving mechanisms	x	x	x	0/x	0/x	0/x
Recirculation pumps	x	x	x	x	x	0
Steam generators	--	--	--	--	--	0
Pressurizers	--	--	--	--	--	0
Isolation valves and safety valves	x	x	x	x	x	0
Emergency cooling system and turbines	--	x	x	x	x	--
Fuel handling equipment	x	0/x	0/x	0	0	0
Rad-wastes disposal facilities						
Gas	0/x	0/x	0/x	0/x	0/x	0
Liquid	0/x	0/x	0/x	0	0	0
Solid	x	0/x	0/x	0	0/x	x
Instrumentation and control						
Nuclear instrumentation	x	x	x	0/x	0/x	0
Process instrumentation	x	0/x	0/x	0/x	0/x	0
Process computers	x	x	x	0	0/x	--
Turbine generators						
Turbines	x	x	x	0	0	0
Condensers	0	0	0	0	0	0
Feed water heaters	0	0	0	0	0	0
Generators	x	x	x	0	0	0
Reactor containers	0	0	0	0	0	0

Note: 0 = indigenous; x = import; -- = not applicable; GCR = gas-cooled reactor; PWR = pressurized water reactor; BWR = boiling water reactor.

Source: Atoms in Japan, May 1971, Supplement I, p. 24. By permission.

CURRENT JAPANESE LAUNCH VEHICLES

The Lambda 4S (Figure D.1) was the launch vehicle
that lifted Japan's first satellite into orbit in February
1970. The first-stage engine has a polyurethane propellant
(solid), is approximately 8.4 meters long, and can produce
a mean thrust of 37 tons for 28.8 seconds.[1]

To provide additional thrust in order to ensure sufficient velocity to enable stability through fin control and
make the rocket less susceptible to wind dispersion, two
subboosters of 13 tons each are strapped to the first stage.
These boosters are jettisoned subsequent to burnout.

The second stage is also of polyurethane, but shorter
than the first stage by two-thirds. Thrust of 11.75 tons
is produced for 38.4 seconds. Stability is provided by
two spin-up motors that spin the second stage (somewhat
like an artillery shell) at 2.5 revolutions per second before the second-stage engine ignites, since fins lose
their aerodynamic effectiveness as the vehicle penetrates
the upper atmosphere.

The third stage has a polybutadien propellant, is only
2.5 meters long, and produces 6.58 tons of thrust over 27
seconds. An attitude control system is connected to the
top of the third-stage motor. Eight hydrogen-peroxide
control jets, providing control for roll, pitch, and yaw
movements, are tied into an attitude reference subsystem
and a supporting electronic subsystem. A two-degree free
gyroscope mounted on a spin-table provides the attitude
reference. The spinning of the vehicle remaining from the
second stage must be eliminated before the attitude control function begins. After the attitude control movement
is over, the spin of the vehicle, provided by the 300-gram
thrust jet nozzles, is begun again at three revolutions
per second.

The fourth stage has a polybutadien propellant motor
that yields 0.81 tons of thrust for 31.5 seconds. The payload weight was 8.89 kg.[2]

Improved performance of the Lambda is planned by in-
stalling thrust vector control systems in the lower stages,
for at this stage in development it represents a rather
sophisticated unguided rocket. It has been estimated that
fin-stabilized rockets or rockets employing spin technique

FIGURE D.1

Lambda 4S Rocket

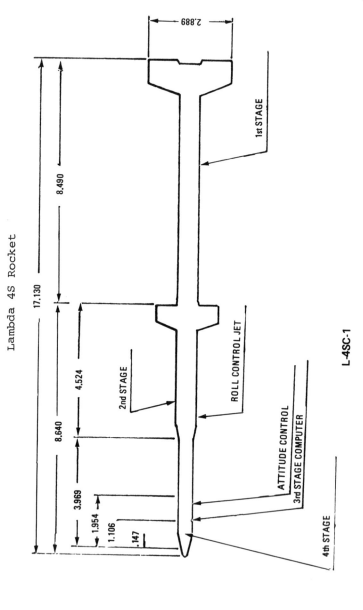

Source: Nihon Roketto Kaihatsu Kyogikai Kaiho, February 1972, p. 31.

for stabilization have a gross CEP of 30 miles. The horizontal firing range of this rocket has been set at approximately 1,000 miles, and as range increases, the probability for greater CEP error increases.[3] Rockets with a total weight of 20,000 pounds of solid propellant can normally carry a 1,000-pound warhead over a 500-mile horizontal range;[4] however, lacking an inertial guidance system and thrust vector controls and being quite susceptible to ground winds--even though the compensation mechanism is sophisticated--the Lambda would not meet the requirements for an effective nuclear delivery system.

THE M-4S

The M-4S rocket (Figure D.a) was the natural outgrowth of the Lambda rocket and uses the latter rocket's technology as its base. It has been used as the standard rocket in the Japanese family of solid propellant boosters for satellites in the weight range of from 60 to 90 kg.[5] Its total weight, approximately 87,600 pounds, puts it in the category of solid-propellant rockets with a 5,000-nm range potential carrying a 1,000-pound warhead.[6]

The overall length of the M-4S or Mu is 23.567 meters. It consists of four stages with four solid motors and eight strap-on boosters. The strap-on boosters deliver an average of approximately 10 tons of thrust each while the main, first-stage, motor (M-10) is rated at an average of 75 tons over a 61-second burn (see Figure D.3).

The second-stage engine (M-20) produces an average thrust of 29.1 tons over an expected burn time of 66 seconds. There are six spin motors that are located in the second and third stage coupling section, which provide a spin rate of 2.6 revolutions per second.

The third-stage motor (M-30) is rated at an average thrust of 13.1 tons over 42 seconds. Four retrofire motors provide safe separation distance between the third and fourth stages. The assorted devices providing attitude control are contained in an aluminum alloy cylinder in the third stage.

Stability for the first stage is provided by the four fins, as in the Lambda; the second stage utilizes a combination of flares and spin. The third stage uses the spin accumulated from the second stage, but two seconds after separation, the third stage despin motors are activated to negate existing spin. At zero spin, the attitude mechanism begins to function. Attitude control is provided

FIGURE D.2

M-4S Rocket

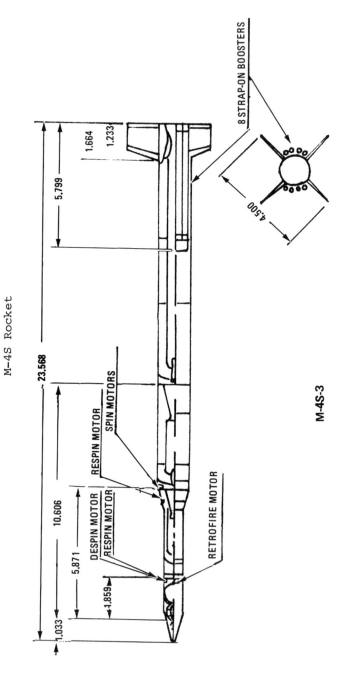

Source: Nihon Roketto Kaihatsu Kyogikai Kaiho, February 1972, p. 19.

FIGURE D.3

Standard Flight Path of M-4S

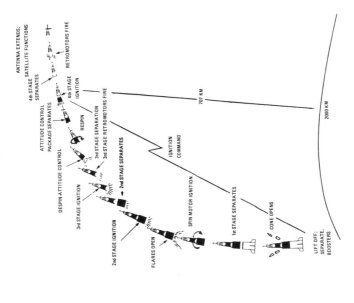

Source: Nihon Roketto Kaihatsu Kyogikai Kaiho, July 1972, p. 24.

by a reference unit plus an electronics package and hydro-gen-peroxide engines.

The reference unit has a two-degree free gyro (note: only one two-degree free gyro), which is mounted on a spin table, which is rotated in the opposite direction of the spin of the vehicle. This maintains the gyro in a station-ary position with respect to inertial space.[7] This device operates after the third-stage motor is jettisoned and de-spinning of the vehicle is accomplished. Once the axis of the rocket has been directed onto a horizontal course at the top of the flight path determined by the gyro (preset), the attitude of the vehicle is corrected and spin is again imparted. At the apex of the flight path, the third and fourth stages separate, and the fourth-stage spherical motor adds the additional velocity necessary to achieve orbital velocity.[8]

The fourth stage houses an M-40 motor, with an average thrust of 2.6 tons for 39 seconds, instruments, and the satellite.[9] The satellite and the fourth stage motor are separated at burnout.

In the launch of M-4S-2, these systems worked to pro-vide control over pitch and yaw so that accuracy of 0.5 degrees was achieved.[10] The M-4S has been used success-fully on three occasions to place satellites in orbit, once in 1971 (Tansei) and twice in 1972 (Shinsei and Dempa). The latter two were scientific measurement satellites.[11] The first Mu carrying a satellite, M-4S-1 (September 1970), failed to achieve orbit when the fourth-stage motor did not ignite. (This event might have played a significant role in plans to revise the entire 1969 space program.) Failure was attributed to excessive centrifugal force pro-duced by a malfunctioning hydrogen-peroxide roll jet, which defeated a mechanical timer related to ignition se-quence.[12]

Mu, although it represents a launch vehicle weighing 43.8 tons with a total thrust at liftoff of 200 tons (in-cluding the eight strap-on boosters), still remains in the realm of "semi"-guided rockets with guidance systems per-mitting considerable errors and control at initial stages still dependent on fins rather than thrust vectoring or gimbaled motors. It has been said that this system could be developed to carry a 10,000-pound payload a distance of 25,000 miles;[13] indeed, with the guidance system permitting a rather broad range of accuracy, a 10,000-pound payload may be necessary to make it a militarily viable delivery vehicle. This point will be addressed at greater length later, but its serious nature was demonstrated in the launch of M-4S3 when upper-air westerly winds were so strong as to cause the actual flight path to be higher than the one scheduled even after the initial vertical launch angle was adjusted in anticipation. The changed attitude of the rocket resulted in the fourth-stage firing at a distance of 982 kilometers rather than 620 kilometers, as was planned; this produced an orbit for Tansei of one hour and 46 minutes vice two hours 18 minutes.[14] The deficiencies in control have not gone unnoticed by Japanese space experts,[15] and it is hoped that a secondary injection thrust vector control system currently being developed might help.

LS-C-5 ROCKET (SPACE DEVELOPMENT AGENCY)

The LS-C-5 rocket (Figure D.4) is a two-stage rocket used to develop a liquid fuel rocket to be used in satellite programs. The first stage is solid while the second stage is liquid. The liquid stage incorporates gimbal controls and gyro and gas jet devices for vehicle revolution. The average thrust developed by stages one and two respectively is 17.8 and 3.38 tons. Burn time is 8.3 and 40 seconds, and the total weight is 2.55 tons.

While the LS-C-5 is admittedly a smaller rocket than the Mu, it is significant in that gimbals are being used on the liquid stage. A rate gyro and an integral gyro have been installed on each of the three axes (note: three one-degree-of-freedom gyros), pitch, roll, and yaw. A programmer was used to alter pitch. It is planned to continue these experiments in LS-C-6, and to add a free gyro as a method to determine the attitude of the vehicle.[16]

THE JCR ROCKET (SPACE DEVELOPMENT AGENCY)

The JCR rocket (Figure D.5), now up to number eight,[17] is a polybutazene-composite-fueled two-stage rocket that was designed further to develop Japanese guidance control technology. The JCR-6 developed an average first-stage thrust of 11.4 tons, and second-stage thrust of 4.8 tons. Burn time was 18.8 and 15.4 seconds, respectively. Launch was accomplished at the Tanegashima Space Center in September 1971.

FIGURE D.4

LS-C-5 Rocket

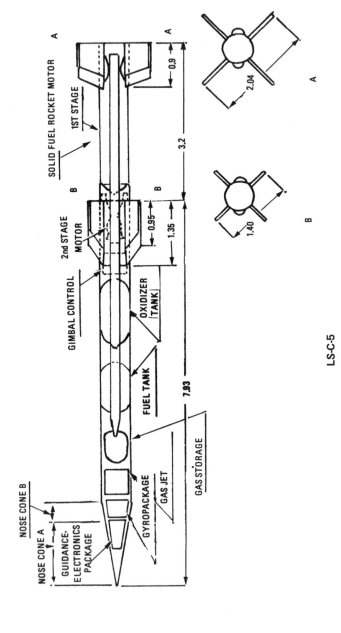

LS-C-5

Source: Nihon Roketto Kaihatsu Kyogikai Kaiho, February 1972, p. 37.

FIGURE D.5

JCR-6 Rocket

(MEASUREMENTS: METERS)

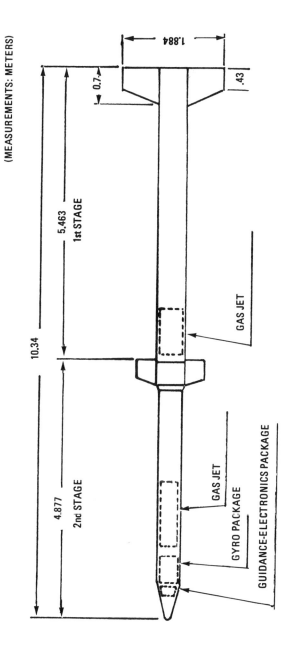

Source: Nihon Roketto Kaihatsu Kyogikai Kaiho, February 1972, p. 42.

Gyro instruments that were on board the vehicle in the second stage consisted of a pitch and yaw integral gyro, free gyro, timer programmer, and inverter. Gas jets were activated to examine roll-control characteristics and used to stop the spinning movement during the flight path of the second stage. The results indicated a steady control "within a precision of plus or minus 1.0 degree until immediately before splashdown 378 seconds after launch" and some 350 kilometers down range.*

The test indicated that gas-jet controls of the test vehicle were within anticipated performance criteria during inertial flight.[18]

THE N-ROCKET

The N rocket (Figure D.6) had been slated originally as an indigenous effort, but "technical" problems and growing user impatience caused the program to be drastically revised so that, at this writing, it has become, more and more, an item of technology transfer, principally from aerospace firms of the United States. Growing user impatience has not been overcome and has surfaced as recently as August 22, 1972, when the Japan Broadcasting Corporation (NHK) and the Nippon Telegraph and Telephone Public Corporation (Dendenkosha) floated a plan to request the United States to launch broadcasting and communications satellites for Japan in 1976.[19] This development came only four months after officials of the space program were chided in the House of Councilors, Committee for Audit, for the faltering execution of the N rocket development program.[20]

The N rocket as currently designed will have a total of three stages, a length of 33 meters, a maximum diameter of 2.4 meters, and a weight of 90 tons.[21] Development costs for this launch vehicle, capable of placing a 1,000-kilogram satellite in a circular orbit of 200 kilometers,[22] are estimated to be approximately 99 billion yen. These costs, however, include developmental costs for the experimental rockets to be used in the initial testing of engines, equipment, and so on, and 77 billion yen will be spent on support equipment.[23]

---

*It should be recalled at this point that a plus or minus one degree course over a thousand-mile trajectory can result in a gross error of a magnitude of plus or minus 60 nautical miles. Guidance is obviously still a problem.

FIGURE D.6

N Rocket

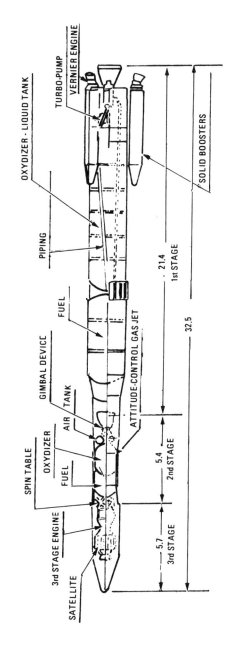

OXYDIZER - LIQUID TANK

TURBO-PUMP

VERNIER ENGINE

PIPING

SOLID BOOSTERS

FUEL

21.4

1st STAGE

32.5

GIMBAL DEVICE

AIR TANK

ATTITUDE-CONTROL GAS JET

SPIN TABLE

OXYDIZER

FUEL

5.4

2nd STAGE

3rd STAGE ENGINE

5.7

3rd STAGE

SATELLITE

Source: After Nihon Roketto Kaihatsu Kyogikai Kaiho, September 1972, pp. 13-14.

The first stage will be the U.S.-designed Thor Delta (1968 model) produced in Japan on a "partial knock-down" basis. This "partial knock-down" formula has been necessitated, as both McDonnell-Douglas Corporation (fuselage builder) and North American Rockwell Rocketdyne Division (engine builders) have ceased production of the 1968 model. Some parts and jigs will be available; others will have to be made in Japan.[24] It will differ from other past Japanese-produced rockets, as it is reported that it will be "fully guided."[25]

On August 21, 1972, the Space Development Corporation announced it was near contract-letting to Mitsubishi Heavy Industries for the production of two N rocket first-stage main frames for a sum of 3,070,800,000 yen. In this contract McDonnell-Douglas Corporation was seen as the technological exporter. Another contract for three N rocket first-stage engines was to be divided between Mitsubishi Heavy Industries and Ishikawajima-Harima Heavy Industries, totaling 2,337,600,000 yen. In this latter case, North American Rockwell will cooperate with Mitsubishi Heavy Industries.[26]

The total contract for two frames and three engines for the N rocket will amount to 5,408,400,000 yen. At 306 yen to the dollar (August 1972 rate), it will cost Japan $5,017,647 for one frame and $2,546,405 for one engine. The cost for a first-stage core of a Model 2914 Delta (the 1973 model) is $1.3 billion.[27] Thus Japan as a technology importer must pay $6,264,052 above the current "shelf" price for a first stage Delta. Obviously, the technology to be transferred must be needed to warrant such a price.

Latest information available to this researcher indicates that the second stage will be produced by Mitsubishi Heavy Industries (MHI) based on booster technology from McDonnell-Douglas and North American Rockwell to include parts, components, and other material.[28] The first second-stage rocket motor was built at MHI's Nagoya aircraft plant,[29] and it underwent burn tests, March 21-27, 1972, at MHI's Nagasaki shipyards.[30] Subsequent performance tests were conducted during July and August 1972 at the NASA White Sands Proving Grounds in the United States. The engine was fired satisfactorily under conditions simulating a 30-kilometer altitude. Four points were confirmed as a result of the summer tests:

1. The combustion situation of this rocket engine is stable, and its relative driving force is more than 285 seconds.

2.   Its driving force is 5.44 tons plus or
minus 0.11 tons.
3.   Its durability against the burning-off
of the engine is 4 minutes and 10 seconds.
4.   The performance of the cooling device is
satisfactory.[31]

For a while, confusion surrounded the choice of a
third stage for the N rocket. Competition existed between
a solid-fueled rocket, the TEM-364, produced by Thiokol
Chemical Corporation, and the SVM-4 of Aerojet General.
However, it was announced that the Thiokol engine was selected and that Nissan Motors would be charged with the
test and adaptation program.[32]
The major role in developing the avionics--guidance--
seems to be allocated to Mitsubishi Electric and Nippon
Electric.[33] It was reported that guidance and attitude
control systems, held by Honeywell, would be sought in
order to "pinpoint orbital position" for the N rocket.[34]
Tentative production schedules for the N rocket show
engine and airframe production were set to begin in August
or September 1972. Engine production would continue until
the end of March 1974 with air-frame production scheduled
to conclude slightly before March. Assembly would begin
in March 1974 and continue through to August 1974, at which
time adjustments would be made prior to final assembly and
project completion of the first N rocket in September 1975.
Construction of supporting launch facilities has already started at the space center on Kagoshima. By August
1972, approximately 2.74 million square meters of land had
been obtained for the launch area. Government allocations
of 700 million yen have been finalized, and work has begun
on the launch pad. Work was also slated over a year ago
for the range control center, block house, and generating
plant. Twenty-two kilometers north of the pad, a medium-
range radar has been constructed, and two telemetry sta-
tions will be built to support the launching. This construction is planned for completion by the end of 1973,
and all supporting facilities are scheduled for completion
in 1974.[35]

TEST ROCKET OR "Q" DASH (NATIONAL
SPACE DEVELOPMENT AGENCY)

The "test" rocket, or, as it is sometimes called, the
"Q" Dash rocket, is to be used in conjunction with final

257

development of the N rocket. The test vehicle, as currently planned, will have a total weight of 37.5 tons, a
length of 22.6 meters, a maximum diameter of 1.4 meters,
and a thrust of 153 tons (73.5 tons first stage and 79.5
auxiliary boosters). This rocket will consist of the M
rocket first stage and be specially configued to test the
flight characteristics of the upper-stage components of
the N rocket with an eye toward developing guidance and
control technology.[36]

SPACE PROGRAM ORGANIZATIONS

While the above data indicate the nature of the recent
operational vehicles, and, of course, the planned N rocket,
it would be worthwhile to consider the scope of the government organizations directing the space program and the
depth of the industrial and technical resources supporting
these numerous projects. A feeling for the future capability of this island nation in the field of space and the
attendant military ramifications can be gained by reviewing
the budget, government agencies, industrial, and manpower
support that exist today.

THE SPACE BUREAUCRACY

As pointed out earlier in this volume, Japan has several governmental and academic bodies involved in space
development. Primary to the overall thrust and direction
of this activity is the long-term planning accomplished
by the Space Activities Commission. This body, within
the Science and Technology Agency, is entrusted with the
overall direction of the space effort and advises the prime
minister of its recommendations. It has attempted to make
a clear-cut delineation of responsibility as to this development, and this position was reflected in the 1968 rule
that the Institute of Aeronautical and Space Technology at
the University of Tokyo (Todai) would be responsible for
the scientific studies in space while the National Space
Development Agency (NSDA) would be charged with the primary
responsibility of practical application. Some funds are
given directly to the Institute of Aeronautical and Space
Technology at Todai while others reach the institute after
being funneled through the Ministry of Education.

The National Space Development Agency, although a comparative newcomer to space research, has come to receive by

far the larger amount of space development funds since it was established on October 1, 1969.

Under the NSDA Law, which was promulgated in June 1969, the NSDA absorbed the former space research organization in the Science and Technology Agency as well as some of the satellite development work of the Postal Services Ministry. The utilization of space for peaceful purposes, and NSDA's role in this was underlined in Article 1 of the NSDA Law:

> The NSDA is established for the purpose of contributing to the promotion of the development and utilization of space, only for peaceful purposes, carrying out the development of artificial satellites and the development and launching of satellite-launcher rockets, as well as the comprehensive, planned, and therefore effective development of space.[37]

While the NSDA is dependent on government funds for its operations, it does have the administrative latitude to accept funds from nongovernmental bodies that use its satellite services such as broadcasting and communications organizations.

NSDA's main responsibilities are in the development of rockets capable of launching satellites, work on satellites themselves, ensuring adequate support facilities and equipment, and the launching of the total rocket/satellite packages. Other organizations that have a parochial interest in a specific satellite are expected to do the basic research considering their own particular requirements. Once development status is reached for the satellite, NSDA assumes the responsibility and moves ahead. In the case of scientific satellites, however, the Todai Institute of Space and Aeronautical Science has been given developmental authority due to its intimate relationship to space science.[38]

The Todai Institute also continues to have developmental authority in regard to rockets, but once reliability of a partial rocket is established, NSDA assumes control. Responsibility for tracking and calculation of satellite orbits has also been centralized in the NSDA.

BUDGETARY CONSIDERATIONS

A close examination of Table D.1--the fiscal 1972 (April 1, 1972-March 31, 1973) budget draft--will aid in

TABLE D.1

Budget for Japanese Space Development Program, Fiscal 1972

Agency Overview	Amount in Yen
Science and Technology Agency	
Funds related to space development	19,811,082,000
Other space-related funds	--
Education Ministry	
Funds related to space development	1,897,957,000
Other space-related funds	1,370,360,000
Ministry of International Trade and Industry	
Funds related to space development	98,000,000
Other space-related funds	--
Ministry of Transportation	
Funds related to space development	220,902,000
Other space-related funds	238,745,000
Ministry of Postal Services	
Funds related to space development	173,000,000
Other space-related funds	257,961,000
Ministry of Construction	
Funds related to space development	--
Other space-related funds	13,535,000
Total	
Funds related to space development	22,200,941,000
Other space-related funds	1,880,601,000
Grand total	24,081,542,000
Selected Program	
Institute of Aeronautical and Space Technology	
Liquid rocket engine research	56,730,000
Guidance sensor research	16,740,000
Solid rocket fuel combustion halt research	25,900,000
Spin combustion research	15,970,000
Rocket engine upper atmosphere test facility	400,000,000
Data control facility	67,900,000
Rental fee for computers and other machinery	329,086,000
Tsunoda Branch and other items	299,451,000
Total	1,213,389,000
Space Development Agency	
Rocket development funds	10,179,752,000
Satellite development funds	1,564,762,000
Rocket launch experiments as well as the Tanegashima Space Center	2,357,127,000
Satellite tracking funds	331,287,000
Experiment control center	1,739,839,000
Funds for other activities	1,123,133,000
General administrative funds	1,444,936,000
Total	19,811,082,000
Education Ministry	
Todai Institute	
No. 4 satellite, M4S for launch of satellite No. 2, M4SC1 for launch of satellite No. 3	1,031,473,000
M rocket development funds	866,484,000
Total	1,897,957,000

Source: Nihon Roketto Kaihatsu Kyogikai Kaiho, February 1972, pp. 2-9.

260

an appreciation of the principal thrust of the overall Japanese space development program and needs to be examined so as to better to understand the number of different institutes and laboratories engaged in space research and receiving government funds.

While the space and related budgets are sizable, and registered a 56 percent increase over that of the previous year, the visible amount spent on guidance was only 0.07 percent of the entire space budget and indicates no unusual stress in that particular area. It was estimated in 1966 that from $50 million to $100 million would be required to develop an inertial guidance system that would be acceptable for use in ballistic missile systems. Due to inflation and the relatively high development costs for onboard electronics in Japanese aerospace, that figure could now be placed close to $200 million.[39]

TECHNICAL PERSONNEL AVAILABLE

The Space Development Agency consisted of 446 persons in fiscal year 1972 (up 100 from the previous year) headed by five directors. The supporting structure consists of a General Affairs Division, Finance Division, System Planning Division, Project Control Division, and a Reliabilitation and Safety Control Division. The bulk of the scientific muscle is found in the following special groups: Rocket Design, Satellite Design, Ground Facilities Design, Guidance Control Design, Structural Development, Engine Development, On-Board Electronic Instrument Development, Ground Equipment Development, and Environment Testing.[40]

This organization has the overall responsibility to see that the space program is executed in as efficient a manner as possible. This program, which has already seen the successful completion of two scientific satellite missions, is shown in Tables D.2 and D.3.

It is clear from the above that a work force of approximately 450 scientists and technicians could not possibly propel the Japanese space program at its current speed without significant industrial support. In fact, it has been stated that in a modern industrial environment, such as Japan, a skilled work force of approximately 10,000 workers, including 2,500 engineers would be necessary for the development and production of a 500-mile ballistic missile.[41]

To judge better the depth and indigenous strength of the Japanese space program, a brief examination of the sup-

TABLE D.2

Proposed Satellite Program

Satellite	Mission	Weight (kg)	Altitude (km)	Inclination Angle	Orbit Type	Launching Year	Launching Rocket
Engineering Test Satellite-1 (ETS-1)	Rocket-launching technology, satellite tracking and control technology, extension of antennas	85	1,000	30°	Circular	1975	N
Ionosphere Sounding Satellite (ISS)	Observation of world-wide distribution of critical frequencies and so on	125	1,000	70°	Circular	1975	N
Engineering Test Satellite-2 (ETS-11)	Stationary satellite-launching technology, attitude control of stationary satellite, and other functions	130	36,000	0°	30°	Synchronous	1976	N
Experimental Communication Satellite (ECS)	Space communications tests, improvement of satellite function	130	36,000	0°	Geostationary	1977	N

Source: H. Shima, "Japan in Space," Nature, November 24, 1972, p. 216. Reprinted by permission.

TABLE D.3

Future Application Satellites

Satellite	Mission	Weight (kg)	Orbit	Launching Year
Meteorological satellite	Continuous meteorological observation from space; collection and dissemination of meteorological data	250–300	Stationary	Projected 1976
Communications satellite	Communication with moving objects and isolated islands; emergency communication	250–300	Stationary	Requested 1976
Television relay satellite	Domestic television relay to Asian countries including Japan	300–500	Stationary	1976
Navigation satellite	Navigational aid, navigation control, communication and other services for airplanes and ships	250–350	Stationary synchronous	--
Geodesic satellite	Establishment of geodesic reference points	60–80	Circular orbit of 1,000 km	--
Earth resources satellite	Technology for earth resources survey by satellites and its application	300–500	Polar orbit	--

Source: H. Shima, "Japan in Space," Nature, November 24, 1972, p. 216. Reprinted by permission.

263

porting rocket industrial base would be useful. According
to a March 1969 report, there were 2,280 technical personnel concerned with rockets in Japan. Of these, 1,663 were
interested exclusively in rocketry, while the remainder
shared their interests probably in some other related aerospace field. A total of 43.9 percent were held to be primarily engaged in guidance, tracking communications and
measurement, and so on, with 21.8 percent devoted to air-
frame work.[42]

If this industrial base is added to the 455 personnel
of the Space Development Agency (who admittedly are not
all scientists) plus the staff or personnel available to
the Todai Institute of Space and Aeronautical Science num-
bering approximately 500;* a figure is developed that com-
prises a capable core of over 3,000. Possibly they are
not all engineers, but their achievements to date have indicated a degree of proficiency.

Twenty-one thousand individuals were employed in Japan's aircraft industry in 1964, and its sales at that
time represented a figure of $202 million.[43] By 1971,
sales, including production and repair, had reached $304
million,[44] or an increase of 50 percent. Trained manpower,
by the current time frame, certainly exceeds the "marginal"
requirement figure, at least by a factor of two.

The Japanese aerospace industry could list six firms
(A) (in 1968) that were capable of research, trail manufacture, and production of rockets (including air-to-air,
surface-to-surface, surface-to-air missiles and so on);
eight companies (B) had experience with rocket bodies,
parts and accessories; 10 firms (C) that produced on-board
electronics, electric, optical equipment, and warheads;
seven enterprises (D) that had manufactured propellants;
and 15 companies (E) that produced support equipment. In

---

*Some 10 universities, four research institutes, and
approximately 60 manufacturing companies participate in the
Institute of Space and Aeronautical Science program. The
10 universities are University of Tokyo, Tohoku University,
Nagoya University, Kyoto University, Osaka University,
Kyushu University, Kobe University, Rikkyo University, Tokai
University, and Osaka City University. Japan National Re-
port on Space Research, April 1970, submitted to the 13th
Plenary Meeting of the ICUS Commission on Space Research;
and Aerospace International, January-February 1973, p. 19.

all, 23 firms have technical personnel related to rockets and rocket production (F).*

The problem of supplying the needed space researchers for both industry and government was addressed directly in the Space Development Plan of 1970. In Chapter 5, "Policies Necessary for Promotion of Space Development," the Space Activities Commission called for expansion of specialist training in the universities and, uniquely, suggested the retraining of personnel with research and technical experience to meet the express needs of space development.[45]

In December 1972, Hanzo Omi underlined one of the continuing problems regarding the trained manpower reserve in Japan, that of the so-called brain drain. Tracing the

---

*The companies, involved by group, are as follows:

Group A. Hitachi Ltd., Kawasaki Heavy Industries, Nissan Motors, Nihon Electric, Mitsubishi Heavy Industries, Mitsubishi Electric.

Group B. Ishikawajima-Harima Industries, Ltd., Kawasaki Heavy Industries, Sumitomo Precision, Tokyo Instruments Manufacturing, Nissan Motors, Nihon Aircraft, Hitachi, Ltd., Mitsubishi Heavy Industries.

Group C. Ishikawajima-Harima Industries, Ltd., Showa Kaseihin, Nissan Motors, Japan Aviotronics, Nihon Electric, Hitachi, Ltd., Fujitsu, Mitsubishi Heavy Industries, Ltd., Mitsubishi Electric, Tokyo-Shibaura Electric (Toshiba).

Group D. Asahi Kasei Kogyo, Showa Kaseihin, Daiseru, Teikoku Kakohin Seizo, Nissan Motors, Japan Oil and Fat, Mitsubishi Heavy Industries.

Group E. Ishikawajima-Harima Industries, Kawasaki Heavy Industries, Jinko Electric Equipment, Tokyo-Shibaura Electric (Toshiba), Toyo Communications Equipment, NAC, Nissan Motors, Japan Aviotronics, Japan Steel Works, Nihon Electric, Nihon Musen, Hitachi, Ltd., Fujitsu, Mitsubishi Heavy Industries, Mitsubishi Electric.

Group F. Ishikawajima-Harima Industries, Oki Electric, Kawasaki Heavy Industries, Showa Kaseihin, Jinko Electric Equipment, Sumitomo Precision, Daiseru (Daicel Ltd.), Tokyo Instruments Manufacturing, Tokyo Aviation Instruments, Toyo Communications Equipment, NAC, Nissan Motors, Japan Aviotronics, Japan Steel Works, Nihon Electric, Nihon Aircraft, Nihon Musen, Japan Oil and Fat, Hitachi, Ltd., Fujitsu, Mitsubishi Heavy Industries, Mitsubishi Electric, Nissho-Iwai. (Nihon Roketto Kaihatsu Kyogikai Kaiho, August 1970, pp. 20-49.)

TABLE D.4

Scientists to United States from Four Developed States

Country	1945	1957	1965	1966	1967
England	515	1,183	1,094	1,443	2,345
Germany	548	517	452	432	558
France	113	119	133	139	188
Japan	21	43	35	107	158

Source: Journal of the Institute of Electronics and Communication Engineers of Japan, December 1972, p. 1571.

comparative flow of scientists to the United States from England, Germany, France, and Japan over the years from 1956 to 1967, Omi noted (see Table D.4) that the real problem could be seen in the rate of scientist emigrants versus immigrants. While the number of English and French scientists going to the United States was high, the overall flow was on a one-for-one exchange basis. However, in the case of Japan the rate is a very unfavorable, and alarming, ten-to-one. Ten Japanese scientists go to the United States for every U.S. scientist entering Japan. Omi called for retention of this scientific power, as without it, "we will be confronted by a danger to the prosperity of Japan."[46]

Overall, the number of researchers available to Japan was dealt with in a more optimistic manner by Hachihiro Nakagawa in a lecture on future planning for space.[47] He pointed out that the total researchers, including technicians in Japan numbered 160,000. This number was compared rather unfavorably with the U.S. number of 500,000, but favorably against Europe's 180,000. Nakagawa also made the important observation that once the nation begins, in earnest, its space program, a "large number of researchers from foreign countries would flow in."

In this 1971 address, it was also stated, in a rather self-deprecating manner, that Japan was 15 years behind the United States in space development. This is a rather revealing comment, actually, if it is recalled that 1956 was the year just prior to the United States beginning its testing of the Atlas and Thor military missiles.[48]

NOTES

1. Tamiya Nomura, "The Lambda 4S Rocket," in Proceedings of the Ninth International Symposium on Space Technology and Science (Tokyo: Agne Publishing, 1972), p. 564.

2. Ibid., p. 565.

3. Browne and Shaw Research Corp., The Diffusion of Combat Aircraft, Missiles, and Their Supporting Technologies (Waltham, Mass.: Browne and Shaw, 1966), p. B-35.

4. Ibid., p. B-27.

5. D. Mori, "The Project of M-4S," in Proceedings of the Ninth International Symposium on Space Technology and Science (Tokyo: Agne Publishing, 1972), p. 569.

6. Browne and Shaw, op. cit., p. B-27.

7. Mori, op. cit., p. 569.

8. Ibid.

9. Nihon Roketto Kaihatsu Kyogikai Kaiho, July 1972, pp. 5-28.

10. Mori, op. cit., p. 572.

11. H. Shina, "Japan in Space," Nature, November 24, 1972, p. 216.

12. Mori, op. cit., p. 571.

13. Stockholm International Peace Research Institute, The SIPRI Yearbook (Stockholm: SIPRI, 1972), p. 323.

14. Flight International, October 14, 1971, pp. 616-17.

15. See especially, N. Takagi, T. Nomura, and S. Saito, "Developmental Research on Space Electronics at University of Tokyo," Electronics and Communication in Japan, June 1967, pp. 162-63.

16. Ibid.

17. Asahi Evening News, February 5, 1973.

18. Ibid.

19. Ibid., August 22, 1972.

20. Nihon Roketto Kaihatsu Kyogikai Kaiho, May 15, 1972.

21. "Initial Movement in N Rocket Development: Equipment Orders for Each Section in April," Rocket News, March 1972, p. 15.

22. Japan Press Exchange Aviation Weekly, January 18, 1971, pp. 11-12.

23. Nihon Roketto Kaihatsu Kyogikai Kaiho, November 1970, p. 23.

24. Rocket News, March 1972, p. 15.

25. Asahi Evening News, August 22, 1972.

26. Nihon Roketto Kaihatsu Kyogikai Kaiho, September 1972, pp. 11-14.

27. W. R. Schindler, C. R. Gunn, "The Delta Launch Vehicle for Scientific and Application Satellites," Pro-

ceedings of the Ninth International Symposium on Space Technology and Science (Tokyo: Agne Publishing, 1972), p. 597.

28. Flight International, March 9, 1972, p. 366.

29. Yasuhiro Kuroda, Nihon Koku Uchu Gakkaishi (Tokyo: National Space Development Agency, 1972), pp. 57-60.

30. Nihon Roketto Kaihatsu Kyogikai Kaiho, March 1972.

31. Asahi, October 18, 1972, U.S. Embassy translation.

32. Japan's Aerospace Newsletter, January 26, 1972, p. 2.

33. JPE Aviation Report Weekly, January 18, 1971, pp. 11-12.

34. Flight International, October 14, 1971, pp. 616-17.

35. Rocket News, March 1972, pp. 15-16; and Kyodo, September 4, 1972. It should be noted that the Japan Rocket Development Council in its development plan for the fiscal years 1974 to 1987 proposed that during this time frame large rockets should be developed. The rockets mentioned for special attention were the "N Remodelled I, N Remodelled II, M-X and O (tentative name) rockets." (Nikkan Kogyo, July 30, 1974, U.S. Embassy translation.)

36. Kuroda, op. cit., pp. 59-60; and Wing International, February 1971, pp. 4-5.

37. Nihon Koku Uchu Gakkaishi, pp. 57-60.

38. Ibid.

39. Browne and Shaw, op. cit., p. B-34.

40. Nihon Roketto Kaihatsu Kyogikai Kaiho, June 1972, p. 7.

41. Browne and Shaw, op. cit., p. 9.

42. Nihon Roketto Kaihatsu Kyogikai Kaiho, August 1970, pp. 20-49. The 43.9 percent rose to 54.6 percent in 1972.

43. G. R. Hall and R. E. Johnson, Aircraft Co-Production and Procurement Strategy (Santa Monica, Calif.: RAND Corporation, 1967), p. 61n.

44. Nihon Keizai, March 1, 1972, U.S. Embassy translation.

45. Nihon Roketto Kaihatsu Kyogikai Kaiho, November 1970.

46. Hanzo Omi, Journal of the Institute of Electronics and Communications Engineers of Japan, December 1972, p. 1572.

47. Hachihiro Nakagawa, "The Purpose and Significance of Drawing up Future Plans," Rocket News, September 1971, pp. 2-10.

48. George H. Quester, Nuclear Diplomacy (New York: Dunellen Corporation, 1970), p. 150.

PUBLIC DOCUMENTS

Japan

Anzenhosho Chosa Kai. <u>Nihon no Anzenhosho--1970 nen e no
Tembo</u>. Tokyo: Asagumo Shimbunsha, 1968.

"The Atomic Energy Basic Law." December 19, 1955. Xerox
copy.

Defense Agency. "Address by Esaki Masumi, Minister of
State, Director-General of the Defense Agency." Tokyo:
Defense Agency, June 1972.

_____. <u>Debates in the Diet, January-May 1970</u>. Tokyo:
Defense Agency, 1970.

_____. <u>Defense of Japan, 1970</u>. Tokyo: Defense Agency,
circa 1970.

_____. "International Environment and Defense of Japan
in the 1970's" (text of a speech delivered at the
Harvard Club of Japan by Nakasone Yasuhiro). Tokyo:
Defense Agency, June 30, 1970.

_____. <u>Kokkai Sanyo Shiryo</u> (Reference Material for
Diet Consultants). A comprehensive interpretation of
the basic policies as related to national defense.
Tokyo: Defense Agency, July 1972.

_____. <u>Nihon no Boei</u> (Defense of Japan). Tokyo: De-
fense Agency, October 1970.

_____. <u>Statistical Data on National Defense and Eco-
nomics</u>. Tokyo: Defense Agency, March 1972. (In
Japanese.)

_____, National Defense College. <u>Kakuto no Anposeisaku</u>.
Vols. 1 and 2. Tokyo: National Defense College, 1973.

Ministry of Finance. <u>The Budget in Brief</u>. Tokyo: Budget
Bureau, 1971 and 1972.

Ministry of Foreign Affairs. <u>Background of SALT</u>. Tokyo:
Arms Limitation Office, June 1972. (In Japanese.)

_____. <u>Kakuheiki Kakusan no Senzai Ryoku</u>. Tokyo: Arms
Limitation Office, July 1972.

_____. <u>The Northern Territorial Issue</u>. Tokyo: Public
Information Bureau, Ministry of Foreign Affairs, 1968.

_____. "Statement by Ambassador Nisibori on Comprehen-
sive Nuclear Test Ban at the Conference of the Committee on Disarmament on March 28, 1972." Tokyo: Foreign Office, 1972.

_____. "Statement by Ambassador Nisibori on Disarmament
at the Conference of the Committee on Disarmament on
22nd June, 1972." Tokyo: Foreign Office, 1972.

_____. "Statement by Ambassador Nisibori to Introduce
a Joint Working Paper on Measures to Improve Tripartite Co-operation among Canada, Sweden and Japan in
the Detection, Location and Identification of Underground Nuclear Explosions by Seismological Means."
Tokyo: Foreign Office, 1972.

_____. "Statement by Ambassador Tanaka at the First
Committee of the U.N. General Assembly on the Question
of Disarmament." Tokyo: Foreign Office, 1971.

_____. "Statement by Mr. M. Nisibori on Disarmament
at the Conference of the Committee on Disarmament."
Tokyo: Foreign Office, 1972.

_____. "Statement of Ambassador Tanaka on the Compre-
hensive Prohibition of Nuclear Weapon Tests at the
Meeting of the CCD on 17 August 1971." Tokyo: Foreign Office, 1971.

_____. "Statement of Ambassador Tanaka on the General
Problems of Disarmament at the Meeting of the CCD on
July 6, 1971." Tokyo: Foreign Office, 1971.

Science and Technology Agency. <u>Atomic Energy in Japan</u>.
Tokyo: Atomic Energy Bureau, Science and Technology
Agency, 1971.

United Nations

Proceedings of the Second United Nations International Conference on the Peaceful Uses of Atomic Energy. Gene-
va: United Nations, 1958.

Proceedings of the Third International Conference on the
Peaceful Uses of Atomic Energy. New York: United
Nations, 1965.

Secretariat. Effects of the Possible Use of Nuclear Wea-
pons and the Security and Economic Implications for
States of the Acquisition and Further Development of
These Weapons. New York: United Nations, 1968.

United States

Air Force, Air University. Fundamentals of Aerospace
Weapon Systems. Washington, D.C.: Government Printing Office, circa 1960.

Arms Control and Disarmament Agency. "Explanatory Remarks
About the Draft Non-Proliferation Treaty." Washington, D.C.: Government Printing Office, 1968.

Atomic Energy Commission. The Effects of Nuclear Weapons.
Washington, D.C.: Government Printing Office, 1962.

_____, news release. "International Implications of
the Nuclear Fuel Cycle." Washington, D.C.: Government Printing Office, 1972.

Congress, House of Representatives. Hearings before the
Subcommittee on Asian and Pacific Affairs of the Committee on Foreign Affairs. United States-China Relations: A Strategy for the Future, 91st Cong., 2d
sess. Washington, D.C.: Government Printing Office,
1970.

Congress, Joint Economic Committee. People's Republic of
China: An Economic Assessment, a Compendium of Papers,
92d Cong., 2d sess. Washington, D.C.: Government
Printing Office, May 1972.

Congress, Senate, Committee on Foreign Relations, Hearings
on the Treaty on the Nonproliferation of Nuclear Wea-

pons, 90th Cong., 1st sess. Washington, D.C.: Government Printing Office, 1969.

Congress, Senate, Hearings before the Subcommittee on Arms Control, International Law and Organization of the Committee of Foreign Relations. ABM, MIRV, SALT, and the Nuclear Arms Race, 91st Cong., 2d sess. Washington, D.C.: Government Printing Office, 1970.

Congress, Senate, Hearings of the Subcommittee on United States Security Agreements and Commitments Abroad of the Committee on Foreign Relations. Japan and Okinawa, 91st Cong., 2d sess., Part 5. Washington, D.C.: Government Printing Office, 1970.

Department of Defense. DOD Annual Report, FY 1974, Secretary of Defense Elliot Richardson. Washington, D.C.: Government Printing Office, 1973.

_____. National Security of Realistic Deterrence, Secretary of Defense Melvin R. Laird's Annual Defense Department Report FY 1973. Washington, D.C.: Government Printing Office, 1972.

Department of State. Department of State Bulletin. Washington, D.C.: Government Printing Office, 1951-73.

_____. Issues in United States Foreign Policy, Profile of Mainland China. Washington, D.C.: Government Printing Office, 1969.

_____. United States Foreign Policy, 1971. Washington, D.C.: Government Printing Office, 1972.

_____. U.S. Treaties and Other International Acts Series. Washington, D.C.: Government Printing Office.

President Nixon. U.S. Foreign Policy for the 1970's: A New Strategy for Peace. Washington, D.C.: Government Printing Office, 1970.

BOOKS

Agne Publishing. Proceedings of the Seventh International Symposium on Space Technology and Science. Tokyo: Agne Publishing, 1968.

_____. Proceedings of the Ninth International Sympo-
sium on Space Technology and Science. Tokyo: Agne
Publishing, 1972.

Asahi Shimbun Sha. Nihon to America. Tokyo: Asahi Shimbun Sha, 1971.

Beaton, Leonard, and John Maddox. The Spread of Nuclear
Weapons. New York: Praeger Publishers, 1967.

Borton, Hugh. Japan's Modern Century. New York: Ronald
Press Company, 1970.

Browne and Shaw Research Corp. The Diffusion of Combat
Aircraft, Missiles, and Their Supporting Technologies.
Waltham, Mass.: Browne and Shaw, 1966.

Chai, Winberg. The Foreign Relations of the People's Republic of China. New York: Capricorn Books, 1972.

Clemens, Walter C., Jr. The Arms Race and Sino-Soviet Relations. Stanford, Calif.: The Hoover Institution
on War, Revolution and Peace, 1968.

Cole, Allan B., George O. Totten, and Cecil H. Uyehara.
Socialist Parties in Post War Japan. New Haven,
Conn.: Yale University Press, 1966.

Couch, William T., ed.-in-chief. Collier's Encyclopedia,
1960 ed. New York: P. F. Collier and Son, 1960.

Emme, Eugene M., ed. The History of Rocket Technology.
Detroit: Wayne State University Press, 1964.

Emmerson, John K. Arms, Yen and Power: The Japanese Dilemma. Tokyo: Charles E. Tuttle, 1972.

Fukui Haruhiro. Party in Power. Los Angeles: University
of California Press, 1970.

Fullard, Harold, ed. China in Maps. London: George
Philip and Son, 1968.

Hall, G. R., and R. E. Johnson. Aircraft Co-Production
and Procurement Strategy. Santa Monica, Calif.:
RAND Corporation, 1967.

_____. Transfers of United States Aerospace Technology to Japan. Santa Monica, Calif.: The RAND Corporation, 1968.

Hashimoto Seinosuke. Nihon no Genshiryoku, 15 nen no Ayumi. Tokyo: Nipon Genshiryoku Sangyo Kaigi, 1971.

Hellmann, Donald C. Japanese Domestic Politics and Foreign Policy. Berkeley: University of California Press, 1969.

Herrick, John W. Rocket Encyclopedia Illustrated. Los Angeles, Calif.: Aero Publishers, 1959.

Hinton, Harold C. Communist China in World Politics. Boston: Houghton Mifflin, 1966.

Hoagland, John H. World Combat Aircraft Inventories and Production: 1970-1975. Cambridge, Mass.: Massachusetts Institute of Technology, 1970.

Hobbs, Marvin. Basics of Missile Guidance and Space Techniques. New York: J. F. Rider, 1959.

Holst, Johan Jorgen. Security, Order, and the Bomb. Oslo: Universitetsforlaget, 1972.

Holsti, K. J. International Policies. Englewood Cliffs, N.J.: Prentice-Hall, 1967.

International Institute for Strategic Studies. The Military Balance 1971-1972. London: International Institute for Strategic Studies, 1971.

_____. Strategic Survey, 1971. London: International Institute for Strategic Studies, 1971.

Jijimondai Kenkyujo. Gensuikyo. Tokyo: Jijimondai Kenkyujo, 1961.

Kaihara Osamu. Nihon Retto Shubitairon. Tokyo: Asagumo Sha, 1972.

Kuenne, Robert E. The Polaris Missile Strike. Columbus: Ohio State University Press, 1966.

Kuryman, Dan. Kishi and Japan. New York: Ivan Obolensky, 1960.

Langer, Paul F. Japanese National Security Policy-Domes-
     tic Determinants. Santa Monica, Calif.: RAND Corpor-
     ation, 1972.

Leondes, Cornelius T. Guidance and Control of Aerospace
     Vehicles. New York: McGraw-Hill, 1963.

Li, Choh-Ming. Industrial Development in Communist China.
     New York: Praeger Publishers, 1964.

Mainichi Shimbun Sha. Japan Almanac, 1972. Tokyo: Maini-
     chi Newspapers, 1972.

_____. Jimintoseiken no Anzenhosho. Tokyo: Mainichi
     Shimbun Sha, 1969.

_____. "Komeitoseiken" ka no Anzenhosho. Tokyo: Maini-
     chi Shimbun Sha, 1969.

_____. "Minshatoseiken" ka no Anzenhosho. Tokyo:
     Mainichi Shimbun Sha, 1969.

_____. "Shakaitoseiken" ka no Anzenhosho. Tokyo:
     Mainichi Shimbun Sha, 1969.

McNamara, Robert S. "A 'Light' ABM System," Readings from
     Scientific American. San Francisco: W. H. Freeman
     and Company, 1969.

Quester, George H. Nuclear Diplomacy. New York: Dunellen
     Corporation, Inc., 1970.

Reischauer, Edwin O. Japan: The Story of a Nation. New
     York: Alfred A. Knopf, 1970.

Sapolsky, Harvey M. The Polaris System Development, Bu-
     reaucratic and Programmatic Success in Government.
     Cambridge, Mass.: Harvard University Press, 1972.

Scalapino, Robert A. Asia and the Major Powers. Stanford,
     Calif." Hoover Institution on War, Revolution and
     Peace, 1972.

_____. The Japanese Communist Movement: 1920-1965.
     Santa Monica, Calif.: RAND Corporation, 1966.

Stockholm International Peace Research Institute. _The Near-Nuclear Countries and the NPT_. New York: Humanities Press, 1972.

_____. _SIPRI Yearbook, 1972_. New York: Humanities Press, 1972.

Stockwin, J. A. A. _The Japanese Socialist Party and Neutralism_. Carlton, Victoria: Melbourne University Press, 1968.

Thayer, Nathaniel B. _How the Conservatives Rule Japan_. Princeton, N.J.: Princeton University Press, 1969.

United Nations Association of the United States. _Safeguarding the Atom_. New York: The Association, 1972.

Weinstein, Martin E. _Japan's Postwar Defense Policy, 1947-1968_. New York: Columbia University Press, 1971.

Williams, Shelton L. _Nuclear Nonproliferation in International Policies: The Japanese Case_. Denver: University of Denver, 1972.

Winter, Sidney G. _Economic Viability after Thermonuclear War: The Limits of Feasible Production_. Santa Monica, Calif.: RAND Corporation, September 1963.

World Policy Research Institute. _Japan's Defense and Security_. Tokyo: World Policy Research Institute, 1968.

ARTICLES, PAPERS, AND REPORTS

Auer, James E. _The Postwar Sea Forces of Maritime Japan 1945-1971_. Medford, Mass.: Ph.D. Dissertation, Fletcher School of Law and Diplomacy, 1971.

Beer, Lawrence W. "Japan 1969: 'My Homeism' and Political Struggle." _Asian Survey_, January 1970.

Brendle, Thomas Marle. "Japan's Ground Self-Defense Force, 1950-1970: Problems Encountered in Developing and Managing an All Volunteer Army." Medford, Mass.: Ph.D. Dissertation, Fletcher School of Law and Diplomacy, 1971.

Brzezinski, Zbigniew. "Japan's Global Engagement." Foreign Affairs, January 1972.

Buck, James H. "Japanese Defense Options for the 1970's."
Asian Survey, October 1970.

Bungcishunju Ltd. "Nihonkyosanto wa Nani o Kangaeteiru
ka." Bungeishunju, March 1973.

Cole, Allan B., et al. Japanese Opinion Polls with Socio-
Political Significance 1947-1967. Medford, Mass.:
Fletcher School of Law and Diplomacy, undated.

Emmerson, John K. "Japan: Eye on 1970." Foreign Affairs,
January 1969.

Endicott, John E. Japan's Nuclear Option. Medford, Mass.:
Unpublished MALD Thesis, Fletcher School of Law and
Diplomacy, 1972 and 1973.

Garwin, Richard L. "Antisubmarine Warfare and National
Security." Scientific American, July 1972.

Gelber, Harry G. Nuclear Weapons and Chinese Policy. Pre-
pared for the Conference on U.S.-Soviet Strategic
Balance and Nuclear Multipolarity, Fletcher School of
Law and Diplomacy, May 3-5, 1973.

George, T. K. "Asian Regionalism and India's Early Initiatives: The Two Asian Conferences." India Quarterly, July-September 1971.

Gillinsky, Victor. Fast Breeder Reactors and the Spread
of Plutonium. Santa Monica, Calif.: RAND Corporation, 1967.

_____. Where Is Nuclear Reactor Technology Taking Us?
Santa Monica, Calif.: RAND Corporation, 1967.

_____, and Paul Langer. The Japanese Civilian Nuclear
Program. Santa Monica, Calif.: RAND Corporation,
1967.

Gregory, Gene. "The Japanese Model: Prospects for the
Future." Asia Quarterly, no. 4 (1971).

Gupta, Bhabani Sen. How Close Is India to the Bomb? Prepared for the Conference on U.S.-Soviet Strategic

Balance and Nuclear Multipolarity, Fletcher School of
Law and Diplomacy, May 3-5, 1973.

Hagi, Jiro. "Japan's Potential for Building Nuclear Weapons." Medford, Mass.: Fletcher School of Law and
Diplomacy, unpublished paper, 1970.

Harootunian, Harry D. "Commentary on Nationalism in Japan;
Nationalism as Intellectual History." Journal of
Asian Studies, November 1971.

Hoag, Malcolm. One American Perspective on Nuclear Guarantees, Proliferation, and Related Alliance Diplomacy.
Santa Monica, Calif.: RAND Corporation, 1971.

Hoffmann, Stanley. "Weighing the Balance of Power." Foreign Affairs, July 1972.

Honma Nagayo. "Something Which Saves America." Jiyu,
July 1971.

Hoover Institution on War, Revolution and Peace. Communist
China and Arms Control 1967-1976. Stanford, Calif.:
The Hoover Institution, 1968.

Horikoshi Jiro. "F-104J Production Program as Viewed from
the Japanese Standpoint." AIAA Paper #65-804.

Hsieh, Alice Langley. Communist China's Military Policies
and Nuclear Strategy. Santa Monica, Calif.: RAND
Corporation, 1967.

Hughes, Michael Bryant. Japan's Air Power Options: The
Employment of Military Aviation in the Post-War Era.
Medford, Mass.: Ph.D. Dissertation, Fletcher School
of Law and Diplomacy, 1972.

Imai Ryukichi. "Changing Nuclear and Disarmament Concepts."
Jiyu, July 1972.

_____. "Japan and the World of SALT." Bulletin of
Atomic Scientists, December 1971.

_____. "The Non-Proliferation Treaty and Japan." Bul-
letin of the Atomic Scientists, May 1969.

_____. "Nuclear Safeguards." Adelphi Papers No. 86. London: International Institute for Strategic Studies, 1972.

_____. "The World after the Nuclear Defense Treaty." Kokubo, May 1970.

Ito Kobun. "Japan's Security in the 1970's." Asian Survey, December 1970.

Iwashima Hisao. Japan's Defense Dilemma-Principles and Realities. Tokyo: National Defense College, March 1973.

_____. Trends of Peace Research and Military Studies in Japan. Tokyo: National Defense College, 1972.

Johnson, Chalmers. "How China and Japan See Each Other." Foreign Affairs, July 1972.

Johnson, U. Alexis. "The Role of Japan and the Future of American Relations with the Far East." Annals of the American Academy of Political and Social Science, July 1970.

Kaihara Osamu. "The Meaning of Self Defense and the International Situation." The Problems of National Security for Japan. Tokyo Colloquium, December 1972.

_____. Real Character of the U.S.-Japan Security Treaty as Seen in the Fourth Defense Build-Up Plan. Tokyo: Undated (circa 1972).

Kemp, Geoffrey. "The Strategic Requirements for European Nuclear Forces." Medford, Mass.: Unpublished manuscript, Fletcher School of Law and Diplomacy, August 1973.

Kishida Junnosuke. "Japan Should Not Have Nuclear Weapons." Jiyu, April 1972.

_____. "Non-Nuclear Japan: Her National Security and Role for Asian Peace." Address delivered at Peace in Asia Conference, Kyoto, 1972.

Komeito. The 10th National Convention. Tokyo: Komeito, 1972.

Kosaka Masataka. _Japan's Nuclear Options_. Prepared for Conference on U.S.-Soviet Strategic Balance and Nuclear Multipolarity, Fletcher School of Law and Diplomacy, May 3-5, 1973.

Kotani Hidejiro. "Nuclear Weapons and Nationalism." _Jiyu_, August 1969.

Kramish, Arnold. _A Reexamination of the Nuclear Proliferation Problems Presented by World-Wide Requirements for Enriched Fuel: Relating the February, 1965 Options to Today_. Santa Monica, Calif.: RAND Corporation, 1968.

_____. "The Watched and the Unwatched." _Adelphi Papers No. 36_, June 1967.

Kubo Takuya. _Concerning the Current Nuclear Armaments of Each Country_. Tokyo: Defense Agency, March 1972.

_____. "The Philosophy of Defense Problems and the Fourth Defense Build-Up." _The Problems of National Security for Japan_, Tokyo Colloquium, December 1972.

Kuroda Yasuhiro. _Nihon Kokuuchu Gakkaishi_. Tokyo: National Space Development Agency, 1972.

Langdon, Frank. "Strains in Current Japanese-American Defense Cooperation." _Asian Survey_, September 1969.

Latyshev, I. "New Foreign Policy Concepts of the Japanese Ruling Circles." _Asian Quarterly_, no. 4 (1971).

Maki, John M. "Japan's Contemporary Conservation." _Polity_, Winter 1971.

Mamoi Makoto. _National Security: Reassessment and a New Concept_. Tokyo: Prepared for Racine Conference, January 1973.

Mandel, Douglas H., Jr. "Japanese Opinion on Key Foreign Policy Issues." _Asian Survey_, June and August 1969.

_____. "Japanese Views of the American Alliance." _Public Opinion Quarterly_, Winter 1971.

Miyata Mitsuo. "Getting Rid of the Nuclear Myth." _Tembo_, 150, 1971.

Murakami Kaoru. "Shifting Responsibility for Nuclear Weapons, Background of Laird's Speech." Asahi Journal, July 23, 1971.

Muramatsu Takeshi. "Is the Security Treaty Effective?" Jiyu, July 1972.

_____. Japan's Choice. Paper delivered at the Fifth International Arms Control Symposium, Philadelphia, Pa., 1971.

Murphy, Charles H. "Mainland China's Evolving Nuclear Deterrent." Bulletin of the Atomic Scientists, January 1972.

Nakama (or Chuma) Kiyofuku. "The Road Toward Big Military Power (Status)." Asahi Journal, January 28, 1972.

Nasu Kiyoshi. "Japan and America--A Special Relationship?" Interplay, December-January 1969-70.

Nikkan Kogyo. "Japanese Scientist Makes Electro-Magnetic Quantum Mechanics Approach to Economical Uranium Enrichment." Nikkan Kogyo, October 7, 1972.

Nishio, Harry K. "Extraparliamentary Activities and Political Unrest in Japan." International Journal, Winter 1968-69.

Niu Sien-chong. "Will Japan Go Nuclear?" Ordnance.

Puchala, Donald J. "Foreign Policy Analysis and Beyond." Comparative Politics, April 1970.

Pyle, Kenneth B. "Introduction: Some Recent Approaches to Japanese Nationalism." Journal of Asian Studies, November 1971.

Quester, George H. "Japan and the Nuclear Non-Proliferation Treaty." Asian Survey, September 1970.

Robinson, Thomas W. The Sino-Soviet Border Dispute: Background, Development, and the March 1969 Clashes. Santa Monica, Calif.: RAND Corporation, 1970.

Royama Michio. "The Asian Balance of Power: A Japanese View." Adelphi Papers, no. 42, 1967.

Schlesinger, James R. <u>Nuclear Spread: The Setting of the Problem</u>. Santa Monica, Calif.: RAND Corporation, 1967.

Scoville, Herbert, Jr. "Missile Submarines and National Security." <u>Scientific American</u>, June 1972.

Sekino Hideo. "How to Defend an Ocean Surrounded Nation (Like) Japan," <u>Kokubo</u>, May 1970.

Sergienko. "Japanese Militarism Raises Its Head." <u>International Affairs</u>, June 1969.

Shina H. "Japan in Space." <u>Nature</u>, November 24, 1972.

Smart, Ian. "Advanced Strategic Missiles: A Short Guide." <u>Adelphi Papers</u>, no. 63 (1969).

Smith, Charles. "Australia and Japan." <u>World Today</u>, February 1970.

Stockwin, J. A. A. "Foreign Policy Perspectives of the Japanese Left: Confrontation or Consensus?" <u>Pacific Affairs</u>, Winter 1969-70.

Subrahmanyam, K. <u>An Indian Nuclear Force in the Eighties</u>? Prepared for the Conference on U.S. Soviet Strategic Balance and Nuclear Multipolarity, Fletcher School of Law and Diplomacy, May 3-5, 1973.

Sueyoshi, H. "Space Programs Round the World." <u>Interavia</u>, October 1971.

Takagi Noboru. "General Review of Japan's Space Activities." <u>U.N. Paper, 68-95563</u>, 1968.

Tanaka, Yasumasa. "Japanese Attitudes Toward Nuclear Arms." <u>Public Opinion Quarterly</u>, Spring 1970.

Ullman, Harlan K. <u>Issues in Chinese Nuclear and Atomic Matters</u>. Medford, Mass.: Fletcher School of Law and Diplomacy, unpublished paper, October 1971.

Ullman, Richard H. "No First Use of Nuclear Weapons." <u>Foreign Affairs</u>, July 1972.

Wakaizumi Kei. "Japan's Role in a New World Order." Foreign Affairs, January 1973.

Weekly Post. "Japan Secretly Developing Nuclear Submarine."
Weekly Post (Japanese weekly magazine), February 25,
1972.

Yamamoto Chisako. "A Threat in Japan after President
Nixon's Visit to China." Unpublished paper, May 1972.

Yamano Masato. "The Japanese Aircraft Industry Today."
Interavia, October 1971.

Yasawa Mitsuo. "The Logic of the Nuclear Defense Treaty
System." Asahi Journal, March 15, 1970.

Yatabe Atasuhike. "A Note on the Treaty on the Nonproliferation of Nuclear Weapons--The Japanese Point of
View." Tokyo: circa 1969.

Young, Elizabeth. "The Control of Proliferation, The 1968
Treaty in Hindsight and Forecast." Adelphi Papers,
no. 56 (1969).

Young, Judith H. "The French Strategic Missile Programme."
Adelphi Papers, no. 38 (July 1967).

Zilbert, E. R. The Chinese Nuclear Explosion, N-Nation
Nuclear Development and Civil Defense. Santa Monica,
Calif.: RAND Corporation, 1965.

NEWSPAPERS AND PERIODICALS

Aerospace International, 1973

Asahi, 1971-73

Asahi Evening News, 1970-74

Asahi Journal, 1970-72

Atoms in Japan, 1970-73

Aviation Week and Space Technology, 1971-73

Bulletin of the Atomic Scientists, 1972-73

Bungei Shunju, 1972-73

Chosa Geppo, 1970-73

Chuo Koron, 1972

Denki Shimbun, 1971-72

Denryoku Jiji Tsushin, 1971-72

Denver Post, 1974

Electronics and Communications in Japan, 1967

Flight International, 1971-73

Genshiryoku Sangyo, 1972-73

Geographical Review, 1973

JAIF Weekly, January-December 1972

Japan Quarterly, 1970-73

Japan Press Exchange Aviation Report Weekly, 1971-73

Japan Times, 1970-73

Jiyu, 1972-73

Journal of the Institute of Electronics and Communication
    Engineers of Japan, 1972

Mainichi, 1971-73

Mainichi Daily News, 1970-73

Kagaku Gijutsucho Geppo, 1973

Kokubo Keizai Tsushin, 1972

Nihon Keizai, 1971-73

Nihon Roketto Kaihatsu Kyogikai Kaiho, 1970-73

Nikkan Kogyo Shimbun, February 1972

Nuclear Engineering, 1972-73

Readers' Digest, 1973

Rocket News, 1970-73

Sankei, 1971-73

Scientific American, 1972-73

Sekai no Kansen, 1972

Shukan Boei Tokushin, 1971-72

Space/Aeronautics, 1968

Survival, 1972-73

Tokyo Shimbun, 1971-73

Wing International, 1971-73

Yomiuri, 1970-73

INTERVIEWS

Interviews were conducted in February 1973 with Japanese government officials in the Ministry of Foreign Affairs, Defense Agency and Diet Library, including consultants to the Liberal Democratic Party. Other individuals of the press, academic community, and atomic industry also were interviewed; these interviews were conducted in Japan.

Interviews were conducted in August 1972 with members of the staff of the Embassy of Japan, personnel of the U.S. Atomic Energy Commission, members of the Defense Department at the Pentagon, and a representative of the U.S. Arms Control and Disarmament Agency. These interviews were conducted in Washington, D.C. and its immediate surrounding areas.

INDEX

JOHN E. ENDICOTT is an Associate Professor of Political Science and the Deputy Head of the Department of Political Science and Philosophy, United States Air Force Academy, Colorado. He serves as chairman of instruction for Core and Defense Policy Courses, teaches Asian politics, international relations, American defense policy, and American government, and is a consultant to the National War College.

Colonel Endicott has lived in Asia for nearly a decade, including two military assignments in Japan and one in Vietnam. During that time he has been a first-hand observer and analyst of political affairs. His area of specialization is Japanese politics and his research language is Japanese.

Lt. Colonel Endicott received his Ph.D. in international relations from the Fletcher School of Law and Diplomacy, Tufts University. He also holds an AM and MALD from Fletcher and an MA, in history, from the University of Omaha.

RELATED TITLES
Published by
Praeger Special Studies

ARMED FORCES OF THE WORLD: A Reference
Handbook
> edited by Robert C. Sellers

THE POSTWAR REARMAMENT OF JAPANESE MARI-
TIME FORCES, 1945-71
> James E. Auer

SCIENCE POLICIES OF INDUSTRIAL NATIONS
> edited by T. Dixon Long and
> Christopher Wright

WEAPONS TECHNOLOGY AND ARMS CONTROL
> W. F. Biddle